Engraved by H. Robinson.

SIR WALTER RALEIGH.
From the original of ZUCCHERO.

SIR WALTER RALEIGH

BY

SIR RENNELL RODD

London
MACMILLAN AND CO., Limited
NEW YORK: THE MACMILLAN COMPANY
1904

CONTENTS

CHAPTER I

CHAPTER VIII

PAGE

CHAPTER IX

CHAPTER X

CHAPTER XI

CHAPTER XII

CHAPTER XIII

CHAPTER XIV

CHAPTER XV

CHAPTER XVI

CHAPTER I

EARLY YEARS

1552-1579

THE lives of few public men have offered more scope
for controversy than has the life of Sir Walter
Raleigh, and yet the uncertainty which at many points
perplexes the story of his adventurous career cannot
be ascribed to any dearth of biographical material.
After he had once emerged from respectable obscurity
he lived continuously in the fierce light of publicity.
No prominent character of an age rich in individuality
was more eagerly discussed by contemporaries; of none
have the conduct and actions been more curiously investigated by historians. State records, as well as the
social and political correspondence of the day, are full
of first-hand evidence of his many-sided activity; while
no less than one hundred and sixty-five letters from
his own hand, bearing on the most important episodes
in his chequered fortunes, have come down to us. So
that here, if ever, it might seem warrantable to assume
that the accumulation of matter should enable the
student, after examining the tangled story from every

E   B

side, with the eye of friend and foe, from the official as
well as from the private point of view, to form an unpre-
judiced judgment on the character and merits of this
remarkable man.   Nevertheless, in spite of the volume
of testimony, so much remains unexplained and intangible to subsequent generations that his numerous
biographers have for the most part been, perforce, content
to state the case, to sum up the evidence, and leave the
final judgment unpronounced.

Not only was the man himself compounded of many
elements and endowed with a versatility which amounted
to genius, but his age and environment were peculiarly
favourable to complexity of character ; and the appreciations of his contemporaries, when not contradictory, are
marked by the subtlety and absence of simplicity to
which all recorded appreciations tend in a dangerous
atmosphere of jealousy and suspicion.   It is perhaps
difficult in the present day to fully estimate the intri-
cacy of life at a Court where so much depended on
caprice, when public opinion was not yet an organised
force, and ambition struggled through a sea of intrigue
in which only the most dexterous swimmer could keep
his head above the wave.   Which of all the leading
figures that occupy the stage at that period can be
credited with motives consistently above suspicion if
judged by the sterner standards of to-day ?   Not one
of the counsellors of an autocratic and very feminine
mistress, not Walsingham, not even Burghley, least of
all the longest in the retention of office, the opportunist Robert Cecil.   Even Drake, direct and straightforward by nature, something of a Puritan by inherited tendency, was forced at times to have recourse

to tortuous methods in order to countermine the eternal intrigues of his opponents.   Perhaps the fact that the nobility of Sidney's character so profoundly impressed his contemporaries, in spite of the brevity of his career, may be accepted as evidence of how rare were those qualities which in him commanded their admiration.

A question of detail confronts us at the outset. What is the proper spelling to adopt of a name for which there are, perhaps, among his contemporaries more variants than there are for any other well-known name in those days of undetermined orthography? Sir Walter himself was not consistent in his own signatures, though after the year 1584 he appears to have finally adopted Ralegh, which recurs in one hundred and thirty-five of his letters.   A deed of the year 1578 exhibits three different spellings, subscribed by his father, his brother, and himself, who sign it Ralegh, Rawlygh, and Rawleyghe respectively.   The accepted spelling of Raleigh, if never employed by himself, has the sanction of use by Lady Raleigh and other members of the family, as well as the contemporary Hooker-Hollinshed chronicles, and it has been so universally adopted by posterity that it appears almost pedantic now to employ any other form.

Again, the very date of his birth cannot be fixed with absolute certainty.   The registers of the church at East Budleigh, where it should be inscribed, do not commence until 1555, three years after the date to which it has been generally assigned ; while the inscriptions on two of his portraits by Zucchero would, if correct, rather place it in 1554.   Inscriptions on portraits, however, are not very satisfactory evidence.   The whole chronology of his early years is uncertain, but it will best accord with such dates as can be approximately established to adopt the popular tradition of the year 1552.

Even as to the place of his birth there has not been complete unanimity. One writer at least has claimed that honour for an old house in the neighbourhood of the palace at Exeter, while others have accorded it to the hereditary manor of Fardell, which is near Ivybridge, on the edge of Dartmoor. The question, however, appears to be decided beyond dispute in favour of East Budleigh by a letter from Sir Walter himself to a Mr. Richard Duke, of Otterton, the owner of the farm of Hayes, where it was long kept and shown to visitors. In this letter, which has now disappeared, but which was duly transcribed by Aubrey, he endeavoured to persuade Mr. Duke to allow him to purchase the farm which had been for many years occupied by his family, adding " for the natural disposition I have to that place, being borne in that house, I had rather seat myself there than anywhere else." The actual name Hayes does not occur in the letter, but there is no room for doubt that Sir Walter referred to the estate of which his father held a lease from the Dukes. The old Tudor farm-house of Hayes, or Hayes Barton, still retains its sixteenth-century character. It is situated between the Otter and the Exe, about a mile from the church of East Budleigh, some six from Exmouth and three from the little port of Budleigh Salterton, from which it is separated by a wood of oak-trees.

The Raleighs came of an ancient stock; in fact the zealous antiquarian, John Hooker, chamberlain of Exeter and a relative of Sir Walter, is at pains to trace his descent, through the marriage of John de Raleigh with the daughter of Sir Roger d'Amerie, back to King Henry the First and so to the Conqueror. Like many of the West-country families the Raleighs appear to have had seats in Wales, as well as in Somerset and Devon, where they gave their name to several towns and villages. There were in the reign of Edward the Third. no less than five branches of Raleighs in Devonshire, in each of which the head of the house had achieved the honour of knighthood. The Fardell branch was descended from a certain John de Raleigh, grandson of Wimund de Raleigh of Bolleham, who in 1303 married Johanna, the daughter and heiress of William de Newton, and thus acquired the estate of Fardell. The family became greatly impoverished in the days of a later Wimund Raleigh, the grandfather of Sir Walter, who had succeeded to other properties, and whose position in the county is sufficiently marked by his having married a daughter of Sir Richard Edgecombe of Cothele. Whether the heavy fines which he was called upon to pay for some constructive misprision of treason had embarrassed him, or whether the too-lavish hospitality of the West-country had dissipated a goodly inheritance, he was obliged to part with his estate of Smallridge; while his son Walter, who followed him, was not only unable to live at Fardell, but was forced to alienate a portion of his remaining property.

Walter Raleigh of Fardell was three times married, and had issue by each of his three wives. The first was a daughter of John Drake of Exmouth, and by her he had two sons, of whom the elder inherited Fardell. These half-brothers, John and George Raleigh, had probably both grown up and passed out of the family circle before the appearance of the younger Walter; in any case they do not appear in the story of his life. His second wife is entered on a pedigree in the Devonshire visitation as daughter of Darrell of London. Elsewhere she is stated to have been the daughter of Giacomo de Ponte, or de Pant,[1] a merchant of Genoa established in England, with whom Walter Raleigh may have had business relations, if, as there is reason to believe, he was interested with partners at Exmouth in the merchant shipping trade. This appears the more probable as his four sons seem to have been brought up to follow the vocation of the sea, for the names of all of them occur in a list drawn up in the year 1585 of gentlemen quali-fied to command Her Majesty's ships, together with such illustrious names as Drake, Hawkins, Grenville, and Frobisher. By his second wife he had one daughter, who married Hugh Snedale of Exeter. His third marriage (to which no certain date can-be assigned), with Elizabeth, daughter of Sir Philip Champernoun and widow of Otho Gilbert of Compton and Greenaway, was more distinguished, and brought the Raleighs into connection with the Devonshire Carews. She was already the mother of three sons, who all distinguished themselves in after life. The eldest of these, Sir John Gilbert, was perhaps separ-ated by many years from the three children of her second marriage, Carew, Walter, and Margaret Raleigh; but the younger sons, Humphrey and Adrian, whose names are so intimately associated with Sir Walter's

---

[1] The name Darrell, which is not very clear in the MS. pedigree, might perhaps also be read Parrett, an erroneous transcription from Ponte or Pante.

fortunes, though upwards of ten years older, were probably the true elder brothers and heroes of his childhood,
which was passed between the Raleigh and Gilbert
houses on the Devonshire coast.

The story of his early years is shrouded in obscurity,
but two little incidents, in which his parents played a
conspicuous part, have come down to us, and are significant as illustrating the home influences under which he
was brought up. The first is told in Hooker's continuation of Holinshed. In 1549, at the time of the
famous rising in the West in favour of the restitution
of the old liturgy, the rising which drove the sturdy
preacher Drake of Tavistock to fly with wife and
child from his burning homestead, Walter Raleigh of
Hayes was riding into Exeter with certain mariners of
Exmouth, whose association with him on this occasion
tends to confirm the supposition that, like so many
other West-country gentlemen, he speculated in maritime ventures. The whole country-side was in a state of
ferment, and all the villages were constructing barricades
to close the road to Exeter against any forces which
might be sent to quell the movement. Overtaking on
the way an old woman, who with her beads in her hand
was making for the church of Clyst St. Mary, Raleigh,
who had warmly embraced the reformed doctrine, stopped
his horse, and, with the zeal of a proselytiser, began to
take her to task for carrying beads. He explained
the new laws, which had been passed against super-
stitious practices, and recommended prompt obedience
to authority, which his own connections, Sir Gawen and
Sir Peter Carew, had been sent to Exeter to enforce.
The woman, frightened but unconvinced, took refuge in

the church where the villagers were assembled for service, and broke forth into angry clamours against the gentry who were threatening on the highroads to burn the poor folks' houses over their heads if they did not give up their beads, their holy bread, and holy water. Inflamed by the incantations of this sibyl the parishioners left the church in tumult, and began to throw up new entrenchments, while a body of rioters pursued the squire, who, had he not been rescued by the Exmouth sailors of his company, was "in great danger of his life, and like to have been murdered." Though he escaped on this occasion, a rumour of his ill-timed advocacy of the new doctrines spread among the excited population, and he was soon after seized by another band of rioters and detained as a prisoner in the church of St. Sidwell, situated in a suburb of Exeter which they held. Here he was many times threatened with death, and it was not until Lord Russell and Lord Grey de Wilton had defeated the insurgents in the bloody battle of Clyst Heath, and compelled them to raise the siege of Exeter, that he was delivered from his precarious plight.

The other anecdote, recorded in Foxe's *Acts and Monuments*, belongs to a period some seven or eight years later, after the accession of Queen Mary had reversed the position of religious antagonists. Among the victims of the Catholic reaction, who lay in Exeter Castle under sentence of death by burning, was a poor uneducated woman, by name Agnes Prest. It is probable that she came from the immediate neighbourhood of Hayes or Greenaway, and therefore the wife of Walter Raleigh went to visit her in prison. John Foxe records their converse together, on the eve of execution, and the deep impression made upon that "woman of noble wit and godly opinion" by the simple, earnest faith of a poor peasant, unable to read or write, who could never so have spoken if God had not been with her. Young Walter Raleigh was at that time about six years old, and the story of the death for conscience sake of the simple countrywoman, who was perhaps a familiar neighbour, may well have made a deep impression on the precocious and reflecting child, and may unconsciously have helped to form that abiding hatred of priest-craft which characterised his later years. Such stories as this would also have early familiarised him with denunciations of the chief temporal supporter of the Church, whose marriage with the Queen had been the signal for the revival of all the persecuting statutes against heretics.

These two anecdotes and old Devonshire traditions which record young Raleigh's habit of cultivating the acquaintance of seafaring men, and questioning them on their experiences in many parts of the world, are all we have to indicate the influences which moulded his boyhood. As regards his early education, we can only conjecture from the reputation which he acquired during his brief university career, as well as from the scholarship and knowledge displayed by his versatile pen, that his grounding in the humanities must have been thorough. The Reformation and the dissolution of the religious establishments had taken education largely out of the hands of the Church, and both Edward the Sixth and Elizabeth endowed a number of grammar-schools to supply a much-needed want in the country.

Had young Raleigh been sent to any of these newly founded establishments there is little doubt some record of so distinguished a pupil would have been preserved there. Winchester and Eton, to which Humphrey Gilbert was sent under special provision in his father's will, were far away, and the famous school at Tiverton, where so many sons of the West-country have been taught their syntax, was not opened till some fifty years after his birth. It seems probable that the young Raleighs pursued their studies under the paternal roof until the time came for them to find their way to one of the great universities.

He had come into the world at a turning-point in the history of the nation, which had just passed through the crisis of the Reformation to endure the fiery ordeal of the Catholic reaction. As he grew to boyhood's consciousness of his environment, he may have realised, young as he was, something of the sense of relief with which those dark times of reserve and misgiving were succeeded by the freer air and more spacious vistas of Elizabeth. The thoughts which were stirring in men's hearts, and the words which fell from their lips, were well calculated to fire the imagination of the sea-born child. Freed from the fetters of routine and the limitations of a conscience held in others' keeping, men in England were learning to rely on their own strength and initiative. The old convictions were not dead nor radically altered, but they had expanded with the intellectual awakening of mankind, to become more powerful incentives to action. With the opening of a new spiritual horizon the material horizon also had widened beyond the dreams of imagination. It is well-

nigh impossible now to fully realise the momentous
influence of the voyages of Columbus, which at the close
of the former century had displayed a new world to
human ken, and promised revelations of infinite extension. With bewildering rapidity discovery had succeeded
discovery. The startled imagination of men dreamed of
great veins of virgin gold sleeping in the unquarried
mines of the new world's mountains, and conceived the
shores of the farther ocean as pebbled with inexhaustible
gems. Fired by the fame and example of the continental
discoverers, adventurous Englishmen followed the irre-
sistible attraction of the mystic West. Sir Hugh
Willoughby turned the North Cape to seek a passage
into the sister ocean, and perished in the ice with
all his men. Encouraged by the first of British
sovereigns who realised the sea kingdom's need of a
navy, William Hawkins went trading to Brazil, and
taught his famous son to follow in his track. The crisis
of the Reformation gave impulse to maritime enterprise,
for the antagonism of Spain to the rising sea-power and
commercial expansion of England turned simple traders
into privateers, and swift reprisals were exacted for a
restrictive policy which was reinforced by the zeal of
the Inquisition. There was a great unrest upon the
world, and whether unconsciously, stirred by the spirit
of the time, or with a dim consciousness of their new
inheritance, the hearts of humble men in England were
drawn towards the sea. The persecutions of the Catholic
reaction brought eager recruits to the ranks of the
privateers, and the younger sons of the great West-
country families,—the Carews, the Horseys, the Tre-
maynes, and the Strangways—supported the cause of the

reformed religion in their ships, harassing communications between Spain and the Low Countries. Such was the quickening spirit of the age, and such were the traditions with which the Gilberts and Raleighs grew. Their boyish games along the river reaches of Dart and Otter were mimic voyages of discovery. Familiar from the cradle with boats and ships and tackle, the friendly sea had no terrors for the hardy lads, who learned from well-tried masters those early lessons of navigation which bore their fruit in after-years.

Anthony Wood, the antiquarian and historian of Oxford, who studied the college records 'little more than a century later, states that Raleigh "became a commoner of Oriel College in or about the year 1568, when his kinsman, C. Champernoun, studied there." He adds that he resided for three years. The date of his matriculation only professes to be approximate, and it is more probable that he went up at the age of fifteen in 1567, and remained there through the whole of 1568 and a part at least of the following year, in which he is known to have left England for France. Students in those days did not wait for manhood to take up their residence at college; his son matriculated at Corpus Christi at the age of fourteen, and Sidney, who must have been a contemporary at Oxford, was still in his fourteenth year when he entered Christ Church, of which college Fuller states that Raleigh also became a member. Like Sidney he appears never to have taken his degree, though, according to Wood, his natural parts were strangely advanced by academical learning, so that he became the ornament of the juniors of his year, and attained proficiency in oratory and philosophy. His ready wit was evidently an Oxford tradition, for Bacon includes in his apothegms a rebuff of Raleigh's to a fellow-student, which was remembered with approval, though its humour does not appear particularly luminous to modern appreciation. His name is found in proximity to that of his kinsman Champernoun, without the distinguishing mark of the graduate, on a list of the members of Oriel College of 1572, three years after he had certainly left Oxford. This, however, is in no way remarkable, if Raleigh and Champernoun were called away from their studies to the field of battle before they had taken their degrees. They may well have kept their names upon the college books with a view to completing the university course upon their return.

How welcome would be a contemporary record of the social life and thought of our English universities during the first two decades of the reign of Elizabeth! Something of the spirit and enthusiasm which stirred the soul of youth in those days of national expansion we may, indeed, conjecture, something also of the external influences which contributed to break down the narrow insularity of former years. Already foreign travel had become almost a fashion, and education was not unfrequently completed by a visit to the celebrated continental universities, or the experiences of the grand tour. The artistic and speculative forces of the Renaissance had penetrated into the dominant classes of England, moulding the tastes and habits of the rising generation, and developing a more complex type of character. A growing tendency to luxury and magnificence attracted hither a number of southern artists and architects, and Italian culture began to cast that siren spell over our northern youth which Ascham deplored in an eloquent sermon.

Among the literary achievements of the first half of the sixteenth century, two books exercised a pre-eminent influence over the generation with which Raleigh grew up. The first was the *Principe* of Macchiavelli, with its cogent, sinister logic, its glorification of practical capacity, that *virtu* which by a strange substitution of language usurps the title of a moral quality, and its scathing contempt for simplicity and guilelessness. The *Principe* was published in 1532, after the death of its author, and its teaching must have formed one of the principal subjects of discussion among the fellow-students of Raleigh, who often refers to it, though not with approval, in the writings of his later years. The second book, the *Cortegiano* of Baldassare Castiglione, first printed in 1528, and translated into English by Thomas Hoby in 1561, pourtrays the ideal gentleman of the Renaissance, and discusses the characteristics which should illustrate the perfect courtier. Courtier and gentleman were indeed in those days in Italy well-nigh synonymous terms, for there was but little scope for culture, or opportunity for intellectual intercourse, outside the privileged atmosphere of court life, while at the same time the multiplication of little courts produced a considerable number of such intellectual centres. It is interesting to enumerate the various qualifications laid down in the *Cortegiano*, and to trace how closely the personality of Raleigh, as presented to us in contemporary records, coincides with the ideal type of Castiglione. It is difficult to refrain from the conclusion that the discussions, so gracefully ascribed by the author to the refined court of Urbino, where Bembo and Bibbiena exchange ideas with the keen-witted wife of Guid' Ubaldo da Montefeltro, had profoundly impressed the precocious student of Oriel.

In the first place the author lays down that the typical gentleman must be well born, and qualified for a fair start in the battle of life by the prestige of race. Now, no sooner had Raleigh emerged from obscurity than he is found occupying himself with the records of the Herald's College, and curious in collecting from Devonshire antiquarians facts for the establishment of his pedigree. His ambition of birth, and his anxiety to trace his descent to the Plantagenets, drew down upon him from John Hooker a sermon on the obligations of nobility, in which he found it seasonable to remind his younger relative, that, if it had fallen to his lot to revive the fortunes of an ancient family, the Lord had only blessed him in order that he might be serviceable to all men. Further, the ideal gentleman must be courageous in the field of battle, not merely skilful in the use of weapons, but he should excel in all manly exercises, while avoiding mere ostentation of athletic prowess. Raleigh, when still almost a boy, abandoned the university to pursue an education in arms, and, although a veil of obscurity hangs over the period of his training in the French wars, and his possible brief period of service in the Netherlands, he early proved himself to be a tried and experienced soldier in the Irish campaigns, where he performed feats of personal valour which would in modern times have entitled him to the most coveted distinctions. In the brilliant scenes of the tilt-yard, which had at that period not yet become extinct, he showed to conspicuous advantage.

Among the other characteristics of the finished courtier
are grace in act and word, freedom and force in speech
or writing, without affectation or pedantry, a knowledge of letters, not to be used for vain display, but
rather employed to illustrate conversation, the accom-
plishments of music and dancing, and a general acquaintance with the arts. He must be full of tact in approaching the prince his master, and modest in tendering him
advice, without ever sacrificing his own liberty of judgment. He should be cautious in forming friendships,
and admit but few to his intimacy. Even such practical
considerations as a proper attention to the choice of
clothes and the suitable equipment of retainers are dealt
with in this curious treatise. It would be difficult in
the whole history of English court life to point out any
well-known character who has so closely realised the
ideal type of the *Cortegiano* as Raleigh, the fearless
soldier, the magnificent Captain of the Guard, the
accomplished man of the world, the most incisive
speaker in a brilliant group of contemporaries.

Not less enigmatical than the rest of his early history
are the circumstances of his long residence in France. It
is expressly stated by Camden in the *Annals* that during
the third civil war in that country, which broke out in
1568, Elizabeth, taking up the cause of the persecuted
Protestants, supplied the Queen of Navarre with
money and men, and permitted Henry Champernoun, a
relation by marriage of the Comte de Montgomerie, to
carry a troop of gentlemen volunteers into France,
amongst whom was Walter Raleigh, then a very young
man. Now, Henry Champernoun was the son of John
Champernoun, the elder brother of Sir Walter's mother.

Her youngest brother, Sir Arthur Champernoun, Vice-Admiral of the West, had a son Gawen, who afterwards married Montgomerie's daughter, and certainly served somewhat later in the Huguenot wars. He may have volunteered also on this occasion, and may even be identical with the C. Champernoun of Wood and the Oriel register. His marriage had not taken place in 1569, but Camden's reference to relationship is not specific, and there may have been a previous marriage connection between the Champernouns and Montgomerie, who took refuge in England after he had the misfortune to cause the death of his king by an unlucky stroke at a tournament.

According to de Thou, Champernoun's contingent arrived in the Huguenot camp on October 5th, 1569, therefore on the second day after the battle of Moncontour. On the other hand, Raleigh, in his *History of the World*, distinctly speaks of himself as having been an eye-witness of the retreat at Moncontour under the Duke of Nassau. To reconcile these two statements we must either assume that Raleigh joined the Huguenot army before the rest of Champernoun's troop, or that he only personally experienced the latter part of the retreat, which is hardly consistent with the general tenour of his observations on the subject.[1] Some historians have inferred from another passage in his *History* that he had actually arrived in the beginning of the year, before the battle of Jarnac, which was fought on March 13th. There, in considering the evil effects of a division of the command between two associates with equal powers, he instances the case of Condé and

[1] *Works* (Oxford Ed.), vi. 211.

C

Coligny, and writes, "I well remember that when the
prince was slain after the battle of Jarnac the Protestants
did greatly bewail his loss "[1]; but he goes on to say they
comforted themselves with the recollection that his rash-
ness had often endangered the solid advantages secured
by his older and more cautious colleague.   That Raleigh
should well remember and record the views expressed
during his service with the Huguenot army with reference
to a recent event, does not necessarily imply that he was
himself present in person at the battle of Jarnac.

His first experience of fighting was formed in a very
rough school.   The third civil war in France was, in
reality, not a war of religion.   The high standard which
had marked the conduct of the Huguenots in their
former campaigns was no longer maintained in this inter-
necine struggle, and in the general demoralisation the
combatants on either side were guilty of the most detest-
able cruelties, as we know from the evidence of Agrippa
d'Aubigné, the soldier, politician, historian, and poet,
who was born in the same year as Raleigh himself, and
who had joined the army of Condé a twelvemonth earlier.
It is impossible to resist the assumption that these two
men, whose lives and characters had so much in common,
learned to know and appreciate one another then, and
eagerly discussed by the camp-fire light, when the brawler
slept and the rattle of the dice was still, the promise and
ambitions of the coming years.   So, also, one is tempted
to reflect how, nearly half a century later, when in the
decline of life the old Huguenot chief was finishing
his *Histoire Universelle* in exile at Geneva, the news
that came from England may have turned the key of

[1] *Works*, vi. 157.

sleeping memories, and carried his thoughts back to
the youthful comrade of his first campaign, who, after a
career not less rich in adventure than his own, had
occupied the weary years of captivity in compiling a
History of the World. But these are mere conjectures
on lines over which it is pleasant to linger. No letters
of Raleigh's are extant belonging to the period of his
service in France, and beyond the notice in Camden and
three references to this campaign in his own writings
there is an entire dearth of biographical material. Nor
have we any evidence as to his subsequent movements,
when in August of the following year both parties, worn
out with the desperate struggle, signed the peace of St.
Germains. That he remained for some time in France,
in fact that his sojourn there extended over a period of
more than five years, is to be inferred from a dedication
addressed to him by the younger Hakluyt, who bears
witness that Sir Walter's residence in France had been
longer than his own, which, as he elsewhere states, had
covered five years. A legend, for which there appears
to be no authority, has included him among the young
Englishmen who, with Philip Sidney, took refuge in
the house of the British ambassador, and thus saved
their lives on the night of St. Bartholomew. Montgomerie, who had escaped to England, returned the
following year, with a squadron equipped in the western
counties under Champernoun, to La Rochelle, but was
compelled to retreat once more. The co-operation of
the Champernouns was now ostensibly, at any rate, disavowed by the Queen, whose tortuous policy towards
the French Court and the Huguenots was at this period
marked by bewildering inconsistency ; and when in 1574

Montgomerie was organising his last fatal expedition from Jersey, the French ambassador in London reported that Elizabeth had taken measures to render the enterprise abortive.   Whether or not Raleigh was associated with these later attempts of the Huguenots to retrieve their position in France must remain uncertain.   The English sympathisers who joined them did so at their own risk and peril, and were studious to keep their own counsel.   He appears, at any rate, to have returned to England not long after the execution of Montgomerie, which took place on June 26th, 1574, and to have taken up his residence in the Middle Temple.   His name is found in a register of the members kept since the beginning of the sixteenth century, entered as : " Walter Rawley, late of Lyons Inn, Gent. Son of Walter R. of Budleigh Co. Devon Esq." under the date of February 27th, 157$\frac{4}{5}$.   It seems probable, though it does not necessarily follow from his residence in the Temple, that he intended at this period to devote himself to the study of the law.   That he, however, did not carry out his intention is recorded by himself in the protest which fell from his lips during his trial: "If ever I read a word of the law or statute before I was a prisoner in the Tower, God confound me!"   Prefacing a satirical volume of verse, *The Steele Glass* of Robert Gascoigne, which was published in 1576, are some commendatory verses by "Walter Rawely of the Middle Temple." They bear the impress of his style, and the concluding lines have a suggestive prophetic application to their author :

> For whoso reaps success above the rest,
> With heaps of hate shall surely be oppressed.

The doubts which have been expressed as to the identity of this Walter Rawely with the young soldier lately returned from the French wars can be scarcely maintained since the discovery of the entry in the Temple register, and further circumstantial evidence in favour of Raleigh's relations with Gascoigne is afforded by his having afterwards appropriated the motto assumed by the latter, and printed under his portrait in this publication, *Tam Marte quam Mercurio*. Gascoigne himself, a soldier as well as a poet, had lately returned from the war in the Low Countries, where he had doubtless known the Gilberts, through whom he became acquainted with Raleigh.

Several contemporaries have alluded to Raleigh's services in the Netherlands under Sir John Norris. There is nothing impossible in such a hypothesis, and the fact that Sir Humphrey Gilbert commanded a regiment there lends plausibility to the supposition. It can be shown that he was in England in December, 1577, as well as at some period previous to the publication of *The Steele Glass* in 1576. But there was ample time between the two dates for a young man of spirit to have won his spurs in the school of the Prince of Orange. It is, however, less probable that he witnessed, as another author has alleged, the famous battle of Rimenant, inasmuch as he was undoubtedly in Devonshire early in 1578, and occupied in the latter part of that year with the equipment of Gilbert's first expedition of dis-. covery, in which his brother had offered him a command. The expedition itself was a failure. Drake's successful raids had made Philip suspicious. A tall ship was lost in an encounter with the Spaniards, and Raleigh himself

fought a critical action, in which his own vessel was
sorely battered. He nevertheless held on for a while
at sea, but was compelled to return in 1579, having
exhausted his supplies, with nothing achieved. It was
the first great disappointment of a life rich in successes
and reverses. From boyhood upwards he had been
waiting for the day when he, too, might follow the
track of the great adventurers into the new world of
promise, and now, when he returned undaunted by
failure, an attempt to reorganise the expedition was
peremptorily checked by the Queen. Sir Humphrey
and his brother were forbidden to embark, and an entry
to this effect in the registers of the Privy Council marks
the first appearance there of Raleigh's name, to which
the complaints of the Spanish government had attracted
attention. He had already, it would seem from an
entry in the Middlesex registers of 1577, been introduced at Court, perhaps in the suite of the Earl of
Leicester, with whom, it is clear from a letter which
Raleigh addressed to him from Ireland in 1581, he had
at some previous period been intimate.

CHAPTER II

1580–1581

THE policy of Elizabeth in Ireland, alternating between extreme severity and premature forbearance, between spasmodic energy and parsimonious neglect, was one for which the most zealous enthusiast would find it difficult to suggest plausible justification, and the bloody annals of those grim years remain a "sullen page in human memories." Her natural instincts were undoubtedly in favour of conciliation; her unstatesmanlike opportunism led only to disastrous failure. It is true that had the country been left to itself its fate would probably have been little better; for while the other nations of western Europe had made mighty strides in progress, and had long since realised the conception of national unity and individual evolution, independent of the tyranny of medieval ideals, Ireland still remained abandoned to the savagery of the primeval Celt,—a savagery not less real because it was coloured with the vivid poetry of a gifted and imaginative race. The chieftains of her rival factions maintained their hordes of lawless kernes, whose sole occupations consisted in raids and cattle-lifting,

23

accompanied by the indiscriminate slaughter of the followers and families of a rival partisan. The bandits of the Burkes, the O'Neils, the Butlers, and the Geraldines perpetuated a condition of anarchy which made true national sentiment impossible ; and the only bond of union was a common hatred for the conqueror and a detestation of the new religion, fostered by as ignorant a clergy as ever maintained ascendency over the superstitions of a constitutionally emotional race. "Under the sun," wrote Sir Philip Sidney, after careful personal observation, "there is not a nation that live more tyrannously than they do one over the other."

The value set on human life varies with social and geographical conditions. We need not go to the wilds of Central Africa to establish an extreme case. Nearer home, in portions of the Turkish empire, the low appreciation of life and relative measure of indignation which its violent extinction evokes can with difficulty be realised by the imaginative faculty of those who dwell among the ordered societies of the West, where an act of violence committed in the immediate neighbourhood produces a shudder of repugnance and resentment. In order to arrive at an unbiassed judgment of the actions of prominent men in other centuries we must endeavour to reconstitute the conditions and the standards which formed their moral environment, and turn back the wheel of evolution. Much that is accepted in our own moral standard of to-day, ideals which we still uphold and actions which we set down to righteousness in contemporaries, will perhaps be incomprehensible to the mind of after generations, who will be astonished at our selfishness and hardness of heart. Such reflections

cannot of course palliate the horror of the methods
employed in repressing the revolt of the Desmonds.
But it is necessary to bear in mind the barbarous and
abject condition of the local population, the intolerance
bred of religious antagonisms, and to take into account
the attitude of earlier ages towards rebellion in general,
in order to understand for a moment how the treacherous
slaughter of the O'Neils and the ghastly massacre of
Rathlyn could have been the handiwork of a man so
cherished and esteemed by contemporaries as Walter
Devereux, Earl of Essex, who on his death-bed deplored
the irreligion of his own countrymen, and only regretted
that his thoughts had been too much with his sovereign
and too little with his God. In the uncompromising
West-country squires of the type of Warham St. Leger
and Humphrey Gilbert, God-fearing and simple-hearted
men in their ordinary relations of life, there could
be no glimmer of sympathy for the wild cattle-lifter of
an earlier stage in human development. To them the
rhymer that celebrated, the harlot that recompensed,
and the priest that gave absolution to the heroes of
lawless brigandage, were only so much scum to be swept
off the face of the earth. Even so honourable and high
principled a man as Sir Henry Sidney, who, accompanied
by his illustrious son, took up the thankless charge of
Deputy in Ireland in 1575, with all his desire for
tolerance and conciliation, only succeeded in the temporary preservation of order by as liberal a use of the
rope and gallows as his predecessors had employed, and
Sir Philip defended him vigorously against the charge
of over-severity. Drury, Malby, Grey de Wilton alike
found all ordinary methods of government unavailing.

Ormonde, as an Irishman himself, had some sympathy for his own countrymen, and at least considered them human beings, so long as they did not belong to the accursed race of Fitzgerald ; and yet he, in his spring campaign of 1580, put to death forty-six captains, eight hundred notorious traitors, and upwards of four thousand other nameless folk.

The moving spirit of the Desmond rebellion was the Jesuit, Dr. Nicholas Sanders, the evil genius of Ireland at this crisis. For years he had been preaching a Catholic crusade against England, which he sought to stimulate by the collection and circulation of every libellous story which malignity could invent. More successful at Rome than at Madrid, where pacific counsels were in the ascendant, he obtained from Gregory his own nomination as Legate to Ireland, a consecrated banner to serve as the oriflamme of the Catholic cause, and the appointment of a papal general in Sir James Fitzmaurice, who had already distinguished himself by a massacre of English settlers. In July, 1579, Sanders and Fitzmaurice landed with a small company of friars, English refugees, and Spanish or Italian adventurers at Dingle, where they proceeded to build a fort. In view of subsequent events and the charges brought against Raleigh for his connection with the affair at Smerwick, in which he played only a subordinate part, it is well to remember the first proceedings of Sanders and his mercenaries, for which that massacre was to some extent a retaliation. They had fallen in with a Bristol trader off the Land's End and had thrown the captain and crew into the sea. The crew of another English barque they carried off as prisoners or hostages, and these were put to death by the Desmonds after the crushing defeat of Fitzmaurice. They now summoned the Earl of Desmond himself to join the holy war. The Earl wavered, but his brother John, to precipitate a crisis and involve the whole race of Geraldine in the quarrel, treacherously murdered in cold blood two English officers, Davell and Carter, who, with a few servants only, had gone to Tralee to gain information as to what was on foot. The rising of the Geraldines in force threw the Burkes into the opposing scale, and with their assistance Sir Nicholas Malby defeated Fitzmaurice in the woods of Limerick. The papal general himself lost his life, and the consecrated banner fell into the hands of the victors. It was then that the Desmonds retaliated by the murder of the prisoners at Dingle. In spite of this defeat the rebellion gathered strength, and the Earl, who still hesitated to take up arms, shut himself up with Sanders and his brothers in his castle at Askeaton, whence he saw the town and the abbey burned to the ground by Malby's troopers. Thereupon he took the field in person and broke into the English town of Youghal, which he abandoned to his kernes to plunder. The wives and daughters of the English merchants were savagely violated, and every man who had not escaped was put to the sword. On either side the wildest passions were aroused, and the most horrible atrocities were now to be anticipated. Early in 1580 Lord Ormonde came over with a commission as military governor of Munster and orders to prosecute the Geraldines, the hereditary foes of his house, to the death. Two armies, one under Ormonde, the other commanded by Sir William Pelham, marched through the rebel countries, killing man, woman, and child, and burning their miserable cabins to the ground, while Sir William Wynter entered the Shannon with a fleet which remained to watch the coast. The fortress of Carrigafoyle, in which Sanders had established his mercenaries, was battered to the ground by the ordnance of the ships, and its garrison annihilated. Desmond in panic deserted his stronghold at Askeaton, and with Sanders took refuge in his island castle in Kerry, where they once more narrowly escaped capture. For a brief moment the strength of the rebellion seemed broken; but the lull was only a temporary one. The Barons of the Pale were seething with discontent, and lamenting that they had not availed themselves of the opportunity to rise with the Desmonds. The desire for an alliance with Spain, the protector of the Church, became a last passionate hope. News of the exploits of Drake on the Pacific shores during his great voyage had slowly filtered home, and the damning confirmations of his privateering triumphs had aroused a storm of indignation among the Spaniards, whose patience was now thoroughly exhausted. If the Queen could not control her free-lances, why should Philip hesitate? An expedition for a descent on Ireland had long been privately preparing at Corunna, and a favourable opportunity for action presented itself when Wynter, short of provisions, with ships too foul to hold the sea, withdrew to England, believing the insurrection crushed. Eight hundred Spaniards and Italians, bringing with them stores, arms, and equipment for some four thousand more, landed during his absence on the Irish coast and occupied Dingle and Smerwick.

It would appear that Raleigh's service in Ireland began under Lord Justice Pelham. What are known as the Raleigh reckonings, a statement of accounts for the little force which he commanded, date from July 13th, 1580. His appointment to command a "foot-band" of one hundred men, to which he added later a small complement of horse, may have been procured through the interest with the Queen of his relative Mrs. Katherine Ashley, or through Sir Humphrey Gilbert, his half-brother, who had served in Ireland and stood in favour at Court. His emoluments were not magnificent; four shillings a day for himself, two for his lieutenant, and eightpence a day for each soldier appear from the reckonings to have been the scale of payment allowed. Soon after his arrival he sat on a joint commission with Sir Warham St. Leger ("Sir Warram" of the Raleigh letters, now Provost Marshal of Munster,) for the trial of the rebel James Desmond, brother of the Earl, who had fallen into the hands of the Sheriff of Cork. The Sheriff's own conduct had not been above suspicion, and in his anxiety to propitiate the authorities he betrayed Sir James, who was executed forthwith. Pelham was relieved in August, 1580, by Lord Grey de Wilton, who brought over six or seven hundred fresh troops. His first operations were unsuccessful, and young Sir Peter Carew, a relative of Raleigh, with some three hundred men, lost his life in an ambush. In spite of this reverse Lord Grey determined to take the risk of attacking the foreign invaders at Smerwick with all his available forces. He was accompanied by Raleigh and Edmund Spenser, who were here first thrown together. Sir William Wynter had received orders to return with

the fleet, and after many delays from contrary winds
he arrived early in November. Lord Grey had reached
Dingle a fortnight earlier. Upon the arrival of the
fleet trenches were dug, siege operations were set in
train, and the fortress was heavily bombarded. According to Hooker, who gives a full account of the siege
in his continuation of Hollinshed, two offers made to
the garrison to yield to mercy were refused, and the
assault continued. The officer in command of the
foreign troops, a certain Don Sebastian, accompanied by
an Italian soldier of fortune, then held a parley with
the Lord-Deputy under a flag of truce, offering to surrender on terms. They confessed that they held no
commission, but the Italian stated that they were sent
by the Pope for the defence of the Catholic faith. Lord
Grey, as it appears from his official despatch, which is
confirmed in the account given by Spenser of this affair,
refused any terms but unconditional surrender, and
declined to entertain even a "surcease of arms." He
at length, however, consented to leave the garrison in
the fort through the night until the following morning,
when Don Sebastian undertook to yield it up, handing
over hostages in the meantime. When morning broke
the Lord - Deputy presented his companies in battle
order before the fort, and the garrison with trailing
banners made sign of submission. "Then," he wrote in
his report to the Queen, "I put in certain bands, who
straight fell to execution—there were six hundred slain."
The officers only, to the number of twenty, were reserved
for ransom. Hooker states that Captains Raleigh and
Macworth entered the castle and made a great slaughter.
The Lord - Deputy does not mention Raleigh's name.

Vice-Admiral Bingham attributes the massacre to a number of marines and soldiers who "fell to revelling and spoiling, and withal to killing." The evidence, however, of Lord Grey's despatch, corroborated by the testimony of Spenser, is conclusive that the massacre of the prisoners was deliberate. There does not appear to have been any hesitation on his part as to the course to be pursued, nor does he make any attempt to conceal the facts. The garrison, uncommissioned soldiers from Spain and ruffians discharged from the papal prisons, were deliberately invading a foreign country in league with rebels in open insurrection. To such, according to the standards of the day, no mercy was due. Moreover a stern lesson was needed, for these foreign troops were only the advanced guard of a more formidable invasion. They were consequently regarded and treated as bandits. Raleigh himself, if the additional information given by Hooker be accepted as true (and it must be remembered that he puts it down to his credit), played only a subordinate part, and obeyed the orders which he received. It is nevertheless matter for regret that his name has been associated with a deed of blood which has remained a sinister memory in the traditions of the Irish people. English writers, from Bacon downwards, have generally represented the Queen as having shown displeasure at the strenuous action of the Lord-Deputy. But a letter which she addressed to him in acknowledgment of his despatch, reporting the capture of Smerwick, makes it apparent that it was the undertaking given to spare the lives of the officers, and not the massacre of the rank and file, which incurred her criticism. " In this late enterprise," she wrote, " performed

by you so greatly to our liking, we could have wished
that the principal persons of the said invaders to whom
you have promised grace, which we will see performed,
had been reserved for us, to have extended towards
them either justice or mercy, as to us should have been
found best, for that it seemeth to us most agreeable to
reason that a principal should receive punishment before
an accessory."

Raleigh and his company took up winter quarters
at Cork, and while there he received a commission from
the Lord-Deputy to take order with the notorious rebel
David, Lord Barry, whose dangerous influence as a leader
of revolt he had himself brought to Lord Grey's knowledge. The expedition was rendered abortive by the determined action of Barry himself, who burned his house to
the ground and laid the country round it waste; but on
his return journey to Cork an adventure befel the young
captain which tried his mettle and enabled him to give
proof of conspicuous gallantry. Between Youghal and
Cork was a ford in the Balinacurra. Here there lay in
ambush, waiting for his passage, a certain Fitz-Edmunds, a
rebel of Barry's faction, known as the Seneshal of Imokelly,
with numerous horsemen and footmen. His little escort
of six men were lagging behind, and Raleigh reached
the river's edge accompanied only by an Irish guide,
when suddenly the whole company of Fitz-Edmunds
sprang from their hiding and held the ford. He cut his
way through and had crossed in safety to the other side,
when he became aware that one of his followers was
unhorsed in the middle of the stream and crying to him
for help. Dashing back into the river he brought the
man safe to land, and then with his pistol cocked stood

firm on the opposite bank, waiting for the rest of his party to come up. The Seneshal, seeing other troopers advancing in his rear, made off in haste, although his force numbered nearly twenty to one. This exploit led to a curious sequel not long afterwards. At a parley held with the rebels Fitz-Edmunds proclaimed his own martial achievements in such a braggart manner, notwithstanding that Raleigh had openly taxed him with cowardice, that Ormonde, the Governor of Munster, challenged him, together with Sir John Desmond and any other four he chose to name, to meet himself, Captain Raleigh, and four others at the selfsame spot. There his lordship undertook that he and his companions would cross the river in the others' despite and determine the point of honour in battle, two to two, four to four, or six to six. It was a chivalrous proposal and one after Raleigh's own heart; but no answer was returned to the challenge, which was a second time repeated in vain.

This was not by any means his only passage-of-arms with Barry's men, or with the Seneshal, whom he cleverly out-manœuvred in his adventurous expedition to Bally to seize the person of Lord Roche and bring him before Ormonde at Cork. The conduct of Lord Roche had afforded considerable suspicion of disloyalty, and some information as to his possible arrest had evidently got abroad, for the Barrys and the Seneshal were out, waiting once more in ambuscade to intercept any force on the road to Bally. Raleigh, by an unexpected night-march, reached Lord Roche's seat at daybreak with his company of foot and a few horsemen; there, however, he found five hundred of the townsmen

D

up in arms to oppose his progress. He disposed his little force so as to hold these in check and occupy their attention without provoking a conflict, while he proceeded with half-a-dozen men to the castle, leaving orders for a second party to follow. He was admitted to parley with Lord Roche on condition that he would dismiss half of his followers. By some device, however, all six got safely within the castle ward, and while he held the master of the house in converse they admitted the second detachment which had followed, so that the gate and the gate-house remained in possession of his redoubtable footmen. Lord Roche, with true Irish hospitality, invited the intruder to share his table, and Raleigh then explained his business and submitted his commission to his host, who, with the best grace he could assume, agreed of his own free will to accompany an envoy who had so obviously the means of compelling him. Raleigh ingeniously persuaded him to select an escort from the town-guard for their protection on the way to Cork, and Lady Roche prepared for a nocturnal ride. It was a wild dark night and the road lay through a dangerous country, admirably suited for surprises and ambuscades. The presence of the town-guard from Bally had, however, perhaps become known to the Seneshal's men, who feared they might not be able to distinguish friend from foe; or it may be that Raleigh avoided the main highway where the Barrys were assembled. In any case he succeeded in bringing his prisoners safely to Cork, with the loss of only one man, who died of exhaustion on the march. Lord Roche, it should be added, was able to clear himself of all the charges which had been alleged against him, and proved himself a loyal subject of the Queen, in whose service three of his sons afterwards lost their lives.

In the spring of 1581 Lord Ormonde, whose administration Raleigh had unmercifully criticised in his letters to Walsingham and Grey, retired from the government of Munster, which was temporarily placed in commission and entrusted to Sir William Morgan, Captain Piers, and Raleigh himself, who continued the work of pacification with energy until August when a new Governor was appointed in Captain John Zouch. The ruthless vigour of his administration was so far successful, that occasion arose to reduce the English garrison and pay off Raleigh's company. The latter had already expressed his anxiety to leave Ireland in a letter written from Lismore to Leicester, in which he declares his readiness " to dare as much " in the Earl's service as any man he might command. He, therefore, no doubt welcomed the opportunity which was afforded him of returning to England in December in charge of Lord Grey's despatches, for which duty he received a sum of £20. It is probable that the period of his active service in Ireland closed at this time, for in the following February an order was sent by the Council to the Lord-Treasurer requiring him to pay £200 to Edmund Denny and Walter Raleigh upon the entertainment due to them in Ireland, which payment was to be notified to the Treasurer at the wars, and by him deducted from the entertainment due to them in his account. Nevertheless, in April, 1582, he received a new Irish appointment as captain of a band of footmen in succession to Captain Appesley, under a warrant from the Queen, in which it is stated that "Our

pleasure is to have our servant Walter Rawley trained
some time longer in that Our realm for his better
experience in martial affairs." He was at the same time
by the terms of his warrant excused from proceeding
immediately to his post, and allowed to leave the band
or regiment of footmen in charge of such lieutenant as
he should depute. It would appear, however, that the
appointment was never officially notified to the Lord-
Deputy, who, when he heard it rumoured, expressed his
disapproval in unequivocal terms. He had had in the
meantime good reason to suspect that Raleigh had
furnished the Lord-Treasurer with material arguments
for criticising his administration in Ireland.

CHAPTER III

1581

THE arrival of Raleigh in charge of Lord Grey's despatches, and the first-hand evidence he was able to give as to the position of affairs in Ireland would alone have sufficed to attract the attention of the Court to a young soldier who had won a reputation for gallantry during his service in Munster, and had already attracted the notice of Walsingham by his vigorous and outspoken correspondence. It may be that he was indebted to Leicester, whom he accompanied, two months later, on a mission to the Netherlands, for a special recommendation to the notice of a Queen ever ready to welcome and advance young gentlemen of good parts and pleasant exterior. It is equally possible, as other biographers have maintained, that the Earl of Sussex, now Leicester's most formidable rival, had taken him under protection, with the intention of securing a promising recruit to his faction. But Raleigh himself was not without interest at Court, and it is more natural to assume that his present favourable reception, as well as his original nomination to a captaincy of infantry, was due to his

family connection with the influential wife of Henry
Ashley, a former favourite of Anne Boleyn, who sat in
Parliament for the county of Dorset, and had received
the honour of knighthood at the coronation of Queen
Mary.   Katherine Ashley, who had acted as governess
to Elizabeth, remained in her service as Woman of the
Bedchamber, and long exercised a powerful influence
over the mind of her royal mistress.   A daughter of
Sir John Basset of Umberleigh, she claimed as great-
grandfather on the mother's side Otho Gilbert of
Compton, whose grandson, Sir Otho Gilbert, was the
first husband of Raleigh's mother and father of his half-
brothers John, Humphrey, and Adrian.   The families of
Raleigh, Champernoun, Grenville, and Gilbert were
intimately connected by frequent intermarriage, and
the clannish feeling which in those days subsisted
between the prominent houses of Devon and Cornwall
was sure to enlist for the young Gilberts and Raleighs
the protection of a relative who had constant access to
the Queen.   She was in all probability responsible for
the first employment of Sir Humphrey Gilbert, whose
brilliant justification of her patronage had already
brought him into prominent notice.

Another account of the circumstances which contributed to his first success at Court, placed on record
by Sir Robert Naunton, a contemporary, if considerably
his junior, must not be passed over without mention,
though it can scarcely be accepted as accurate in the
form in which he has presented it.   He states that
Raleigh, upon his return from Ireland, was summoned
to appear before the Queen and Council to answer
interrogations respecting a dispute which had arisen

between himself and Grey, and that his bearing and eloquence on that occasion first attracted the favourable notice of Her Majesty. Naunton is, however, particular to mention that both Grey and Raleigh were drawn to the Council table, whereas it is demonstrable that the Lord-Deputy did not return to England until August, 1582, long before which date Raleigh had received signal proofs of royal favour. The Council records, moreover, contain no reference to such an affair. At the same time there is undoubtedly some foundation for the story told by Naunton, and it is evident that Raleigh had on his return made his views on the situation in Ireland known to Burghley, and through the Lord-Treasurer's influence obtained the ear of the Queen. For already in January, 1582, the Lord-Deputy wrote to Burghley that he had "lately received advertisement of a plot delivered by Captain Rawley unto Her Majesty for the lessening of her charges in the province of Munster, and the disposing of her garrisons according to the same"; and he put forward a plea for the favourable consideration of his own judgments, formed in accordance with the best advice available, rather than of the advice of "those, which upon no ground but seeming fancies, and affecting credit with profit, frame plots upon impossibilities, for others to execute." That the captain's opinions secured a favourable hearing is evident from a memorandum, dated October 25th, 1582, written partly in Burghley's and partly in Raleigh's own hand, entitled—*The opinion of Mr. Rawley upon motions made to him for the means of subduing the Rebellion in Munster*,—in which he strongly urges the policy of winning over the smaller Irish chieftains. How unwelcome were these views, and the attention which they received, to the Lord-Deputy, is clear from the manner in which he commented on the news that Raleigh had been appointed to succeed to a command in Ireland vacated by Captain Appesley. "For mine own part," he wrote to Walsingham, "I must be plain: I neither like his carriage nor his company; and therefore, other than by direction and commandment, and what his right can require, he is not to expect at my hands."

That Mistress Katherine Ashley should have bespoken the Queen's favour for her relative, and that a bold expression of opinion on the burning Irish problem, involving criticism of superior officers which he succeeded in justifying, should have afforded convincing proof of his ability is probable enough, and it is not necessarily inconsistent with the famous story of his first introduction to the Queen, which has been contemptuously dismissed by recent biographers, apparently because it has no better authority than that of Fuller, who recorded in his *Worthies* a popular tradition of one whose tragic end must have made a deep impression on his own early years. The account of Raleigh's chance meeting with the Queen as she was walking abroad and of the chivalrous service which he rendered, is best told in Fuller's own words:—"Her Majesty meeting with a plashy place made some scruple to go on; when Raleigh (dressed in the gay and genteel habit of those times) presently cast off and spread his new plush cloak on the ground, whereon the Queen trod gently over, rewarding him afterwards with many suits for his so free and seasonable tender of so fair a foot-cloth. Thus an advantageous admission into the notice of a prince is more than half a degree to preferment." The incident had its sequel when Raleigh, now welcomed at Court, scratched with a diamond on a window, where they could not escape the royal eye, the words :

Fain would I climb, yet fear to fall.

To which the Queen in due course engraved the re-joinder :

If thy heart fail thee, climb not at all.

Raleigh's employment on occasions of State for con-fidential personal service began at any rate immediately after his return from Ireland. The Duke of Anjou, who was now an apparently prosperous suitor for the hand of the Queen, arrived in England in November. The preliminary negotiations had been skilfully conducted by his agent Simier ; but the envoy had inevitably incurred the jealousy of Leicester, who, although now privately married to the widow of the Earl of Essex, resented his advocacy of a rival in the Queen's affections, if indeed Simier had not actively provoked his anger by disclosing the secret of his marriage. On the arrival of his master in person the agent returned to France, presumably in the month of December, and Raleigh was selected as one of his escort. If Camden is to be believed, Simier stood in need of protection, for he speaks of bravos hired by the Earl to assassinate the ambassador. In an anonymous contemporary publica-tion it is stated that Flushing pirates were suborned to sink the boat which conveyed him ; and that, although this plot miscarried, the English gentlemen of his escort

were held in chase for four hours on their return journey
from the French coast, "as Master Raleigh well knoweth,
being there present."

In the following February Anjou left England for
Antwerp to assume the government of the United
Provinces as Duke of Brabant.   The Queen herself
accompanied him to Dover, and Leicester, with a
magnificent train which included the Lord High
Admiral and Philip Sidney, was deputed to introduce
him to the allied government.   Raleigh was now
attached to the suite of Leicester, whose intrigues
against the French prince's envoy he had been recently
employed to counter.   He alludes in his essay on the
Invention of Shipping to this visit to the Netherlands,
where he remained behind after the special mission had
returned, and held converse with the Prince of Orange,
who delivered into his hands letters for the Queen,
and bade him say to her "*Sub umbra alarum tuarum
protegimur,*" a message for her private ear, which would
afford him an opportunity he was not the man to
neglect.   Then followed his appointment to the command
of Captain Appesley's band, which has already been
referred to, with a special dispensation to remain for
the present at Court, where his advice was found useful,
while his personal attractions and his ready wit soon
made his position assured.

Elizabeth was now approaching that critical period
in the life of a woman when the desire which she still
retains of attracting is intensified by prophetic misgiving as to the endurance of her powers to please.   It
gratified her intense personal vanity to believe that she
could still exercise as a mistress a hold over the

affections of those gallants whose interest it was to pay court to her as a queen. So much may at least be said without transgressing an injunction which has become proverbial, in which shape its formulation is not without significance. This weakness the handsome young Devonshire squire, inordinately ambitious and unusually observant, was not slow to discover and turn to account. His own utterances on the subject of his relations to the Queen are eminently discreet,—for the hyperbolical diction of his letter to Sir Robert Cecil, written from the Tower when he was out of favour in 1592, is obviously a mere assumption of the conceit and affectation of the day. If so grave a critic as Bacon could find it excusable in the Queen that she suffered herself to be caressed, and celebrated and extolled with the name of love, and wished it and continued it beyond the suitability of her age, because "gratifications of this sort did not much hurt her reputation and not at all her majesty," the voice of scandal was nevertheless by no means silent at the time in its reflections on the "English Cleopatra" and the man who pleased her too well. It is recorded, moreover, that the comedian Tarleton was forbidden the royal presence for some too free utterance respecting the position and influence of the new favourite.

The manly bearing and cultured address of the young soldier, who first appeared on the scene during the visit of the latest suitor for the Queen's hand, offered a striking contrast to the ill-favoured and empty-headed Anjou, whose pretensions were not long afterwards finally rejected. His portraits, of which not a few have been preserved, fully bear out the evidence of

early authorities as to his personal appearance. He
was tall, about six feet in height, well compacted and
proportioned, with strong regular features. His dark
hair and beard were in early life thick and curly, his
eyes blue, the forehead high, the mouth resolute, while
the whole expression of his face betokened self-reliance
and a certain assurance. Aubrey, who wrote more than
fifty years after his death, but who recorded a living
memory, speaks of him as "sore eye-lidded," but his
information was probably based on the recollection of
those who had only seen him after long confinement
in the Tower and years incessantly occupied in study.
Elsewhere he says of him, "He was a tall handsome
and bold man, but his naeve was that he was damnable proud"; and again, "He had an awfulness and
ascendency in his aspect over other mortals." Obedient
to the precepts of Castiglione, he expended no small
proportion of his then slender means on the sumptuous
apparel which was the fashion of the day at Court;
and as early as 1583 we find in the Middlesex register
the record of a certain Pewe, who was tried for the
theft of a jewel worth £80, and a hat-band of pearls,
the property of Walter Raleigh. The extravagance of
his taste in armour, dress, and jewellery is attested by
the portraits painted at the period when he was at the
height of his prosperity; but the aforesaid chronicler
of curious detail has also recorded a gossip of old
servants to the effect that the real pearls were not
so big as the painted ones. The broad Devonshire
dialect, from which he never quite emancipated his
speech, amused the Queen, who from the first delighted
in his conversation and regarded him as a kind of

oracle; for the young courtier, whose adventurous experiences in the Huguenot wars and conspicuous gallantry in Ireland had attracted jealous attention, had ideas of his own which he expressed with epigrammatic incisiveness. Such characteristics appealed inevitably to Elizabeth, who dearly loved a proper man. Translated into the terms of poetry, the romance of Belphœbe and Timias in the *Faery Queen* is admitted by the author himself to describe in the language of allegory the fortunes of his friend. Without pursuing so delicate a subject to unnecessary lengths, it may safely be asserted that the extraordinary rapidity of Raleigh's advancement in royal favour could scarcely be accounted for without due allowance for a strong personal attraction, such as he was by no means the first to exercise upon a sovereign fully conscious and perhaps unduly proud of those physical charms to which contemporaries have borne witness.

If there is no record of any definite appointment to office, or of any special privilege accorded to Raleigh earlier than in March, 1584, it may nevertheless be assumed that he immediately received and continued to enjoy exceptional proof of royal patronage. For, when in the early months of 1583 Sir Humphrey Gilbert was organising his fatal expedition, he was able to adventure £2000, and to contribute the famous *Ark Raleigh* of two hundred tons burden, which afterwards became the flag-ship of the Lord High Admiral in the great fight with the Armada. There is indeed mention, in a letter addressed by Raleigh to the Solicitor-General in April, 1583, of two leases granted to the Queen by All Souls' College at Oxford, and transferred to him as beneficiary, which leases he promptly disposed of, no doubt on favourable terms. In March, 1584, he was granted a very remunerative license to export woollen broadcloth, and this license was periodically renewed and extended in subsequent years, conditionally upon the payment of a rent to the Crown. About the same time the patent for the colonisation of remote heathen lands not actually possessed by any Christian prince, hitherto held by his illustrious half-brother, was transferred to Raleigh, and, perhaps in order to assist him in meeting the great expenditure which its execution would entail, the Queen further granted him a patent for licensing the sale of wine, which entitled him to receive a fee from every vintner throughout the kingdom. These rights he underlet to a certain Richard Browne for a term of seven years for an annual payment of £700, and before that term had expired, realising that his lessee was receiving an undue share of the profits, he induced the Queen to revoke the old patent and grant him a new one for a term of thirty-one years. This profitable monopoly, however, led him into disputes, and his rights were contested by the University of Cambridge, whose chancellor finally established, to the satisfaction of the Lord-Treasurer, a claim to regulate the sale of wines within the radius of University jurisdiction. Nor were his differences with the lessee Browne satisfactorily terminated by the revocation and reissue of the patent, as appears from the recurrence of suits before the Privy Council. The maximum of revenue which he eventually received from this source was about £1200 a year.

A suitable residence in town was also found for him by the surrender for his use of the greater portion of

Durham Place, the London palace of the Bishop, which
the Crown had appropriated.   The palace was a
castellated building with turrets opening on the river,
occupying the extensive Adelphi area to the west of
the Savoy estate upon which stood the house of the
Bishop of Carlisle.   The river bank beyond the actual
city boundaries in the direction of Westminster had
been from early times occupied by religious foundations,
whose sacred character enabled them to avail themselves
of sites outside the shelter of the city walls.   The
grounds and outhouses at the back communicated with the
Strand, the highway between London and Westminster.
Durham Place appears to have become a royal residence
even before the accession of Henry the Eighth, and was
used as a hostel for distinguished guests.   Cardinal Pole
claimed and obtained the restoration of the house to
Bishop Tunstall in Mary's reign, but it does not seem
certain that he ever resided there, and the estate
remained at Elizabeth's disposal until her death, when
Raleigh was turned out and it was restored to the
Bishop of Durham, to be by him again ceded to Robert
Cecil, who made much profit by turning the Strand
frontage to account.

   In 1854 Raleigh was chosen to represent the county
of Devon in Parliament, and towards the end of that, or
in the beginning of the following year, he received from
the Queen the honour of knighthood.[1] In July, 1585, he
was appointed Lord Warden of the Stannaries, in succession to Francis, Duke of Bedford, an office which involved

---

[1] On the seal prepared for him as Governor of Virginia, and
bearing the date of 1584, which has lately been presented to the
British Museum, he is still described as *Miles*, not as *Eques*.

the regulation of the mining industry in the two counties of Devon and Cornwall, and conferred upon the holder the privileges which belonged to the western Dukedom, now in suspension, including the command of the Cornish Militia. In this capacity he presided over the Stannary Parliament, and during his tenure of office he reduced the unwritten law of custom to a reformed code of rules which remained in vigour many years after his death. Before long his influence in the West was rendered paramount by his appointment to the Lieutenancy of Cornwall and the Vice-Admiralty of the two counties. In six years the young soldier of fortune had thus accumulated a number of offices and monopolies which ensured his social and material position ; but a still more conspicuous mark of royal favour was to follow in 1587, when Sir Christopher Hatton, the Captain of the Guard, was raised to the post of Lord High Chancellor, and Raleigh was called upon to take his place in immediate attendance on the Queen. The office itself conferred no salary, but it appears from an entry in the Warrant Book that "six yards of tawney medley at thirteen shillings and fourpence a yard, with a fur of black budge rated at ten pounds," were provided out of the royal purse for his uniform. His place was henceforth in the royal ante-room, where he was close at hand whenever counsel was required.

About the same time this portionless younger son became one of the largest landowners in the United Kingdom, by the Irish grant of confiscated Desmond estates conferred upon him in 1586, and by the acquisition of a great portion of the property forfeited to the Crown by the attainder of the unfortunate Babington.

The latter grant was made a pretext by the enemies of
Raleigh, whose numbers increased with his prosperity,
to fix upon him an odious charge·for which there is no
particle of evidence. He was accused of accepting a
bribe for intercession on behalf of a condemned conspirator, by whose death he was materially to benefit.
The Elizabethan age saw nothing discreditable in the
traffic of pardons, and there seems no doubt that Raleigh,
when at the height of his influence after the conspiracy
of Essex, received substantial acknowledgment from
suspects who obtained the royal clemency through his
agency. Babington had undoubtedly endeavoured to
secure his intervention. That his advances were entertained or encouraged by Raleigh is unsupported by
any evidence, and it is inherently improbable that he ·
would, at this early period in his career, have pleaded
for the pardon of a convicted conspirator against the
life of the Queen. The reckless charge may, therefore,
be dismissed. He succeeded, however, to nearly all the
forfeited estates in Lincoln, Derby, and Nottingham-
shire, with all rents and profits, goods, personals, and
movables.

Another piece of gossip, which has been recorded to
his discredit, may perhaps be most appropriately disposed
of at the same time. Sir John Harrington, godson of
Elizabeth, poet, courtier, and sycophant, is responsible
for a charge, made at a time when Raleigh was a prisoner
in the Tower at the King's pleasure, against a former
"chief favourite," whose identity, though he is not
actually named, can scarcely be doubtful, of having
during Elizabeth's reign circulated scandalous stories
respecting Thomas Godwin, Bishop of Bath and Wells,

E

in order to coerce him into surrendering the lease of a valuable manor. In refutation of this story it has been pointed out by Oldys that the bishop's own son, Dr. Francis Godwin, himself a bishop and therefore interested in the preservation of episcopal property, makes no mention in his father's biography of a charge which he could neither have ignored nor overlooked. Harrington, who, when symptoms of the Queen's approaching end were plain to all the Court, did not scruple to send a fantastic Christmas gift to James inscribed, "Lord, remember me when thou comest into thy kingdom!" was not likely to be scrupulous in sifting the evidence for a story to the discredit of the new King's enemy. He was essentially a time-server, but elsewhere has done Raleigh better justice. While stories resting on so slender a foundation of evidence may be dismissed by disinterested critics, it must nevertheless be admitted that Raleigh displayed a somewhat grasping spirit in his accumulation of wealth. But if he appreciated magnificence, it was as the outward sign of success and ascendency. If he aimed at riches, it was in no mean or miserly spirit, and he spent the money, which at this time flowed into his coffers, royally in the realisation of his illimitable dreams. The plantation of Virginia cost him £40,000, and the expedition to Guiana well-nigh ruined him. In the days of his prosperity he was a generous patron and an open-handed contributor to public objects, and when misfortune overtook him there was little left to sustain him in his long adversity.

The Irish grant, under which he took over a portion of the vast estates escheated from the Desmonds, limited

the area to be held by a single undertaker to twelve
thousand acres, but in the case of Raleigh this limitation
was expressly suspended. Two other undertakers, Sir
John Stowell and Sir John Clyston, were associated with
him, and three seignories, each of twelve thousand acres,
with an additional seignory of six thousand acres, were
assigned to the three. A rough survey of these lands
which had long lain waste was completed in 1587, when
Raleigh began to grant leases with a view to repeopling
the desolate province of Munster, but it was not till
some years later that he was able to devote personal
superintendence to the problem of their development.
The thoughts of every man in England were now fixed
on graver issues. The execution of the Queen of Scots
in February precipitated the preparations of Spain for
war, and towards the close of the year Raleigh was fully
occupied at the Council of War or in levying troops for
the defence of the menaced kingdom.

Once admitted to royal favour he soon became, for a
time at least, omnipotent. Already in the year 1583 so
tried and trusted a servant of the Crown as Burghley
craved the exercise of his good offices with the Queen,
when he had fallen under temporary displeasure, perhaps
on account of the unruly behaviour of his son-in-law
Oxford. Not long after it once more fell to his lot to
intercede with his royal mistress' on behalf of the old
favourite Leicester, whose conduct in the Netherlands
had given dissatisfaction, and he was able to write and
inform the Earl that he had succeeded; the Queen was
now "well pacified, you are again her sweet Robin."
Nevertheless, in spite of his dominant personality, there
was in Raleigh some intangible characteristic which

qualified confidence if it did not actually inspire mistrust,
and while he could command the devotion of adherents,
he was never able to compel the regard of his equals.
Adroit, contriving, adventurous, he was, like the man of
many resources, the Ulysses of Homer to his friends, the
Ulysses of the dramatists to his enemies.   It is evident
that the Queen, who allowed herself to be influenced by
his persuasive charm, and recognised the soundness of
his judgment in moments of emergency, never reposed
in him the unreserved confidence which her most trusted
councillors enjoyed.   She never appointed him to any
important office of State, and his ambition to be admitted
to the Privy Council remained unsatisfied till her death.
In the meantime, however, his rise to power was pheno-
menal in rapidity, and his unpopularity with Court and
country was commensurate with his success.   "His
naeve was that he was damnable proud," and his contemporaries never forgave that air of ascendency which
was innate perhaps rather than assumed, and the conviction of superiority with which he asserted his opinions.
The energetic vitality which helped him to outstrip all
competitors was an offence to his would-be rivals, and
his very versatility gave colour to the insinuation of
imposture.   Five hours of his day were at this period
devoted by him to sleep, four to reading, two to relaxa-
tion, and the rest to business.   It is characteristic of his
economy of time that he gave his leisure on board ship
during his voyages to the study of chemistry, in which
his half-brother Adrian Gilbert was a proficient, and he
returned to the pursuit of this science during his long
sojourn in the Tower.   Thus he made time suffice to
cultivate his many-sided nature.   He was an accom-

plished musician according to the standards of his day, and the testimony of contemporaries is unanimous as to his powers as an orator. Small as is the volume of verse which can with any degree of probability be attributed to his authorship, it suffices to stamp him as a poet, and the quality of imagination inspired and elevated the practical side of the man of action. Unpopular as he was with the masses, his friendship with men of science and letters was sincere and cordially reciprocated. Spenser, Hakluyt, Hariot, and Hooker were among those who frequented the study overlooking the river, in the turret at Durham Place. Foreign writers and artists sought and readily obtained his patronage. It was to Raleigh that Jacopo Castelvetri, the critic of poetics, dedicated the edition of Stella's epic on Columbus, which he published in London in 1585, and to him also Martin Basanière dedicated the history of the discovery of Florida by Laudonnière, published in the same year at Paris. He was brought into close relation with all the erudite and cultured, who had flocked to a court which had assimilated the traditions of the Renaissance, by a scheme which he had deeply at heart, namely, the institution of a kind of encyclopædic bureau, where students might obtain information on all kinds of subjects at first-hand from experts. Unfortunately but little is known of this public-spirited enterprise, which must have filled a pressing want in the days when books of reference were scarce, beyond what may be derived from an allusion to it in a letter from Evelyn to Lord Clarendon, as a plan suggested by Montaigne, and actually put into practice by the efforts of Raleigh. It is pardonable to conjecture that Bacon may have contemplated the co-operation of its correspondents for the realisation of the system developed in his *Novum Organon*; and perhaps a later outgrowth of this association of the learned may have been the intellectual club, which held its meetings at the Mermaid Tavern in Friday Street, with the foundation of which Raleigh has also been credited. Here Shakespeare, Ben Jonson, Donne, Beaumont, Fletcher, and Cotton, with many other "souls of poets dead and gone," met in unrestrained and congenial intercourse. Here men of thought and men of action were brought together in a fellowship to which few periods of the world's history can afford a parallel; and we may well assume that many a shrewd and pithy saying, gleaned from the encounters of wit which took place in such surroundings, many an experience of strenuous life here recounted to eager listeners have passed into the familiar texts in which genius has incorporated them.

A horror of persecution and a genuine love of toleration were characteristic of Raleigh throughout his public life, and as a consequence he was perhaps more unpopular with the clergy of his day than with any other class. It was in this spirit that he undertook the defence of Udall, who, once a minister of the Established Church, had become a Nonconformist, and was condemned to death for having published a book which was most unjustifiably represented as libellous to the Queen. Raleigh induced Elizabeth to reprieve the sentence, but release was deferred till Udall died in prison. So, again, in the Parliament of 1593 he contested the expediency of expelling sectarians from England, pleading even on behalf of the troublesome and aggressive congregation

of the Brownists. He was in advance of his age
in opposing an enactment making the attendance of
public worship compulsory under pain of banishment.
"What danger may grow to ourselves," he urged,
"if this law pass, were fit to be considered. It is to be
feared that men not guilty will be included in it; and
that law is hard, that taketh life, and sendeth into
banishment, when men's intentions shall be judged by a
jury, and they shall be judges what another man meant."
It is not strange that Raleigh, who was diligent to
promote the spirit of free inquiry, should have been the
object of violent attacks from the Jesuits. The pro-
clamation suppressing their seminaries in England was
issued upon Raleigh's advice, and his action was never
forgiven by that uncompromising and vigilant Order.
Having offended the hierarchies of either religion, he
was inevitably branded with the name of Atheist. His
constant association with Hariot, who was known to
reject many portions of the Old Testament, and was
popularly reported to be a Deist, lent colour to the
charge of unorthodoxy; and it is possible that he had
held conferences with the notorious Giordano Bruno,
who between 1583 and 1585 visited England, where he
dedicated a dialogue to Sir Philip Sidney. Such a
charge would be readily made against so original a
thinker in days when the slightest departure from
accepted traditions was stigmatised as heretical. There
are, however, many passages in Raleigh's written works
which illustrate the real devotional attitude of his mind,
especially in the *Treatise on the Soul*, in his *Instructions
to his Son*, and in what Charles Kingsley with pardonable enthusiasm has described as the most God-fearing

and God-seeing history known.   He may have explored
fields of speculation forbidden to the narrow theology of
his time, but his last words upon the scaffold, uttered
when he stood at the dark brink of death, remain as
an eloquent and convincing profession of faith.

Such was Raleigh at the zenith of his influence and
favour.   He came, he saw, he conquered.   But his
rapid advancement, his proud, unyielding, and impulsive
temperament raised up around him a crowd of jealous
ill-wishers, and like all royal favourites he incurred his
full share of popular antipathy, so much so in fact that
he was described in 1587, perhaps without exaggeration,
as the best-hated man in court, city, and country.
Leicester was still absent from England, and Hatton
had withdrawn with offended dignity into the country.
He had met with scarcely an obstacle on his triumphant
progress.   Suddenly a shadow crossed his path.   The
young Earl of Essex, who had joined Leicester in the
Low Countries, where he was knighted on the field of
Zutphen, after the famous charge in which Sir Philip
Sidney lost his life, returned to Court.   Young, handsome, brilliantly endowed and born in the purple, he
was recognised as a fit successor to the lamented Sidney,
and the intriguers at the palace at once combined to
set him up as a rival to the detested Captain of the
Guard.   The antagonism of Essex and Raleigh was
immediate, and, if at times they dissembled their mutual
antipathy, it none the less remained irreconcilable.

CHAPTER IV

VIRGINIA

1585

FROM childhood's days the young Gilberts and Raleighs had been familiar with the sea. The little port of Budleigh Salterton is only some three miles distant from Hayes Barton. Compton is but an easy walk from Torquay, and the manor of Greenaway, the favourite residence of the Gilberts, is situated on a headland running out into a deep-water reach of the river two miles above Dartmouth. There is little doubt that their parents, like so many of the Western gentry, had adventured their fortunes in the sea, and that the boys were early trained in all that belongs to a sailor's calling. These little harbours of the West-country were the playground of their youth, and the advent of the homeward-bound with tales of the world beyond the sky line, was the event which broke the monotony of isolated country life. Not a village in that pleasant moorland country leaning to the Dart, but had sent forth some of its sons on the path of adventure with Strangways or Tremayne, and there such knowledge of the great new continents as had been brought home to

England, mingled with fable and fancy, could be picked up at first-hand from veterans who had sailed with the elder Hawkins. A sailor boy of humble origin from the neighbouring parish of Sandridge, whose name is for ever written large across the map of the world, may well, as has been suggested with picturesque plausibility, have acted as henchman to the Squire's sons in their expeditions down the green river reaches, to explore the mysteries of the ships and the magic of the sea. Indeed, they could hardly have failed in such close proximity to have drawn into their circle that John Davis whom in after years men vied in eager rivalry to follow, for the love of his generous heart and the smile that lurked behind his ruddy beard, beyond the limit of Arctic snows and across the burning tropic seas. The circumstances of youth and the spirit of the age thus alike prepared them for great enterprises, and when at length opportunity came they embraced it with an eager zest.

Sir Humphrey, the second of the three Gilbert sons, whose career in many respects anticipates that of his illustrious half-brother, was destined for the profession of the law, but early abandoned the studies for which he had prepared himself at Eton and at Oxford to follow the more active life of arms. He served in France and Ireland, where he acted as Governor of Munster, and again in the Netherlands. But his thoughts had never ceased to flow in the channel of early associations, and he had continually occupied his mind with the problems of navigation and the study and amendment of sea-cards, as the early charts were then called. The fruits of these studies and the real object of his ambition were revealed by the premature publication, without Sir Humphrey's consent, of the famous discourse *To prove a passage by the north-west to Cathay and the East Indies,* which concludes with those memorable words : "Give me leave always to live and die in this mind, that he is not worthy to live at all that for fear or danger of death shunneth his country's service and his own honour, seeing death is inevitable and the fame of virtue immortal. Wherefore in this behalf, *mutare vel timere sperno.*"

He had obtained in 1578 a royal charter, authorising him to discover heathen and barbarous lands not actually possessed by any Christian prince or people, to have, hold, occupy, and enjoy them ; but a clause was inserted in the patent limiting the duration of its powers to six years, if during that period no territories had been taken into occupation. The abortive expedition of 1579, in execution of this charter, has already been mentioned. It was not until 1583, when the term of his patent had nearly run out, that a new expedition was equipped, to which his half-brother contributed the famous *Ark Raleigh*, built for this voyage at a cost of £2000. At the last an unexpected difficulty arose from the opposition of the Queen. Her anxiety to retain the new favourite at Court, and withdraw him from the dangers inseparable from a long voyage into those unknown seas in which all save the subjects of the king of Spain were proclaimed trespassers, may account for the peremptory orders given to Raleigh to renounce his intention of sailing in person. In her endeavour to deter Sir Humphrey also from the project, for which he had so long been preparing and in which he had embarked a great portion of his fortunes, it is probable that she was moved by political considerations, having experienced the difficulty of explaining away the reprisals which Drake had exacted from the Spanish settlements in the New World, and the premature publication of Gilbert's discourse justified her misgivings.   She feigned, however, to be actuated only by care for his well-being, and urged him to remain at home, as a man "noted for no good hap by sea." Her scruples were at length overcome through Walsingham's intervention, and on the eve of his departure she sent him by the hand of Raleigh a jewel in the form of an anchor guided by a lady, bidding him have care of himself, and wishing him as great good hap and safety to his ship as though she were present in person.   She expressed, moreover, a desire to have his portrait to keep by her.

The tragic yet glorious story of Humphrey Gilbert's death needs no re-telling.   Stimulated to action, rather than daunted, by the fatal news, Raleigh determined to resume the enterprise.   He obtained from the Queen a charter similar to that granted to Gilbert, but with somewhat larger powers, and, for the further encouragement of maritime exploration, he founded, in association with his youngest half-brother Adrian, Master William Saunderson, and others, the Fellowship for the Discovery of the North-West Passage.   The charter granted to Raleigh, the advocate and apostle of a colonial empire, which is too long to quote in its entirety, contemplated the permanent occupation of the new country, to be held under homage by himself and his heirs, with a reserve to the Crown of a fifth part of all the gold and silver ore found there, and it secured to future inhabitants of British origin all the privileges of free denizens and persons native of England. The comprehensive terms of this charter, and the provisions made for the future status of the colonists, reveal the real aims of Raleigh, as distinguished from those of the filibustering captains who had preceded him on the path of exploration. The guiding principle of all his effort, the fixed idea of his life, which it was not granted him to realise in person, had already taken root. It was his avowed ambition to give the Queen in permanent possession "a better Indies than the King of Spain hath any."

A month after the issue of this charter two vessels, equipped and provisioned at his cost, under the command of Captains Philip Amadas and Arthur Barlow, sailed for the Canaries, and a month later made the West Indies. Their instructions were to work up from the south, as Gilbert's expedition had done from the north. In the beginning of July they were greeted by a land breeze from the shore they were seeking, and sighted what they believed to be the continent. Entering, as they thought, the estuary of a river, they went ashore, and found indeed a promised land, a country rich in animal life, yielding grain and spices, where the vines laden with grapes clung to tall cedar-trees or strayed luxuriantly over the sands towards the sea. It was not long, however, before they discovered that they were upon an island, and that there lay before them "another mighty long sea," enclosing "about one hundred islands of diverse bigness." The first of these islands upon which they landed was in fact Wokoken, off the coast of North Carolina. It was two days before they set eyes

on a human being; but on the third day a boat with
three natives appeared, one of whom immediately established friendly relations with the seamen.   He was
despatched with cloth and simple gifts, and on the
following day a chief called Granganimeo, brother of the
king of the islands, who had himself recently been disabled by a wound, came across with many attendants.
A visit from his wife followed, a comely and modest
lady, clad in a mantle of deerskin lined with fur and
wearing long chains of pearls as big as peas, who took
the strangers under special protection.   The friendliest
relations were established, and the English visited the
neighbouring island of Roanoke, where Granganimeo
himself lived, and other portions of the kingdom of
Wingandacoa.   Then, having bartered some of their
possessions for pearls and valuable skins, and having
persuaded two of the Indians to accompany them to
England, they set a straight course for home, where they
arrived without mishap in the middle of September.

Meanwhile a fellow-enthusiast and life-long associate
of Raleigh, one Richard Hakluyt, who had lately been
appointed chaplain to the British Ambassador in Paris,
returned to London with a paper, which was laid before
the Queen, urging the plantation by Englishmen of such
parts of America as were still no man's land.   This
paper had for its title, *A particular discourse concerning
western discoveries, written in the year 1584, by Richard
Hakluyt, of Oxford, at the request and direction of the right
worshipful Mr. Walter Raleigh, before the coming home of
his barks.*   Hakluyt, who was born within a year of
Raleigh, graduated at Christ Church in 1574.   It is
probable, therefore, that he did not go into residence

until after the brief college career of his patron had
closed with his departure for the Huguenot wars.   If,
however, it be true that Raleigh at some period, perhaps
after his return from France, became a member of Christ
Church, it is possible that the man of action and the man
of letters discovered their mutual affinities at Oxford,
where Hakluyt gave lectures on geography.   His earliest
publication in 1582 of *Divers Voyages touching the Discovery
of America* was in any case sure to have attracted Raleigh's
attention, and to this date at any rate the origin of their
long and fruitful intimacy may be assigned.

After the return of Amadas and Barlow Raleigh at
once prepared a larger expedition to colonise the newly
discovered regions, to which by the Queen's special
desire the name of Virginia was given.   By spring of
the following year a fleet was in readiness, and in April
seven ships sailed from Plymouth under the command
of his kinsman Sir Richard Grenville as general-in-chief,
carrying Ralph Lane, the governor designate of the new
colony, with Philip Amadas as deputy.   Among many
others well known in the annals of the time who went
out full of enthusiasm to lay the foundations of a new
England beyond the seas were Raleigh's devoted friend
Thomas Hariot, the philosopher and mathematician, and
Thomas Cavendish, who afterwards followed the track
of Drake through the Straits of Magellan into the
Great South Sea, and became the second Englishman to
circumnavigate the globe.   The two Indians, Manteo
and Wanchese, were also carried back to their native
country to report to their tribesmen on the wealth and
majesty of England.   Some valuable captures were made
at Porto Rico on the outward journey, and in June the

squadron reached the old anchorage off Wokoken, whence they sent messengers to Roanoke to apprise the chiefs of their arrival. Explorations were carried out on the mainland, and Manteo escorted their first ally Granganimeo to Hatorask, where he was received on board the admiral's ship, the *Tiger*. Every facility was afforded to the settlers, and upwards of a hundred men were left under Lane to start a plantation. Towards the end of August Grenville set sail for England, having pledged himself to return not later than the following Easter with stock and supplies for the colony.

This was not the only enterprise in which Raleigh had an interest during the year 1585. About two months after the departure of Grenville's squadron the Fellowship despatched two barques to follow in the tracks of Frobisher, under the command of John Davis. The equipment of this expedition was entrusted by the joint adventurers to Master William Saunderson, a merchant of London and a great authority on sea-cards, who also contributed the greater portion of the funds for the undertaking. It was on this occasion that Davis, having anchored in 66° 40' N. latitude "in a very fair road under a very bare mount, the cliffs whereof were as orient as gold," named it Mount Raleigh in honour of his friend and patron. The voyage was repeated in the following summer, and again in the summer of the year after; and it is stated by Hakluyt that Raleigh was a liberal contributor to each of the three expeditions. He appears also to have maintained privateering cruisers at sea, for captures of Spanish ships by his officers near the Newfoundland fisheries are referred to in the minutes of the Privy Council for this year.

The reports brought home from the new colony were
full of promise; the climate was admirably adapted to
European settlers; the soil of the mainland was rich,
and stretched away over boundless areas to the unknown
west; the people were gentle and guileless, living after
the manner of the golden age.   So they believed at any
rate in these first weeks of their experience.   Unfortunately our forefathers had not yet learned the lesson
which later years have taught at heavy cost, the secret
of winning the attachment of native races.   Few of the
early navigators, with the notable exception of Drake,
perceived instinctively that firmness and prompt decision,
combined with patient forbearance and inexhaustible
good temper, and above all a rigid sense of justice, are
the qualities which the savage immediately learns to
respect and even to worship.   It was not long before a
too rigorous punishment for a petty crime aroused a
sullen spirit of resentment among the Indians.   The
chieftain of the north-western provinces of Chawanok
was detained as a hostage in chains, and during his
captivity successfully imposed upon the credulity of the
settlers, whose avaricious dreams had filled the unknown
world with all the treasures of romance.   Granganimeo,
the white man's friend, was now dead, and while Lane,
with half the colonists, marched away into the wilderness in search of a fabulous country where the houses
were studded with pearls, his brother Wingina, the
king, who had since become secretly hostile, organised
a massacre.   Lane, to whom the plot had been discovered during the expedition, returned with a starving
company, reduced to "dog's porridge," a broth made
from the flesh of their two English mastiffs, just in time

to defeat the conspiracy, and the king with his principal chiefs were put to death at an interview to which they were summoned. The natives, realising that they were no match for the powerful strangers, and seeing no other hope of deliverance, abandoned the cultivation of the land. Food began to run short, and Easter came without a sign of Grenville and the relief ships. The unexpected appearance of a squadron under Drake, who was led by curiosity to visit the new colony on his return from the sack of St. Domingo and Carthagena, delivered them from an extremely critical position. He furnished them with supplies and ammunition, as well as a barque and pinnaces. But a violent storm which broke upon the coast destroyed these vessels, and once more despondency prevailed. Lane was evidently not of the fibre which goes to form the pioneers of empire, and, moved by the appeals of his dejected followers, he prevailed upon Drake to give the whole company a passage to England. Thus tamely, almost without a struggle, the infant colony of Virginia was abandoned, and on the 27th of July, 1586, Lane returned to Portsmouth with a record of failure to Raleigh's infinite disappointment. Scarcely had the colonists turned their backs on the coast when a vessel of a hundred tons, despatched in advance of Grenville's squadron, arrived at Roanoke with stores for their relief; and a few days later Sir Richard himself, who had been delayed by other cares, sailed in with three ships, only to find the settlement deserted. After a vain search for his countrymen Grenville, tenacious and resolute by nature, persuaded fifteen volunteers to remain as an outpost and evidence of occupation in Roanoke, furnishing them with supplies for two years, and then sailed for the Azores. This little company was all that remained to represent the energy and capital which had been expended. Something had, however, been accomplished; the coast had been explored for eighty miles to the south and one hundred and thirty to the north, and at least two new vegetables of infinite service to mankind were imported from Virginia to England, the potato and the tobacco plant, called by the inhabitants of Wingandacoa *ypponoc*, which Hariot had tried and found to his liking. The latter plant, which had been discovered in Cuba during Columbus's first voyage, was brought to Europe from Florida by the Portuguese in 1560. From Portugal Jean Nicot, whose name is immortalised in its generic appellation, sent the leaf to Catherine de Medici, and it soon became popular in France under the name of the Queen's Herb. It is not impossible that Raleigh therefore had first become acquainted with the use of tobacco in France. In any case tradition has connected his name with its introduction into England in two familiar anecdotes, one of which points to his having been among the first smokers in this country, while the second is evidence of the rapidity with which the habit became popular. It was told that his servant entering his study one day with a tankard of ale, and perceiving smoke issuing from his master's lips as he sat intent upon his books, endeavoured to extinguish the fire by flinging the contents of the tankard in his face, while he summoned the household with his cries of alarm. The other anecdote records a wager between Raleigh and his royal mistress, who refused to believe that he was able, as he professed to be, to ascertain the

exact weight of the smoke produced by a given quantity
of tobacco. Raleigh accordingly carefully weighed a
selected quantity of the leaf and smoked it in his silver
pipe, preserving all the ashes, which he then proceeded
also to weigh. He was thus able to prove, to the
Queen's satisfaction at any rate, that the weight of the
smoke was equivalent to the difference between the
weight of the ashes and that of the unconsumed tobacco.
The Queen duly paid her stake, observing at the same
time that she had heard of those who turned their gold
into smoke, but never before had seen the man who
could turn smoke into gold.

A practical state of war with Spain had been initiated
by the embargo laid on British shipping in that country
in 1585, and Raleigh had welcomed these developments
with enthusiasm. In 1586 he contributed a pinnace to
the first expedition undertaken by the Earl of Cumberland, which failed in an attempt on Bahia, but wrought
considerable havoc on the coast of Brazil. Again in
June he commissioned and despatched two vessels, the
Serpent and the *Mary Spark*, under his captains Jacob
Whiddon and John Eversham, to the Azores, where
they fought a running fight for thirty-two hours against
a Spanish fleet of twenty-four sail, and brought home
three valuable prizes. Grenville was also in action off
the Azores on his homeward voyage from Virginia, and his
squadron there secured a valuable prisoner in the person
of the great navigator Pedro Sarmiento de Gamboa,
who, some years before, had endeavoured to bar Drake's
anticipated return from the South Sea by blocking the
Straits of Magellan, while that elusive captain was
setting his course for the Cape of Good Hope to

complete his voyage round the world. It has generally
been assumed that Sarmiento was brought home by
Whiddon and Eversham, but there can be little doubt
that the credit should be given to Grenville, for the
time of his capture coincides with the arrival of the
latter at the Azores, and Sarmiento especially mentions
in his narrative that between Terceira and San Jorge
he encountered three English vessels, the exact number
of the Virginia squadron, while he makes no reference to
a heavy action such as was fought by the *Serpent* and the
Mary Spark.   Don Pedro complained of rough handling
received on board the *Capitana*, where it was assumed
that he and his men were concealing the knowledge
of treasure.   After their arrival at Plymouth, however,
he was conveyed to Windsor, and handed over to the
care of Raleigh, who conversed with him in Latin
and showed him every regard and attention.   By
Sir Walter's influence he obtained an audience of the
Queen, during which Elizabeth displayed the elegance
of her Latinity for two hours and a half.   Conversations
with the Lord-Treasurer and the Lord High Admiral
followed, and Sarmiento was apparently entrusted with
some official message for the King of Spain, which may
have been intended to serve as a basis for negotiation.
At any rate a passport was issued to him, with permission to proceed to Spain and return once more to
England should the object in view render it desirable.
Not only was no ransom demanded, but a present of a
thousand *escudos* was bestowed upon him, and he took
his leave after receiving great courtesy from all sorts
of people.   On his arrival in France, however, he was
once more made a prisoner, and detained there until

1589, after the Armada had sailed and had been destroyed, so that the message remained undelivered.

The failure of a first attempt in no way abated Raleigh's enthusiasm for the Virginia enterprise, and after the publication of Hariot's report on the country he had no difficulty in enlisting fresh volunteers for a settlement. A new expedition was despatched in the spring of 1587 under Captain John White, with whom were associated a board of twelve members, under the title of the Governor and assistants of the city of Raleigh in Virginia. On his arrival at Roanoke White could find no trace of the fifteen Englishmen whom Grenville had left behind. The whole band had fallen victims to the treachery of the Indians, as they afterwards learned from the faithful Manteo, who was now created a chief and became influential in restoring friendly relations. This little unrecorded tragedy, far away and long ago, was perhaps even at the time too remote to stir profoundly the imagination of their countrymen at home, whose minds were preoccupied with graver issues. And yet the massacre of those fifteen pioneers, the protomartyrs of Imperial expansion, cut off from hope on the edge of the great unexplored continent, has the peculiar pathos, after all this lapse of years, which ever belongs to the first to fall in a great cause, greater than themselves suspected. How many a time the round world over has the tale been told again ; how many a despairing cry of the forsaken and forgotten has gone out on the west wind, since they fought their last fight on those shores, where teeming millions now load the freight ships of the nations with the harvest of prosperity and peace ! Already the

wild growth of tropical vegetation had invaded the
ruins of the fort which sheltered the dwellings of the
first colonists, and the zeal of the new settlers was
damped by a profound sense of discouragement.   Dissensions arose among them, and when White was persuaded
against his better judgment to return to England for
further supplies, things went from bad to worse.   The
impending struggle with Spain for a time rendered all
undertakings in distant seas impossible, and no shipping
was allowed to leave England without a special authorisation from the Council.   Only after the defeat of the
Armada was Raleigh able to obtain permission for three
ships to sail to the Indies, and he contracted with their
owners for the transport of stores and passengers to
Virginia.   The contracts, however, were not carried
out, and the voyage only ended in disaster.   Still he
never relaxed his efforts nor abandoned faith in the
destiny of his nursling.   Five expeditions to Virginia
were equipped by him between 1587 and 1602.   With
his attainder his interests passed to the Crown, but even
from his prison he still devoted to colonial enterprises
what he could save from the wreck of his estate.   " I
shall yet live to see it an English nation," he wrote to
Cecil just before the great eclipse of his fortunes ; and
he did live to see his vast dream realised in part, by the
permanent establishment of his countrymen in Virginia.

Baffled again and again in his early endeavours, cut
off at last, in the full vigour of his manhood and his
powers, from active co-operation with the scheme, he
clung with the tenacity of genius to the great design
which has since become the inheritance of his countrymen and received a development beyond his own most

sanguine anticipations. Whatever judgment may be
passed upon the achievements of this remarkable man,
whose errors like his gifts were great, he was at any
rate the first who dared to conceive the expansion
of England, and he adhered with a passionate faith to
the conviction that the unpeopled shores of earth were
the inevitable inheritance of his own hardy race. To
him his countrymen, accepting their high mission and
proud of their world-wide dominion, must ever grate-
fully look back as the pioneer and prophet of empire.
To him the great kindred people, blood of his own
blood, whose genius of energy has quickened the vast
northern continent from sea to sea, must ever pay due
honour as the first who opened to civilising influences
the threshold of their limitless domain.

CHAPTER V

THE Queen and her far-seeing statesmen had long
realised that war with Spain must be the inevitable outcome of the growing rivalry between the two countries,
which typically represented the opposing forces of
progress and reaction. The genius of Elizabeth for
temporising had secured for her people a long period of
peace in which to develop their material resources, but
this end once gained, she sanctioned a policy which
could hardly fail to end in war. While the people
of England were genuinely convinced that the real
grounds of quarrel with Spain were religious, and that
Philip was the chosen instrument of the Catholic League
for reimposing on this country the fetters of a spiritual
domination which they had endured so much to shake
off, there were in reality other and more substantial
grounds of dispute, clear enough to the enlightened
spirits of the age, working inevitably towards a crisis.
The exclusive mercantile monopolies enforced by Spain
in the new regions thrown open to human enterprise
throughout a century of discovery, had naturally led

to infringements which were sternly repressed. Such repression provoked reprisals, which men, convinced of their title to a share in the benefits of an extended horizon, upheld as legitimate and just. The children of the Reformation could scarcely be expected to accept without protest a theory of possession which, though it undoubtedly rested in part on priority of discovery, was extended into the illimitable areas of an unknown world on the mere authority of a bull issued by a Spanish pope. Moreover, the dread of seeing this exclusive mercantile system applied to the neighbouring Dutch ports was ever present to men whose living was gained upon the sea, and while the rebellious subjects of Philip in the Low Countries received constant and avowed encouragement from the Queen and her subjects, English harbours were ever open to shelter and support the Dutch privateers, whose presence in the Narrow Seas was so galling to Spanish commerce. As a growing sea-power the English people were also violently opposed to the absorption of Portugal by Spain, and the claims of the disinherited Don Antonio, who had taken refuge in England, were supported without regard to his religion. Drake's exploits on the Spanish Main and in the Caribbean Sea, officially disavowed but privately encouraged, were followed by his astounding achievements in the Pacific, where he broke the lock of the secret treasure-house, to circumnavigate the globe with an empire's ransom in his hold. The fevered protests of Philip's envoy, put off with evasive subterfuge so long as want of information could be pleaded, were at length met by open defiance, when the Queen publicly bestowed the coveted honour of knighthood on the successful privateer.

But provocation was not all on one side.   The encouragement afforded by Philip to the rebels in Ireland
struck a blow near home in England's most vulnerable
spot.   He had plotted against the throne and even, her
subjects were earnestly convinced, against the life of the
Queen.   The fear that Spain would obtain control of the
Channel by fortifying the harbours of the Netherlands
was immediate and justified, and when Elizabeth entered
into an alliance with the States, Philip retaliated by
laying an embargo on British shipping in Spain.   With
this arbitrary action in May, 1585, a practical state of
war began.   Drake, as the Queen's Vice-Admiral, carried
it into the enemy's camp, and the Spanish arsenals
advanced their preparations for the invasion of England.
Raleigh threw themself into the struggle with his usual
enthusiasm and, in the following year, two of his ships
fought the brilliant action at the Azores.   The execution
of the Queen of Scots, whose adherents had unconsciously played into Philip's hands, precipitated the
crisis.   There was, however, no lack of warning.   The
restless activity prevailing in Spanish ports, the accumulation of material, and the movements of the victualling
ships were duly reported, and at last, after many misgivings and hesitations, the Queen determined to let her
sea-dogs loose.   In April, 1587, Drake sailed with a free
band in command of a fleet of some thirty sail, which
included four ships of the royal navy.   On the 19th he
entered the road of Cadiz with characteristic daring, and
for thirty-six hours burned, sank, and plundered the
shipping massed in a strongly fortified haven, crowded
with victuallers and men-of-war equipping for the
projected invasion of England.   He followed up this

bold stroke by the destruction of the fishing craft in all the harbours between Cadiz and St. Vincent, thus ruining the tunny industry, upon which the provisioning of the fleet largely depended. The immediate result of this brilliant exploit was to postpone the sailing of the Armada for a year, and to afford England ample time to complete her preparations for defence. But it had another indirect result, no less important at a moment of crisis. It stirred the patriotism of Drake's fellow-countrymen to a pitch of enthusiasm, and by revealing the vulnerability of the enemy, dispelled to a great extent the prevailing myth of Spain's overwhelming power.

The Council had caused full information of the Spanish preparations to be circulated, and the nation, taken into confidence, with one accord responded to the call. A scheme of defence was drawn up by a committee on which the most experienced soldiers and administrators were invited to serve. Raleigh took a leading part in the deliberations of this Council of War, and with him were associated Lord Grey (who at such a moment thought well to forget old differences in Ireland), Sir Thomas Leighton, Sir John Norris, Sir Richard Grenville, Sir Richard Bingham (whose acquaintance with Raleigh also dated from the siege of Smerwick), Sir Roger Williams, and Ralph Lane of Virginia. The committee directed their attention to the various places where the Spaniards might attempt a landing, either by disembarking troops from the fleet which was to enter the channel from the south-west, or with the forces collected under the Duke of Parma in the Netherlands. They recommended that Plymouth should be strengthened by defensive works and garrisoned by the levies

of Cornwall and Devon. Portland was to be fortified
and held by a garrison drawn from Wiltshire and
Dorset. Milford Haven, the Isle of Wight, the Downs,
Margate, and the Thames were also regarded as
practicable landing-places for the enemy ; and suitable
garrisons, to be drawn from the neighbouring counties,
were indicated for all these vulnerable points. A similar
scheme of defence was extended to the eastern coast.
Certain broad rules for the disposition and concentration
of troops were laid down, while the course of action to
be pursued in the event of a landing was . left to the
discretion of the general in command. A special force
was to be provided for the defence of the Queen's
person. Another army was to watch the northern
border in case the enemy should effect a landing in
Scotland. The general scope of the plan was to enable
a force of twenty thousand men to concentrate rapidly
at the spot selected by the enemy, and to impede his
advance by laying the surrounding country waste.

Raleigh himself was actively concerned with raising
the levies of Cornwall and Devon, and a State-paper
from his hand addressed to the Lord-Treasurer points
out how the complements of horse and foot in those
two counties should be selected. His own headquarters
were at Portland Castle, for the equipment of which he
made special provision. While, however, his energies
were devoted in the first place to the organisation of
military measures for resisting invasion, he was far
from advocating reliance on such measures alone, and
his views are expressed in a memorable passage in his
History of the World, where he was perhaps the earliest
to place on record the opinion that the first line of

defence for England must ever be at sea. Thanks to
the energetic administration of the navy by Hawkins,
and the training which both captains and crews had
received in privateering enterprises, the maritime resources of the kingdom could be relied upon, and the
Queen's ships no less than those of private adventurers
were in a high state of efficiency. Lord Howard of
Effingham, whom the Queen had placed in supreme
command at sea, disposed of some sixty-six sail in the
west, where Drake was watching the highway south;
while Lord Henry Seymour, who commanded the eastern
squadron of thirty-three ships, had orders to blockade
the coast of Flanders, intercept any flotilla attempting
to convey Parma's troops from Dunkirk, and keep communications open with the Commander-in-chief. Lord
Howard himself hoisted his flag in the *Ark Raleigh*,
which had been built for Sir Walter by Richard
Chapman, a Deptford shipwright, to take part in the
expedition in which Sir Humphrey Gilbert lost his life.
The ship was acquired for the royal navy for £5000;
the money was never actually paid, but a similar sum
was struck off a debt to the Crown which he incurred
in fitting out an expedition in 1592. The purchase was
much criticised at the time, and was made an excuse for
attacking his administration of the navy by the enemies
of John Hawkins, who insinuated that the ship had been
built out of timber from the Queen's yard. Howard,
however, strongly approved of the purchase, and wrote
to Burghley: "I pray you tell Her Majesty from me
that the money was well given for the *Ark Raleigh*, for
I think her the odd ship in the world for all conditions;
and truly I think there can no great ship make me

change and go out of her.   We can see no sail, great or
small, but how far soever they be off we fetch them and
speak with them."   Another ship of Raleigh's, the
Roebuck, under Whiddon, whose action in the Azores
has already been mentioned, took an active part in the
fighting, and assisted Drake in the *Revenge* to capture
Don Pedro de Valdez and the huge *Rosario*.   It was also
one of his scouts, as appears from a letter of the Admiral,
who brought in news of the Armada off Ushant.

During the winter months there was little prospect
that the great Armada would attempt the boisterous
seas, and Raleigh took advantage of this lull before the
storm to pay a visit to Ireland, where he was appointed
Mayor of Youghal for the year 1588.   A rough survey
of the vast estate which had been assigned to him was
now completed, and his energetic nature was eager to
set to work on what promised to be an absorbing and
remunerative task.   Among the properties which had
fallen to his share was the Dominican monastery at
Youghal.   The old buildings were destroyed in 1587, in
obedience to the policy of the day, which contemplated
the forcible suppression of the Catholic religion in
Ireland.   How far he was responsible for this destruction
is uncertain.   In the same year the castle and manor of
Lismore, the residence of the bishops of that see, was
transferred to him for an annual rent, with the consent
of the Dean and Chapter.   Here he took up his residence
and began to work out a scheme for the development of
the estate.   But his stay was of brief duration, for he
was recalled to England by the news that the Duke
of Medina Sidonia was preparing for sea.

The plan of defence for the English coast had by

now been put into practical execution, and, in addition to
the levies mustered in the southern and eastern counties,
a force of twenty-two thousand foot and two thousand
cavalry, under the Earl of Leicester, with Essex as master
of the horse, was in camp at Tilbury, where the Queen
inspected them and kept up their spirits by assisting at
tiltings and tourneys. A second army of twenty-eight
thousand men under the Earl of Hunsdon was entrusted
with the special care of Her Majesty's person. The
eastern and western squadrons, manned by upwards of
eleven thousand men (mostly trained mariners), were at
their posts of observation. Throughout the length and
breadth of the country her sons, with one mind and
one will, had proved themselves worthy of this great
occasion; and confident in the strength of their patriotic
ardour and in the justice of their cause, they calmly
awaited the inevitable onslaught of the overwhelming
armament which Spain and the Catholic league had
equipped for their destruction. Seldom since the world
began had opposing nations met in such a memorable
contest, and never was a graver issue in the balance.
On the one side were all the forces of the Old World,
trained in the iron discipline of passive obedience, and
blessed by the hand that claimed to hold the keys of
death and hell. On the other was all the promise of the
New World; the strong individuality of men who had
passed through the ordeal of the Reformation to win
that freedom of conscience and liberty of judgment
from which now they would only part with their lives.
Common to both was the deep and earnest conviction
that the God of battles was on their side.

The Armada sailed on the 24th of May amid scenes

of indescribable enthusiasm. If by the death of the
Marquis Santa Cruz the chief command had devolved
upon less competent hands, the seven squadrons were
led by the most experienced of those great captains
which the maritime expansion of the vast Spanish
empire had produced, and, in addition to some eight
thousand sailors and two thousand oarsmen, she carried
a fighting force of nearly twenty thousand soldiers of
that formidable Spanish infantry whose reputation
stood second to none in the world.   In the Netherlands
thirty thousand more, under the orders of the Duke of
Parma, awaited the propitious moment to cross the
channel in a flotilla of transports, collected there for
their conveyance.   The Duke of Guise had a further
army in readiness on the coast of Normandy, to be
transhipped to England in Spanish bottoms.   The
voyage began inauspiciously.   Off Cape Finistere a
violent storm sank many of the smaller craft, and dispersed the great fleet, which was compelled to put
back and refit at the Groyne.   Exaggerated reports
of disaster reached England ; it was assumed that the
expedition would be indefinitely delayed, and Elizabeth,
whose characteristic economy manifested itself even
in this supreme moment of national crisis, ordered
the Lord High Admiral to place four of his largest
vessels out of commission.   This instruction, however,
Howard, to his eternal credit, took the risk of disobeying,
and on the 12th of July the Armada once more put
to sea.   A week later, while his men were enjoying a
short spell of leave on shore, news reached the Admiral,
during the famous game of bowls on Plymouth Hoe,
that the enemy was entering the Channel.

The number of ships of which the Armada was composed has been variously estimated. The fleet which assembled in Corunna was very far from realising the grandiose project conceived by Santa Cruz. According to Spanish authorities it consisted of one hundred and thirty ships in all, not a few of which were mere transports unfitted to take any active part in an engagement at sea. Of the fighting ships, moreover, some were left behind at Corunna, and others were disabled in the storm off Finistère. It seems probable, therefore, that the total force which entered the Channel did not exceed one hundred and twenty sail. The enemy's battle-ships were heavier in tonnage, but there is ground for believing that the English were better armed, and the proportion of sailors to soldiers among the latter was much greater. The Spaniards, still under the influence of old traditions, trusted to sheer weight in hand-to-hand fighting; the English, or rather the moving spirits among them, rested their hopes on skilful manœuvring and loose action. To the former the cannon appeared an ignoble weapon, only to be used at sea to arrest and disable a hostile vessel; their real object was always to grapple and board. The English, on the other hand, had given great attention to the manufacture of ordnance and training in artillery fire, and it is not the least merit of the Lord High Admiral that he perceived the advantage of the new tactics which old-fashioned sailors had not yet fully realised. In a passage in the *History of the World*, where he records the lesson of this experience, Raleigh gives the Lord High Admiral all the credit which his firmness and judgment deserved. The lesson may, perhaps, have guided his own conduct in the fight

at Cadiz, where he appears to have deprecated close
action so long as the artillery duel continued, though
he was the first to grapple and board when the crucial
moment came.

Raleigh himself was certainly not present at the first
engagement on the 21st of July.   As, however, the
great fleet advanced through a succession of skirmishes
farther into the Channel and appeared off Portland,
where it now became clear they could not attempt a
landing, he left his post of observation, and, with a
company of gentlemen, put out in a volunteer squadron
to swell the numbers of the Lord Admiral.[1]

As the stately pageant of battle rolled eastward,
every successive day revealed more clearly the advantage
of the tactics adopted by the Admiral, whose smaller
and more manageable vessels were ever in motion, advancing to discharge their broadsides and then retiring

[1] Some doubts have been expressed as to whether Raleigh did
actually take part in the repulse of the Armada. It may therefore
be well to quote the authorities upon which this statement rests.
Van Meteran, one of the earliest and fullest chroniclers of the war,
in his history of the Low Countries, quoted by Hakluyt, mentions the volunteers from Portland, and specifies Sir Walter Raleigh
among the foremost of those whose contingents increased the
English fleet to 100 sail.   Camden also describes the volunteer
squadron, and mentions Raleigh with the noblemen whose ships
joined the flag, though he does not definitely refer to Portland.
The writer of a despatch sent to Mendoza, Spanish ambassador
in France at this time, also corroborates the statement in a passage
in which he reports that the Earl of Oxford went to sea and
served the Queen in this engagement, "as did Robert Cecil,
Lord Dudley, and Sir Walter Raleigh, a gentleman of the Queen's
privy chamber, and in his company a great number of young
gentlemen, among whom were William Cecil, Edmund Darcy, and
Arthur Gorges."   Oldys, moreover, states in his biography that
he had looked through a foreign history in the copy which had
once belonged to Sir Walter, where many passages relating to himself were corrected in his own handwriting, but the affirmation
that he had joined the fleet had been allowed to stand uncor-
rected.

out of range. When the wind fell slack they were
easily towed in and out of action by their long-boats,
while the unhandy galleons lay helpless on the summer
calms. The flagship of the Andalusian squadron, with
Pedro Valdez on board, had struck to Drake in the first
day's engagement, and a second great ship had been
fired and burned to the water-line. Off Portland a
Venetian and several transports were captured. On the
25th, off the Isle of Wight, Richard Hawkins secured a
Portuguese galleon, which had fallen astern, and the
San Martine, Medina's flagship, was in imminent danger
of capture, when Recalde and Mexia came to the rescue.
Shortness of ammunition alone prevented the English
from pushing their advantage home. The new tactics
invoked an unprecedented consumption of powder and
shot, for which the majority of the captains had made
no adequate provision. In spite of these losses, however,
there was no sensible weakening of the mighty armament, which took up a well-chosen position under the
guns of Calais on the 27th. But the English had gained
confidence from the experience of five days' fighting,
and the Count of Nassau's fleet was investing the harbours, where Parma's transports, hastily put together
for the emergency, lay leaky from long inaction. Before
he had had time to concert a plan of action with the
generalissimo, the fire-ships, steered by two brave
Devonians, Prowse and Young of Bideford, into the
heart of the enemy's anchorage, scared the Armada from
its fancied security, and drove the great ships in confusion out to sea. Then, ere they could rally, the English
adroitly secured the weather gage and barred the way
to Calais road, where they were ordered to reform. So

ensued, on the 29th of July, the memorable battle of
Gravelines, continuing from nine in the morning till six
in the evening, during which, according to Howard's
report, three Spanish galleons were sunk and four or
five driven ashore. The rest, no longer a fleet but
a confused rout of half-disabled shipping, bore away
to the north-east as evening fell, to encounter the
violent gales which wrecked many more on the Scottish
and Irish coasts, and completed the disaster for which
the furious battery of the British guns had prepared
them. The story of those memorable days is aptly
summed up by Raleigh himself :—

It was manifested to all nations, how the navy, which
they had termed invincible, consisting of a hundred and
forty sail, was by thirty of the Queen's ships of war and a
few merchantmen beaten and shuffled together, even from
the Lizard Point in Cornwall to Portland, when they shame-
fully left Don Pedro de Valdez with his mighty ship ; from
Portland to Calais, where they lost Hugo de Moncada, with
the galleys of which he was Captain; and from Calais,
driven with squibs from their anchors, were chased out of
the sight of England round about Scotland and Ireland ;
where, for the sympathy of their barbarous religion, hoping
to find succour and assistance, a great part of them were
crushed against the rocks ; and those other who landed
(being very many in number) were notwithstanding broken,
slain, and taken, and so sent from village to village, coupled
in halters to be shipped to England ; where Her Majesty, of
her princely and invincible disposition, disdaining to put
them to death, and scorning either to retain or entertain
them, they were all sent back again to their own country,
to witness and recount the worthy achievements of their
invincible navy.

Various explanations have been put forward to
account for the miserable failure of an enterprise which

at the time appeared so formidable. Too little credit has, however, been given to the foresight and skill of the English mariners, who were in advance of their contemporaries in adapting the lines of their ships, and in modifying their tactics at sea, so as to give full advantage and play to the ordnance which they had perfected as a weapon of offence, and which enabled them with comparative immunity to harrass, disorganise, and finally to disable an enemy which clung to the old traditions of naval warfare. Raleigh, in his *Discourse of the Invention of Shipping*, recognised the preponderating advantage which his countrymen possessed, and might have retained by a monopoly of their iron guns, and laments the issue of licenses for the export of English ordnance abroad.

After the defeat of the Armada the privateers redoubled their activity; and Raleigh, involved on several occasions in suits brought before the Admiralty Courts for unlawful seizures, was bold enough to complain of the "great charge" which the duty of reprisals entailed on Her Majesty's subjects. The charge was, we know, not unfrequently balanced by very ample material compensations. In the following year an expedition was fitted out under the joint command of Drake and Norris, with six of the Queen's ships and twelve volunteers, to attempt the restoration of Don Antonio to the throne of Portugal. Raleigh joined the expedition in a ship of his own, without any definite commission or command. There are some grounds for assuming that he was anxious at this time to absent himself from Court. It is possible that the rapid advancement of Essex in royal favour, which became the more noticeable after the

death of Leicester in 1588, had already begun to make
his position less assured, and before that year was over
their antagonism had led to a challenge from Essex,
which only the intervention of the Council prevented
from taking effect. The expedition to Portugal was a
failure so far as its ostensible object was concerned,
though Norris was able to march six days through the
country to Lisbon, where he was compelled to re-embark
his men, decimated by some sudden epidemic of sickness.
Raleigh, however, maintains, in his *History of the World*,
that had Norris been in command of a royal army,
and not a mere company of adventurers, he would have
succeeded in driving the Spaniards out of Portugal; and
he adopts the sound conclusion that " it is impossible
for any maritime country, not having its coasts admirably
fortified, to defend itself against a powerful enemy that
is master of the sea." A strange fatality now once more
brought him into conflict with Essex, who had stolen
away from the Court and joined the expedition without
the Queen's knowledge, in company with his old friend
Sir Roger Williams, who had a share in the adventure.
On the voyage homeward the fleet made a successful
capture of sixty Hanseatic vessels bound for Spain with
provisions and munitions of war. One of the prizes
which fell to Raleigh was manned by men lent him for
the purpose by Roger Williams, who then claimed the
ships as his by right of salvage. This led to a dispute,
which was ultimately settled by the Privy Council in
Raleigh's favour, but the claim put forward by a partisan of Essex no doubt served to embitter the feeling
between the rival favourites. After his return from
Lisbon, Raleigh went to Ireland. The gossip of the day

reported that Essex had succeeded in driving him from
the Court, and such a rumour seems to have reached his
ears, for he hastened to repudiate it in a letter to his
cousin Sir George Carew.   Whether or not it be true
that the support given by Essex to the pretensions of
Williams had led to a rupture which imperilled his
influence with the Queen, there is evidence from an
unexpected quarter that some misunderstanding with
his royal mistress actually did take place about this
time.   ·

A grant of some three thousand acres from the
confiscated lands in Cork had been bestowed upon
Edmund Spenser as the reward of his services under
Lord Grey de Wilton.   He had settled in the castle
of Kilcolman, amid scenery of surpassing beauty congenial to his appreciative nature, at no great distance
from Raleigh's Blackwater property.   The acquaintance
between the two poets dated from the bivouac under
the walls of Smerwick, and time had ripened their
mutual regard.   At the beginning of the year Spenser
had sent Raleigh for perusal a portion of his *Faery Queen*,
accompanied by the letter, which is now commonly
printed as a preface to the poem, explaining its scope
and intention.   Raleigh now paid a visit to Kilcolman,
and urged Spenser to return with him to England, to
be presented to the Queen.   He persuaded him to
publish immediately the first three cantos of the *Faery
Queen*, and expressed his appreciation of their author's
genius in a sonnet which has been deservedly inscribed
on the roll of English classics.   This memorable visit
has been immortalised in the exquisite pastoral allegory
which Spenser dedicated, under the title of *Colin Clout's*

come home again, to his patron and friend.   Here at
Kilcolman, in the peace of the well-watered woodland
country, it was that the Shepherd of the Ocean from
the Main-deep sea, borrowed the poet's rustic pipe,
"himself as skilful in that art as any," and here it seems

> His song was all a lamentable lay
>   Of great unkindness and of usage hard
> Of Cynthia the Lady of the Sea,
>   Which from her faultless presence him debarred.

The Queen's passing displeasure seems, however, to
have been of short duration, for it was not long before
the two poets set out together for the Court, and sailing
past Lundy landed at St. Michael's Mount.   In the
following year the three cantos of the *Faery Queen* were
given to the world, and their author was assigned a
pension of £50 a year, in spite of the opposition
of the Lord-Treasurer, whose opinion of the value of
literature is summed up in his characteristic protest,
"All this for a song!"   In Raleigh's restless, strenuous
life of activity and ambition, spent, until the shadow
of the Tower closed round him, in the distracting
atmosphere of Court intrigue, amid the noise of battle,
or the uncertainties of travel and adventure, this visit
to a kindred spirit in the green solitudes of Kilcolman
stands out in bright relief, suggestive of many pleasant
associations.   It is perhaps not amiss that the only
record of their intercourse which has come down to us
should be framed in the language of poetry.

CHAPTER VI

IF Raleigh's Irish undertaking ended in failure it was
not from any want of energy on his part, although
circumstances and the multifarious nature of his interests
and occupations precluded his personal superintendence.
For the Irish themselves he had little sympathy, and the
conditions of his tenure compelled him to ignore their
very existence. He had, it is true, in earlier days during
the rebellion, suggested the expediency of attempting
to win over some of the lesser Irish chieftains, who had
been drawn to the Desmond faction rather by fear
than sympathy. The proposal was, however, purely
opportunist and not inspired by any confidence in the
character or intentions of these representative men. If
Lord Grey, under whom he first served, had declared
himself in favour of a Mahometan conquest of Ireland,
Raleigh was equally consistent in advocating, and
perhaps in unduly urging the policy of *Thorough*. It
is difficult to-day to see through the eyes of three
hundred years ago. No kindlier soul, no more sensitive

spirit than the poet Spenser was ever connected with
the thankless task of Irish administration, and yet he
could see no hope for better things but in the depopula-
tion of the country.   Burghley indeed had other views.
He opposed the distribution of the forfeited lands, and
would perhaps have ultimately contemplated the administration of their own local affairs by the Irish.   But
it was the stern repressive policy of Gilbert and Carew,
which secured the Queen's approval and Raleigh's un-
questioning commendation.   To Ormonde, who, himself
an Irishman, was less uncompromising, save when
dealing with the hereditary foes of his race, Raleigh was
throughout strongly opposed.   In two years of his rule in
Munster traitors had, he said, multiplied by a thousand,
and his employment only intensified the bitterness of
rebellion, since a Geraldine would rather die a thousand
deaths than be subdued by a Butler.   Not less vigorous
in later days was his opposition to the policy of Essex,
who, with no previous experience of Irish government,
inaugurated his assumption of office with a promise of
amnesty and restitution.   A man of Raleigh's temperament could not understand a policy which alternated a
merciless use of the curb with a reckless abandonment of
the reins.   Rightly or wrongly he was firmly consistent
to the view which from the first he had deliberately
formed, and like the majority of his contemporaries he
admitted no extenuating plea for rebellion.

Holding these views it is perhaps not surprising,
however deplorable such an opinion may seem to us
to-day, that he was by no means troubled in his
conscience as to the means by which rebels might
legitimately be removed.   The ceaseless harassing

guerilla war, maintained against the Government and
the new settlers, had hardened men's hearts to a pitch
of ferocity, which we may understand without excusing;
and the continual menace of foreign invasion, facilitated
by the internal enemies of the realm in Ireland, had
extinguished their natural scruples as to methods of
repression. It was not merely that a price was set on
the heads of rebels openly proclaimed : in the sixteenth
century no man would have questioned the expediency
of such procedure ; but the practice of secret assassina-
tion had come to be condoned and countenanced. Even
the pious Earl of Sussex is convicted, by a damning
letter to the Queen, of having suborned a messenger
from Shan O'Neill to kill his master for a reward ; and
the self-confessed perpetrator of a second attempt to
remove him by poison escaped without punishment
under the same administration. On this subject some
correspondence passed between Raleigh and Sir Robert
Cecil, who avowed an antipathy to the use of poison,
but otherwise was not much troubled with scruples.
Raleigh's letter, in reply, it would seem, to one asking for
his advice, has been preserved. No date is affixed, but
it has generally been assigned to the autumn of 1598.
The wording and reference are not clear, but its meaning
cannot be misinterpreted or explained away. There are
many spots in the sun of his great reputation, and if by
his enemies this letter has often been quoted in malice,
his admirers can find nothing to urge in extenuation,
save that such views were common to many of his
contemporaries. It can only be quoted as it stands.

Sir—It can be no disgrace if it were known that the
killing of a rebel were practised ; for you see that the lives

of anointed Princes are daily sought, and we have always in
Ireland given head-money for the killing of rebels, who are
evermore proclaimed at a price.   So was the Earl of Desmond,
and so have all rebels been practised against.   Notwithstanding, I have written this enclosed to Stafford, who only
recommended that knave to me upon his credit.   But, for
yourself, you are not to be touched in the matter.   And for
me I am more sorry for being deceived than for being
declared in the practice.—Your Lordship's ever to do you
service,   W. RALEIGH.

He hath nothing under my hand but a passport.

One of the conditions of the vast grants made to the
undertakers in Ireland was that the country should
be re-peopled with well-affected Englishmen.   Raleigh
sought in Somerset, Devon, and Cornwall for such
colonists, whom he established with their wives and
children in Cork, Waterford, and Tipperary.   Discover-
ing that the climate of the southern portion of the island
was favourable to the growth of tobacco, he established
a plantation in his garden at Youghal.   He introduced
the potato, with other plants and trees whose cultivation
was new to Ireland.   He also brought over miners from
Cornwall to prospect.   But the principal industry which
he endeavoured to foster was the utilisation of the ample
timber which Irish forests produced.   This scheme commended itself on political, no less than on economical
grounds, for the dense forest districts had become hiding-
places for the hunted population, and were a source of
permanent danger in time of rebellion.   An opening for
a profitable trade was found in the manufacture of
barrel-boards, pipe-staves, and hogsheads for the continental wine-trade, and he employed one hundred and
fifty skilled labourers and workmen in their manufacture.

The Privy Council, however, soon interfered with this promising industry, and prohibited the exportation of pipe-staves. It was not until 1593 that a conditional license was obtained for export to England, with a proviso that so much timber only should be felled as could conveniently be spared, that none should be cut on lands escheated to the Queen, and that the Lord High Admiral should have a right of pre-emption for the public service. It is therefore a palpable absurdity to endeavour to make Raleigh responsible, as a recent able but partisan writer has done, for the disafforesting of the whole island.

The survivors of the original Irish population had retired into the hills, and it was not long before their presence on the borders of his estate became a menace to the immigrants, whom they regarded as their natural enemies and supplanters. Unfortunately also for Raleigh's schemes, the first years of investment and organisation had not yet been succeeded by a period of realisation when he fell into disgrace. The jealousy and dislike which Sir Walter had long aroused among the majority of his contemporaries were then revealed in all their intensity. It would appear that Sir W. Fitzwilliam, who was Lord-Deputy in 1592, had also personal grounds for making the hand of authority lie heavily on the fallen favourite. In July of that year Raleigh wrote from the Tower to Lord Robert Cecil, protesting against the treatment which his tenants had received. For a debt of fifty marks, which was paid upon application, and that moreover the first rent paid to the Crown by any undertaker, the Lord-Deputy had substituted a claim for £400, and had sent an

order to the Sheriff to distrain upon the tenants' cattle
if the money were not paid the same day.   Five
hundred kine were accordingly seized by the Sheriff
from these unfortunate people, who had but a cow
or two apiece to support their wives and families
in a strange country, where they had only recently
arrived.   Nor was this the only complaint he had to
prefer.   In this and in a subsequent letter he prophecies
a recrudescence of rebellion if the administration be not
seriously taken in hand, and protests against the levity
and indifference with which his warnings were received
at Court.   It was indeed not long before his predictions
were verified.   Meanwhile he realised that the consequences of his disgrace were making themselves felt
across the sea; and his difficulties were not with the
central authorities alone.   He appears to have fallen into
the hands of an unsatisfactory agent, one Henry Pine,
whose illegal appropriations he invited the Privy Council
to restrain.   The Council registers, moreover, show that
he was involved in constant disputes with his English
lessees.   In the end he became discouraged by the
difficulties which the reclaiming of this "lost land"
presented to an absentee, and was glad to sell the
whole of his Irish property, with the exception of one
old castle and demesne, which remained in the occupation of the famous centenarian Countess of Desmond, to
Richard Boyle, afterwards Earl of Cork, under whose
personal management the estate soon began to prosper.
Nor was the experiment of his friend Spenser destined
to be more fortunate.   The historic house at Kilcolman
was burned to the ground and the estate devastated by
the rebels in Tyrone's rising.   One of his children

perished in the fire, and it was this calamity which
finally broke the poet's heart and hastened his untimely
death.

If some temporary cloud had in the year 1589
threatened the fair prospects of Raleigh's position at
Court, the malignant influence was of short duration,
and after his return to London with Spenser he at once
recovered his ascendency. The restoration to favour
was no doubt accelerated by the disgrace of Essex, who
in 1590 incurred the Queen's deep displeasure by his
secret marriage with Sidney's widow, Frances Walsingham, which she stigmatised as a misalliance. There
was never room at once for both these ardent spirits
at the Queen's right hand, and it was inevitable that as
one advanced the other should decline. It was at this
period that Raleigh took up so warmly the defence of
Udall, and a more congenial occupation was the equipment of a new expedition to intercept the Spanish Plate-
Fleet at the Azores, on its return from the Main. Once
again, however, his ambition to distinguish himself
as a sailor was thwarted, and his appointment as Vice-
Admiral cancelled. His presence at Court could not be
dispensed with. The command of the squadron was
entrusted to Lord Thomas Howard, for Drake was at
present also out of favour, the victim of jealous intrigues,
and Raleigh's place was taken by his cousin, the
immortal Sir Richard Grenville, who sailed in the
Revenge. On this occasion the Spaniards had timely
news of the presence of the Queen's ships at the Azores,
and a powerful fleet of fifty sail, despatched to cover the
movements of the Plate ships, surprised Lord Thomas
in the islands. Of the six battleships and six victuallers

which composed his little squadron, eleven cut their cables or weighed anchor in haste and got clear away. Grenville, however, who refused to believe that the approaching fleet was any other than the Indian *flota*, weighed at leisure, or was delayed in re-embarking the numerous sick, who had been put ashore from the "pestered and rummaging ships," when the hostile fleet bore down on them.

Lord Thomas had got the wind of the Spaniards and was secure from attack; but Grenville, finding the Spaniards on his weather side, greatly determined to maintain the honour of Her Majesty's ship and pass through the enemy's two squadrons in their despite. The well-nigh incredible story of the action which ensued is told by Sir Walter in his report of the *Truth of the Fight about the Isles of the Azores*, published in the year 1591, which thus constitutes his first appearance before the public as a writer of prose. The simple beauty of the narrative in which he records the heroic death of his kinsman, who though "of great means, was also of unquiet mind and greatly addicted to war," would alone have sufficed to make the name of its author memorable, and it is not its least merit to have directly inspired one of the noblest ballads in the English language.

Grenville's conduct, which resulted in the loss of one of the Queen's ships, the first actually taken in war by the Spaniards, had been severely criticised; and dearly bought as it was, the action was credited in Spain as a victory to Alonzo de Bazan. Monson, who writes from the point of view of the professional sailor, charges Grenville with a breach of the discipline of war. Richard

H

Hawkins, who acquits him of deliberate disobedience to orders, nevertheless observes that "the best valour is to obey and follow the head, seem that good or bad which is commanded." The general opinion in England was that expressed by Monson, and it was to defend his cousin from these criticisms that Raleigh wrote the memorable pamphlet, which at the same time furnished him with an opportunity for justifying in public the war policy with which he was identified. He speaks with entire approval of Lord Thomas Howard's decision to refuse action with his little squadron. Undoubtedly he was right in making the safety of the Queen's ships his first care. But Sir Richard Grenville,—who will venture to assert that he was not right also, if "out of the greatness of his heart he could not be persuaded"?

Upon the glowing text of this immortal action Raleigh elected to preach his undying hate of priest-craft and of Spain, compared with whose yoke "the obedience even of the Turk is easy and a liberty."

For matter of religion [he wrote] it would require a particular volume to set down how irreligiously they cover their greedy and ambitious practices with the veil of piety; for, sure am I, there is no kingdom or commonwealth in all Europe, but if reformed, they invade it for religion's sake; if it be, as they term, catholic, they pretend title; as if the kings of Castile were the natural heirs of all the world; and so, between both, no kingdom is unsought. Where they dare not with their own forces invade, they basely entertain the traitors and vagabonds of all nations; seeking by those and their renegade Jesuits to win parts; and have by that means ruined many noble houses and others in this land, and have extinguished both their lives and families. Let not therefore any Englishman, of what religion soever, have other opinion of the Spaniard, but that those whom he seeketh to win in our nation he esteemeth base and traitorous, unworthy persons, or inconstant fools ; and that he useth his pretence of religion for no other purpose, but to bewitch us from the obedience of our natural prince ; thereby hoping in time to bring us to slavery and subjection.

And yet the writer of this uncompromising philippic was one day to be tried for conspiring with Spain "to alter religion and bring in the Roman superstition."

The action at the Azores stimulated the prosecution of the war at sea. It was believed that Philip, realising that his argosies would never be safe while the English fleets were free to roam abroad, was preparing for a new attack on the English Channel, and the Queen's far-sighted councillors continually urged the policy of keeping the enemy occupied with the defence of his own coasts and oversea possessions. Raleigh was permitted to equip a fleet on the model of the successful expeditions organised by Drake, who was still under the shadow of royal displeasure. He exhausted his own available resources, and was obliged to borrow heavily in addition, to complete the equipment of his squadron. But there was a ready response to his call for volunteers. Sir John Hawkins was one of the chief adventurers, and the City of London contributed two ships with a round sum of money. Six vessels of the Earl of Cumberland joined his flag, and the royal navy was represented by the *Garland* and the *Foresight.* In March, 1592, the fifteen sail of his command had mustered in the Thames, but contrary winds delayed them there till the beginning of May.

We are now confronted with one of the many enigmas in the perplexed story of his life. It is evident that up to the moment of his departure his influence over the Queen was undiminished, and that he was in full enjoyment of the royal favour, which, with one temporary break in 1589, had continually advanced his fortunes; for in January of this year the estate and castle of Sherborne, which he had long coveted, was assigned to him.   Sherborne belonged to the see of Salisbury, and, by one of those not very creditable arrangements which were countenanced in Tudor times, its surrender to the Crown on a ninety-nine years' lease was, probably at Raleigh's suggestion, made a condition of the appointment of Dr. Coldwell to the bishopric. Moreover, in spite of his appointment as general of the fleet, Elizabeth had urged him not to leave the Court, and extracted from him a promise to return after the ships were safely got to sea, if he could persuade the adventurers to sail under Sir Martin Frobisher as his substitute.   The gossips, however, whispered that Sir Walter had good reasons for wishing to absent himself from Court.   He sailed on the 6th of May, and on the following day was overtaken by Frobisher, bearing the Queen's orders for his return.   He did not at once obey her commands, believing himself bound, under the arrangement made with his royal mistress, to ascertain how far his fellow-adventurers were disposed to acquiesce in the transfer of leadership.   It was late in the season to contemplate the proposed attack on Panama, and advices received at sea suggested a change of plan.   He divided the force into two squadrons, one of which, under Frobisher, was directed to cruise off the Spanish coast and check the despatch of any armament, while the other, under Sir John Borough, was to take up a station at the Azores with a view to intercepting the carracks from the Indies on their homeward voyage. Having completed these dispositions he set his own course for England, and on his arrival was immediately committed to the Tower. He now realised the meaning of his peremptory recall. He had justly incurred the Queen's deep displeasure. A dispassionate examination of the scanty evidence which has come down to us leaves little doubt that he had sinned against the social law in a manner not uncommon among the courtiers of the time. In similar circumstances, however, both Leicester and Essex found forgiveness more readily than Raleigh did. If the wrong with which he stands charged was unlike his chivalrous nature, at least he was prompt in repairing it, and the whole story of his after-life makes it easier to pardon than explain. Sir Nicholas Throgmorton, one of the Queen's most devoted servants and formerly her ambassador at Paris, had now been in his grave some twenty years. His orphan daughter, named after the Queen and perhaps her god-daughter, had, as soon as years permitted, been adopted at Court as one of the maids of honour, among whom she was pre-eminent for her gifts of mind and person. The brilliant Captain of the Guard, who in his rest-less busy life seemed to have found no time for love, unpopular as he was among the group which surrounded the throne, found favour in the eyes of the tall fair lady who staked her all to win him. In spite of the malice with which his enemies were ever ready to attack him, only one written record has come down to us which need imply any more heinous offence than a secret marriage, if we except a vague reference in Sir

Robert Cecil's letters to Raleigh's " brutish offence "; but
the authority of Camden, whose Annals were published
during the lifetime of Sir Walter and Lady Raleigh,
must be admitted to have the gravest weight.   In a
letter addressed to Cecil on the eve of his departure
with the fleet, he wrote : "I mean not to come away as
they say I will for fear of a marriage, and I know not
what. . . I beseech you to suppress, what you can, any
such malicious report.   For I profess before God, there
is none on the face of the earth that I would be fastened
unto."   While it is difficult to accept the theory put
forward by Raleigh's most conscientious biographer that
here the word "sooner" or "rather" is omitted before
"fastened unto" and to admit that the passage as it
stands is obviously incomplete ; it is also difficult to
believe that, if the relations between Raleigh and
Elizabeth Throgmorton were already in March matter
of comment at Court, some echo should not have reached
the Queen's ears before his definite supercession in May.
Again, while it is not impossible, as some biographers
have suggested, that, in spite of his letter to Cecil, a
secret marriage may already have taken place before he
sailed, it can hardly be assumed that the Queen, jealous
of all rivalry and high-handed as she could be when
offended, would have committed both the lovers to the
Tower for what at worst could only be regarded as a
violation of the respect due to Her Majesty as the
mistress of her Court.   It is easier and more logical to
adopt the accepted theory that the marriage was an act
of reparation, which probably took place in the Tower.
A possible clue to the origin of their intimacy may be
traced in the *Faery Queen* where, as we have already

seen, Spenser admittedly recorded current events under
the veil of allegory.   The poet there tells how Amoret,
walking alone in the woods, was assailed by a savage
monster, who was carrying her away when Timias came
to her rescue and engaged him in deadly combat.   The
monster relinquishing his victim, but still unsubdued,
flies at the approach of Belphœbe, who follows in
pursuit and slays him.   But on her return she finds the
faithless Timias kissing the eyes of Amoret and softly
handling the hurts she had received from the savage.

> " Is this the faith ? " she said,—and said no more,
> But turned her face and fled away for evermore.

Save for this brief reference, suggesting some
romantic episode in which their association took its
rise, and Raleigh's own words of passionate retro-
spection, addressed to his wife, "I chose you and I
loved you in my happiest times," the rest is silence.   It
can only be assumed, if Camden's ominous sentence be
founded on fact, and it is almost impossible to set it
aside, that Elizabeth Throgmorton, whose consistently
noble character, whose fearless and unshaken devotion
to her unhappy husband, entitle her to all men's respect,
is equally entitled to their indulgent judgment for the
very human error to which she yielded to secure his
love.   It may also fairly be assumed that Raleigh, who,
assailed by every form of criticism in the course of his
public career, has, nevertheless, escaped the charges of
gallantry and infidelity so common in his age,[1] had

[1] There is in a letter to his wife, which he believed to be his
last, an allusion which points to the existence of an illegitimate
daughter, but there is nothing to connect her existence with any
particular period of his life.

only deferred an open avowal to a more favourable
moment, from a knowledge that the Queen's consent to his marriage would not be granted, and that
the proposition would only thwart his immediate
ambitions.

It was many years before he was restored to royal
favour.   The erring maid of honour was never received
again by the Queen, who, much as she might resent a
scandal at Court, was still less able to pardon the
affront to her own paramount claims to a monopoly of
admiration.   The marriage, begun in these inauspicious
circumstances, proved, nevertheless, the happiest of
unions, and Arthur Throgmorton, Lady Raleigh's
brother, became one of Sir Walter's few fast friends.
She herself gave him not only the woman's sympathy
which his life had hitherto lacked, but she brought with
her a masculine brain and breadth of view, which made
her at once the trusted confidant and coadjutor of her
ambitious husband.   Every mention of her from his
pen has a note of genuine tenderness, which, in the
course of a correspondence often inevitably artificial
and diplomatic, never fails to ring true ; and the letter
which he addressed to her, when at the outset of his
misfortunes he had resolved upon a desperate course, is
a human document which, after the lapse of three
centuries, illuminates their inner life with a great and
touching pathos.   The story of Lady Raleigh is one of
a long devotion to a man she had chosen and of an
ungrudging self-sacrifice to his hopeless cause, which
secured her the respect and admiration of his more
fortunate contemporaries.   Her best days were spent
in sharing the hardships and humiliations of his long

imprisonment, and after his death she devoted the remaining years of her life to the defence of his memory.

While Raleigh lay fretting in the Tower, the fleet which he had organised had won a very notable success. Frobisher had duly kept the Spanish warships occupied on the coast, and Borough's squadron had, after a sharp action, taken the great carrack of Portugal, the *Madre de Dios*, of seven decks and sixteen hundred tons, the richest prize ever brought to England, containing spices, musk, amber, ebony, precious stones and pearls valued at £500,000.

Meanwhile he was not ashamed to indulge in any artifice to secure his release, protesting that his heart was never broken till the day on which he heard of the Queen's departure from town, writing letters in the extravagant manner of the day, loaded with the hyperbolical phrases in which her courtiers were accustomed to address their flattery-loving mistress, or feigning madness because the keeper of the Tower refused to allow him on the river when the Queen's barge was passing. It was an age of conceits and extravagance, and no one understood his royal mistress better than Raleigh. His object was to escape from durance, and he was little troubled at having to play the part which he thought best calculated to attain this end. But his despairing appeals were vain, until the arrival of the great carrack at Dartmouth created a diversion, which served, if not to restore him completely to liberty, at any rate to release him from a restraint which to his restless nature was irksome as well as humiliating. The expedition had in reality

been a privateering enterprise, in which the Queen was
only a part adventurer with Raleigh, Hawkins, and the
rest, undertaken at their joint risks and for their common
profit.   The Earl of Cumberland had also placed his
squadron under the Queen's officers, and the rule had
been laid down that there should be no pillage of prizes
until all captures had been brought into port.   There
was considerable conflict as to who was entitled to the
credit for the capture of the carrack.   The action had
lasted from ten in the morning, through the afternoon, and on into the night, and the Earl's men had
boarded and finally taken the ship.   Borough claimed
possession in the Queen's name, but, in the brief
space during which Cumberland's men held her, they
had laid hands on a great deal of the more portable
wealth which she carried in pearls and precious stones,
and while Raleigh's ships furnished the *Madre de Dios*
with sails and cables, and stood by to escort her on a
perilous journey in stormy weather to Dartmouth, they
made their way to other harbours, and disposed of their
plunder unobserved.   Plenty of loot was also offered for
sale in the markets at Dartmouth and Plymouth, and
the adventurers realised that their valuable prize would
soon be considerably lightened if strong measures were
not promptly enforced.   Orders were sent to Cornwall
and Devon that all baggage from the western ports
was to be examined, and Robert Cecil was despatched
in haste as a commissioner for the apportionment of
interests, while Burghley persuaded the Queen to grant
Raleigh permission to leave the Tower in proper charge,
and journey west to superintend the division of the
spoil.   Cecil reached Dartmouth only a few days

before the Queen of England's poor captive, as Raleigh styled himself. Great as was his unpopularity in London, his own people in the West knew him and appreciated his worth. "I assure you, sir," wrote Cecil, "his poor servants, to the number of one hundred and forty goodly men, and all the mariners came to him with such shouts and joy, that I never saw a man more troubled to quiet them in my life." Of the more precious freight of the carrack, little was recovered, but there remained five hundred tons of spices, besides ebony, silks and tapestries. The total value of the cargo disposed of by the commissioners came to under £150,000, which must, however, be multiplied by five to represent its approximate value to-day. Raleigh had anticipated that the carrack would be worth £200,000, and in a letter to the Lord-Treasurer he refers to a suggestion which he had made that the Queen's share, which he calculated at a tenth part only, that is to say £20,000, should be set down at £100,000, his own share being sacrificed, apparently as the price of his release from captivity. The correspondence as it stands is enigmatical, but the following passage seems clearly to indicate such a proposal. "Instead of £20,000 if I had made it £100,000, and done injury to none but myself, I hope it may be thought that it proceeded from a faithful mind and a true desire to serve Her. Fourscore thousand pounds is more than ever a man presented Her Majesty as yet. If God hath sent it for my ransom, I hope Her Majesty of Her abundant goodness will accept it." This letter was written before his journey to Dartmouth, and is dated from the Tower. His calculations were rather too sanguine, but by whatever casuistry

Elizabeth may have justified to her conscience a solution which satisfied her avarice, the final apportionment was approximately on the scale of Raleigh's proposal. Out of a total of £141,000, £36,000 were assigned to the Earl of Cumberland, whose disbursements were only estimated at £19,000, and whose men had already annexed a large share of the spoils ; £36,000 again were assigned to Raleigh and his fellow-adventurers, out of which it was stipulated that the City of London should receive £6000 clear profit. The result for the other partners who claimed to have made the royal ships good for sea was a net loss, which was not wiped out by a deduction of £3000 from the Queen's share. The balance, it would seem, or nearly half of the total profit went to the Crown, and restrictive measures in the public markets were promptly enforced to prevent competition with the sale of the plunder. Raleigh had thus fairly paid his ransom, and he did not return to the Tower. In December he dates his correspondence from Durham House, and some six month's later he withdrew to Sherborne, where he seems to have resided for the most part during the two following years, engaged in planting and developing his estate, or in preparations for his famous expedition to Guiana. There is a letter from Lady Raleigh to Robert Cecil, with whom she remained through life on terms of friendly and confiding intercourse, endorsed February 8th, 1593, which throws a pleasant sidelight on that domestic life, and reveals her anxiety in those first years of marriage to retain her husband at her side, even at the expense of his ambition. It seems to indicate that his plans for the voyage were already maturing, and warrants the assumption that her influence contributed to defer the enterprise for a while.

I hope for my sake you will rather draw Sir Walter towards the east than help him forward toward the sunset, if any respect to me or love to him be not forgotten. But every month hath his flower and every season his contentment, and you great counsellors are so full of new counsels, as you are steady in nothing ; but we poor souls that hath bought sorrow at a high price desire, and can be pleased with, the same misfortune we hold, fearing alterations will but multiply misery, of which we have already felt sufficient. I know only your persuasions are of effect with him, and held as oracles tied to them by love ; therefore I humbly beseech you rather stay him than further him.   By the which you shall bind me for ever.

And for two years she had her way, but it was toward the sunset that his heart was drawn, and the dream of his life was now at last to be realised.

CHAPTER VII

GUIANA

1595

HAD the Queen shown any disposition to relent in her treatment of the banished favourite, it is possible that Sir Walter might never have embarked upon the voyage which entitles him to rank with the pioneers of discovery. He never relaxed his efforts to retrieve his forfeited position, and as he was never formally deprived of office, he was encouraged to believe his eclipse was only temporary. Meanwhile he could not be idle. As one door of ambition closed, he cast about for some new outlet for his indomitable energy. It was his resolve, Naunton truly said of him, never to forget himself or suffer himself to be forgotten. Hitherto he had done the work of exploration by deputy, but now at last he was free to choose his own path towards the sunset, and realise a lifelong dream which promised restoration to the favour of a mistress whose anger was swift to melt before her glowing admiration for resolve and enterprise.

The stories which had become associated with the fabled land of El Dorado, whither the princes of Peru had withdrawn into a world of mystery, guarded by impenetrable jungles, and enmeshed by unnavigated streams, appealed to his eager imagination, while his practical ambition thirsted to disprove, by adding an empire to the narrow bounds of British sovereignty, the monstrous claim of Philip to all the unconquered lands beyond the ocean. In the dedication to his *Discovery of Guiana* he refers to a treatise which he composed on the West Indies, in which the possibility of invasion is discussed. His present design, however, was rather to open a new region, which had baffled the patient virtue of the Spaniard.

The credulity with which he has been charged in countenancing the fables with which the sixteenth century associated the name of Guiana, he shared with his contemporaries, who readily accepted what Hume has unjustly stigmatised as deliberate falsehoods invented to popularise his scheme. Indeed, the legend which for upwards of two centuries continued to lure new dreamers to follow the quest of the golden city in the fever swamps and silent forests of the West, was based on some foundation of reality. In the year 1535 an Indian, sent by the Cacique of Bogotà to visit the Inca of Peru, arrived at Quito, and found the land in possession of a new white race, who bestrode strange animals of marvellous swiftness, and carried mysterious weapons which dealt death from afar. From the lips of this Indian the strangers who had come from the sea heard the tale of a great chieftain in his own land who on appointed festivals betook himself with all his people to a solitary tarn in the mountains. There he was anointed with perfumed resin and powdered from

head to foot with dust of gold. Thus equipped he
embarked in his canoe, and putting out into the middle
of the lake plunged into the sacred waters, and
figuratively, with the gold-dust, washed away the offences
of his people. The story, repeated with circumstantial
detail by the historian Orviedo to Cardinal Bembo, was
no idle invention of the brain. Three hundred years
later an English traveller found the tradition still preserved among the degenerate population in the ranges
north of Bogotá, near the holy lake of Guatavita.
They believed, moreover, that, when the land was
conquered by the Spaniards, the old inhabitants had
thrown all that remained of their wealth into the lake,
and that the portion of the Cacique was the burden of a
hundred men laden with gold-dust. A further legend,
based on no reasonable foundation, made its way to
Europe not many years after the story of the golden
king. On the death of the last Inca some still surviv-
ing member of the royal house was said to have led
his people across the Andes, to found a new empire
beyond the white man's ken. The name of El Dorado,
the gilded chief, was transferred to this undiscovered
land, which ever receded before the advance of the
explorer, while its visionary horde grew with every
repetition of the tale. Somewhere between the Andes
and the Atlantic, the Terra Ferme and the Amazon, on
a lake two hundred miles in length, there lay a great
city called Manoa. There a new Inca had revived the
glories of the ancient court of Atahualpa, where Pizarro
found, when he weighed the loot of precious metals,
"52,000 marks of good silver, and 1,326,000 and 500
pesoes of gold."

The earliest attempt to enter Guiana was, however, undoubtedly anterior to the visit of the Cacique's envoy to Quito, for the Germans, the pioneers of colonisation in Venezuela, had already in 1530 advanced westward under Ambrose von Alfinger, and about the same time Diego de Ordaz first essayed the exploration of the Amazon. Alfinger perished at the hands of the Indians, whom he treated with savage severity, and some years later another expedition under Nicholas Federman led to no result; but in the mountains of Bogotá, he, coming from the north-west, joined hands with Gonzalo de Quesnada, the conqueror of New Granada, and Sebastian de Belalcazar, who had marched from Quito in the south. In 1540 Gonzalo Pizarro, setting out from Quito, reached a branch of the Amazon. Dividing his forces he despatched Orellana in a hastily constructed vessel to explore two thousand leagues of unknown waterways to the Atlantic, and himself continued his march through trackless wilds, only after two years to return with a remnant of his force, gaunt with famine, savage, unrecognisable. Well might Raleigh testify of the Spaniards that never had any nation endured so many misadventures and miseries, and yet persisted with invincible constancy in their Indian discoveries. Philip von Hutten was the next to follow with a band of Germans and Spaniards from Coro in Venezuela, to be defeated after wandering for a year among baffling streams and forests. But his faith in the phantom gold led the chivalrous Hutten to set out once more on the path of doom with such few followers as his persuasive eloquence could enlist. Far south in the land of the Omaguas he is reported to have

I

beheld a great city spreading beyond the range of sight, in the midst of which, his guides assured him, arose the palace of the golden colossi.   There he was attacked by the Omaguas, and compelled to retire severely wounded, only to be murdered at his journey's end by the Spaniards who had meanwhile seized the government in Coro.   Twenty years passed before the viceroy of Peru organised a new expedition under Pedro de Ursua. Among his three hundred volunteers was a certain Lope de Aguirre, one of those monsters who from time to time appear in the records of savage exploration. He murdered his captain and the fair Donna Inez, who for love of Ursua had followed him into the wilderness, and led a band of desperadoes, in a wild carnival of blood and debauchery, through Guiana into Venezuela, where he met with a just fate at the hands of the Spanish authorities.   Rumours of these and succeeding voyages, coloured by the imagination and superstition of the old mariners, had inspired the day-dreams of Walter Raleigh's youth, and affected unconsciously the reasoning of later years.   Of more recent adventurers who had essayed the quest, two only call for mention here. The first was the Portuguese, Pedro de Silva, who in 1569 and again five years afterwards, penetrated into the interior.   Of his second ill-fated expedition one solitary survivor, Juan Martin de Abazar, returned after years spent as a prisoner with the natives of the Orinoco.   The second was Antonio de Berreo, Raleigh's immediate predecessor, who was collecting material for a second attempt to reach the mysterious capital, in virtue of a patent from the King of Spain, when the English arrived in Trinidad, of which he was acting as Governor.

In 1594 Raleigh despatched Captain Jacob Whiddon to make a preliminary survey of the mouths of the Orinoco. Berreo received him with outward courtesy, and gave him an undertaking that his men should water and cut wood without molestation. During Whiddon's absence, however, on a visit to the *Elizabeth Bonaventure*, which had come in from the West Indies, his ship's company landed by invitation to kill a doe, and in the woods a number of them were set upon by Berreo's men and held as prisoners. Weakened by this treachery Whiddon was obliged to return with little accomplished, but Raleigh had now an account to settle with the Governor which his lieutenant would not allow him to forget. At the end of the year, Robert Dudley, Leicester's son, arrived in Trinidad, and thence despatched a boat up the Orinoco, which explored three hundred miles of river, while he waited some time in the hope of seeing Raleigh, of whose projected expedition he was aware. In spite of its priority his journey did not attract much attention. He lacked the magic of the pen, which enthralled the readers of Raleigh's vivid narrative.

Sir Walter set sail from Plymouth on the 6th of February, 1595, with a commission in which the customary form of "trusty and well beloved" was significantly omitted. He had full powers to offend and enfeeble the King of Spain and his subjects to the uttermost, to take possession of unoccupied lands, and to resist by arms all who should attempt to establish themselves within two hundred leagues of his settlement. Cecil had a share in the venture, in which all Raleigh's own available resources were invested, and the Lord

High Admiral contributed a ship, the *Lion's Whelp*, which joined him in Trinidad. Here he also expected Amyas Preston and Summers, but these two captains abandoned Guiana for their famous raid upon La Guayra. The number of his companies is not recorded, but nearly one hundred composed the exploring party up the Orinoco. Among the gentlemen adventurers were John Gilbert, his nephew, a son of Sir Richard Grenville, and Butshead Gorges, another cousin. After some profitable captures in the Canaries they made Punto de Gallo in Trinidad in March, and found that Berreo had forbidden the Indians to trade with the English under pain of being hanged and quartered, a threat which it is asserted was actually put into execution. Here he was joined by Captain Keymis, a lifelong friend and follower, whose ship had parted company off the coast of Spain, and by Captain Gifford in the *Lion's Whelp*. Having learned from some garrulous Spanish soldiers that Berreo had sent to Margarita and the Terra Ferme for reinforcements, meaning to have given him a *cassado* at parting, he lost no time in enacting vengeance for the treachery done to Whiddon's men last year. A night attack on the newly built station of St. Joseph met with little resistance. Berreo was brought as a prisoner on board the flagship, and the town was burned at the instance of some Indian chiefs who were found there, attached five to one chain, in the last extremities of starvation. Having by this somewhat high-handed act of reprisal anticipated any further aggression, Raleigh treated his prisoner with every courtesy, and Berreo does not appear to have shown any special resentment at this incident of *buona guerra.* Berreo gave his captor a full account of his first attempt to enter Guiana, with seven hundred horsemen from New Granada. He had followed the Meta to its confluence with the Orinoco : he had waged long war with the people of Amapaia, who gave him images of fine gold upon the conclusion of peace; and assisted by native pilots he had found a way through the bewildering mouths of the Orinoco itself to Trinidad. The images he had sent to Spain, by his camp-master, Domingo de Vera, of whose projects Raleigh had doubtless received information in Europe, and who was, it would seem from the Spanish accounts, already outward bound with a new and well-equipped expedition, to which Philip had liberally contributed, for the conquest and conversion of Guiana. From Berreo he also obtained a copy of the relation of the mysterious Martinez, the one European reported to have set eyes on Manoa, which was preserved in the archives of S. Juan de Porto Rico. By Raleigh, as by Berreo himself, Martinez was believed to have been master of the ordnance to Ordaz, whose voyage up the Orinoco was undertaken in 1531, that is to say, before the death of Atahualpa, and before the tradition of a new Inca kingdom could have arisen. It must be assumed, therefore, if there is any real foundation for the story, that this Juan Martinez was in reality the solitary survivor of Pedro de Sylva's expedition, who had lived long in captivity with the Indians, and that the monks of Porto Rico had built up from his deposition the story which Sir Walter found among Berreo's papers. According to their version, after Ordaz had penetrated some three hundred miles inland, his powder took fire and exploded. Martinez, who

was in charge, was held responsible and condemned to
death.   But the soldiers pleaded for his life, and instead
of being executed, he was placed with his arms in a
canoe and set adrift on the Orinoco.   Some natives, who
had never seen a white man before, intercepted the boat
and carried him to Manoa, the residence of the Inca.

The emperor after he had beheld him, knew him to be
a Christian (for it was not long before that his brethren,
Guascar and Atabalipa [Huascar and Atahualpa], were
vanquished by the Spaniards in Peru), and caused him to
be lodged in his palace, and well entertained.   He lived
seven months in Manoa, but (was) not suffered to wander
into the country anywhere ; he was also brought thither all
the way blindfold, led by the Indians, until he came to the
entrance of Manoa itself, and was fourteen or fifteen days in
the passage.   He avowed at his death that he entered the
city at noon, and then they uncovered his face, and that he
travelled all that day, till night, through the city, and the
next day, from sunrise to sunsetting, ere he came to the
palace of Inga.

During his sojourn he learned the language, and
when at length he obtained permission to depart, he
was presented with as much gold as his guides could
carry to the river.   There he was robbed of all his
treasure by the borderers, and only saved two gourds
filled with golden beads which escaped notice.   He
made his way down the Orinoco to Trinidad, and thence
reached Porto Rico, where he died while waiting for a
homeward-bound ship, leaving his calabashes to the
monks to pay for masses.   It was Martinez who gave
the name of El Dorado to the city, because of the
abundance of golden images, plates, and armour which
he beheld there.   Such was the story which Vera had

circulated in Spain, and which Raleigh repeats in his
Discovery of Guiana.

When his prisoner had told him all he had to tell,
Sir Walter admitted that Guiana was also the goal of
his journey. Berreo became greatly depressed, and did
all he could to dissuade him from the enterprise, en-
larging upon the difficulties of obtaining supplies from
the natives, and the impossibility of navigating the
streams, now beginning to swell with the approach of
winter. Many of Berreo's arguments he found later on
to his cost were sound enough, but he kept his own
counsel, that his men might not be discouraged. An
old gallego was cut down till it drew only five feet of
water, and fitted with oars. In this improvised craft,
two wherries, and a light boat from the *Lion's Whelp,* he
embarked one hundred men and a month's provisions.
Meanwhile captains Whiddon, King, and Douglas had
completed a rapid survey of the opposite coast, and
had discovered the mouths of four rivers discharging
into the bay of Guanipa, which the boats made in
safety after battling with wind and current across some
twenty miles of open sea. Their Indian pilot seems
to have had little knowledge of the intricate network
of wooded streams and islands formed by the many
mouths of the Orinoco, and there they might have
wandered interminably, lost in nature's labyrinth, had
it not been for the fortunate capture of an old man, a
native of the deltas, who being well treated by his
captors, became their willing guide through the country
of the Tivitivas, to which tribe he himself belonged.
These were a nation of hunters, who neither sowed nor
reaped, but lived on the produce of the chase and the

wild fruits of the land, having their cabins in the trees
when the annual floods invaded their hunting-grounds.
Beyond, lay the country of the Arwacas who, like the
wife of Mausolus, drank the powdered bones of their
dead chieftains in pine-apple wine. At length, after
toiling against heavy currents and grounding on
treacherous shoals, they entered a broad channel,
known as the Amana, and soon afterwards the influence
of the sea-tides ceased to be felt. Progress was slow,
the heat intense, and before long the daily ration had
to be reduced. The pioneers of discovery had neither
water-proof coverings nor preserved provisions; when
rain fell their wet clothes dried upon their backs, steam-
ing in the tropic sun; they cooked and slept in their
boats, and their drink was the troubled water of the
river. Some edible fruits were found on the banks,
and fish and fowl served to eke out their decreasing
stores, but as the days went by in their laborious
progress the danger of famine increased. Their pilot
gave them assurance of human habitations up a shallow
tributary, which only the lighter craft could navigate.
Forty miles up this narrow stream they toiled, in the
barge and the two wherries, often cutting their way
through the tangled vegetation with their swords.
Then night overtook them and, had they been sure of
their way back, they would have hanged the pilot, who
still entreated them to persevere. It was an hour after
midnight when at length they reached an Indian settlement where they were able to relieve their wants and
secure a provision of bread and fowls. With daybreak
the whole aspect of the country seemed changed. The
jungles of the river banks opened out into wide grassy

plains, dotted with clumps of forest, where the deer were feeding in the unscared security of a primeval world. The stream itself was the haunt of innumerable wild-fowl, and teamed with alligators.

Once again as they travelled up the great solitary river they were at the last extremity for food, when four canoes were sighted and chased. Two of them escaped by some side channel. The other two, whose occupants fled into the woods, were laden with bread, and contained, moreover, a certain quantity of gold-dust and mining tools. They learned from the Arwaca boatmen, who were eventually captured and treated with kindness, that these canoes were conveying from up-country three Spaniards who, having heard of Berreo's discomfiture, were making their way to the coast. An Arwaca chief, who had been christened by the Spaniards, now became their guide, and the old pilot who had brought them thus far was sent back in a canoe with suitable presents and a letter for the ships. Like Drake, Raleigh was ever considerate in his treatment of the natives, and was eminently successful in winning their affection.

On the fifteenth day, to their great joy, they saw the mountains of Guiana. Friendly Indians supplied them with fish and tortoise eggs, and they halted at the parting of the Amana with the main stream of the Orinoco itself, which Keymis, on his second visit to the country, named the Raleana, in honour of his chief. In the morning Toparimaca, the lord of that land, warned of their presence, came to the boats with a gift of bread, fish, flesh, and pine-wine. They visited his town, and caroused there till some of the captains grew "reasonable pleasant." Now the wind began to help them against the stream, and conducted by Toparimaca's brother, they reached two great islands which parted the main river into three channels. Still sailing due west they observed a great plain spreading northward, which a party was despatched to explore. Their guide told them that these plains extended to Cumana and Caraccas, and were tenanted by four nations, one of which, the black Arora, used arrows of the deadliest poison. To Raleigh was communicated the secret of the antidote, which had been jealously withheld from the Spaniards.

Five days after entering the great river they reached the province of Aromaia and the port of Morequito, which took its name from a cacique whom Berreo had put to death. His uncle and successor, Topiawari, now occupied a station some fourteen miles inland. The ancient King, reported to be a hundred and ten years old, came to the river with copious stores of provisions, having covered the distance before noon, and returned the same evening. Among the presents which he offered was a beast called *armadilla*, "barred over with small plates, somewhat like to a rhinoceros, with a white horn growing in his hinder parts, as big as a great hunting-horn, which they use to wind instead of a trumpet." From him Raleigh gleaned much information as to the people of Guiana and the region beyond the mountains. In the days of his youth, he said, there came down to the lowlands a nation from so far off as the sun slept, called Epurimei, subjects to the Inca, and distinguished by their crimson headgear. They had expelled the old inhabitants, and made themselves masters over all the river tribes, save two only, and in that great war perished his own eldest son, "whom he most entirely loved." Of late, however, all the native populations had united in a common cause against the menace of the Spaniard. Raleigh confirmed the report that he had come thither at the bidding of a Queen, who in her charity to all oppressed nations would deliver his people from tyranny. When he took his leave the venerable cacique promised, though he was weak and "daily called for by death," to pay him a second visit upon the return of the expedition.

Pursuing his journey westward, Sir Walter had intended to ascend the Caroni (or Caroli as he calls it) to the rapids, but the force of the current baffled them. The chief of the district, to whom messengers were sent. came to their camp, and with him as with Topiawari, he concluded what a modern African explorer would call a treaty of protection. Whiddon and others went to prospect for minerals, while the Admiral with a small following marched overland to the falls, where the Caroni dropped from the heights, in a succession of twelve cataracts, "every one as high as a church tower." They seemed to have reached the Happy Valley, where the waters ran in many channels through fair grassy plains, "the deer crossing in every path, the birds towards evening singing on every tree with a thousand several tunes, cranes and herons of white, crimson and carnation, perching on the river's side; the air fresh with a gentle easterly wind; and every stone that we stopped to take up promised either gold or silver by his complexion." Moments such as these coloured the convincing optimism of Raleigh's faith in Guiana, and Whiddon had indeed found stones which were identified as *Madre del oro*, and crystals which they believed to be sapphires. In these regions they heard of the mysterious Ewaiponoma, a race whose heads do not appear above their shoulders, and whose mouths are in the middle of their breasts. These tales, like those of the Amazons, Raleigh repeats, without suggesting any rationalistic explanation, such as a peculiar form of head-dress. The world was not yet old enough to have done with its childhood's dreams, and stranger tales than these found credence still. That they were not held too improbable for belief is revealed by the evidence of the Dutch map published by Hondius in 1598, soon after Raleigh's return, on which may be seen engraved the picture of an Ewaiponoma warrior, side by side with an Amazon in martial equipment. His own conclusion is, "whether it be true or no, the matter is not great, . . . for mine own part I saw them not, but I am resolved that so many people did not all combine or forethink to make the report." There is no trace here of the premeditation of falsehood of which Hume has most unjustly accused him.

The junction of the Caroni in 8° 15′ N. latitude was the farthest point reached. Heavy rains made the daily routine of life unbearable, and the rapid rise of the rivers warned them that it was time to turn back. The defection of Preston and Summers made it impossible to contemplate conquest and occupation, but the experience gained justified the resumption of the enterprise on a larger scale. The rivers traversed had been carefully charted, and friendly understandings concluded with the inhabitants. Their investigations of the mineral wealth of the country were admittedly superficial, but Raleigh's faith in its potential resources has since been

amply vindicated. The journey down the swollen
stream was rapidly accomplished. A second visit was
paid to Topiawari, with whom two volunteers remained
to learn the language and collect notes, and Raleigh took
leave of the venerable chief in full expectation of returning the following year. Keymis was despatched overland to inspect a reported gold-mine, under the guidance
of a chief called Putyma, who was afterwards to conduct
him to a rendezvous on a tributary of the Cararoopana
branch of the Orinoco, by which Raleigh himself
proceeded to visit Emeria and its powerful chief
Carapana. While exploring another tributary stream
they saw from afar a mountain reported to be formed
of crystal, appearing in the distance like a white church
tower. From its summit there fell a mighty river,
thundering to the ground with the reverberation of "a
thousand great bells" clanging together. Carapana
having retired into the mountains, scared by the reports
which the Spaniards had spread abroad of the English,
they continued their journey to the sea, leaving a party
to wait for Keymis, who returned with a more highly-
coloured estimate of the resources of the mine than his
cursory inspection justified, but which readily convinced
the adventurers whose imaginations had been captivated
by the stories of Guiana gold. Baffled by strong head-
winds in the Amana, they found a way through the
Capuri channel to the broad estuary, where their tiny
boats had much ado to live in the boisterous sea which
they encountered ; but profiting by a lull at midnight,
they made the nearest point of Trinidad in safety, and
coasted to Curiapan, where to their great joy they found
the ships. Save for that of one negro servant, killed by

alligators while bathing, no life had been lost; and in spite of continued hardships, exposure, and cramping, sickness had been almost unknown. Raleigh, therefore, was justified in his testimony to the salubrious qualities of Guiana.

Not all, however, of those who embarked for the West were destined to return, and in the island of Trinidad they buried the faithful Whiddon. Raleigh's brief record is his only epitaph: "Whom afterward, to my great grief, I left buried in the said island, after my return from Guiana, being a man most honest and valiant." We would fain know more of the good seaman who fought so valiantly at the Azores, who commanded the *Roebuck* in the great fight with the Armada, and who left his bones in the tropic island at the sea-gate of the mysterious region he had explored. But alas, with few exceptions, over the grave of the valiant and honest, as over that of the coward and the knave, oblivion draws the same impartial veil.

Sir Walter intended, before returning, to visit his plantation in Virginia, but boisterous weather drove him from the coast, and thus he never saw the settlement to which he had devoted his energies and fortune. He revictualled by forced levies in the Spanish colonies, and set his course for home, in full confidence that his countrymen would enthusiastically acclaim the new field he had opened to British enterprise. But his detractors had meanwhile turned his long absence to account, and not a few had even had the effrontery to assert that he had been in hiding and had never sailed for Guiana. Others had proclaimed that he had gone to transfer his services to the flag of the enemy. His return gave the lie to such malicious inventions, but the Queen continued to avert her face; the general public received the news of his discoveries with mistrustful suspicion, and gossips proclaimed that his specimen ores had been purchased in Barbary.   The bitterness of his feelings at this reception is expressed in the Dedication to his *Discovery of Guiana*, addressed to Robert Cecil and the Lord High Admiral.   The publication of this work, however, created a revulsion in public opinion, and a second edition was issued within a few months of the first.   The fame of his voyage is in no small measure due to that literary gift which enabled him to carry his readers with him beyond the horizon of their own familiar seas.   Not a few had penetrated more deeply into the labyrinths of the great southern continent.   Some had found their graves in the wilderness; others had come back, but "could not tell the world."   The sympathetic interest thus aroused enabled him to fit out a second small expedition, under the command of Keymis, to keep touch with the natives and prove that the enterprise was not abandoned.   The report brought home by his lieutenant, who explored a large area of new country, showed that, though the ambitious expedition of Domingo de Vera had ended in disastrous failure, the Spaniards had been able to establish themselves at the mouth of the Caroni.   Here they barred the passage to the mine, whose fabled wealth kept alive the tradition of Guiana gold, and became the ostensible justification for that last unhappy venture which, twenty years later, was destined to prove fatal both to Keymis and to his master.

CHAPTER VIII

CADIZ

1596

THE crisis of the Armada had called every energy of the country into play, and the Queen herself, when decisive action had become inevitable, rose to the height of a great occasion and nobly led her people. But once the imminent fear of invasion was removed she turned a cold ear to the advice of those who urged that the first successes should be followed up by a disabling blow. Her sincere desire for peace, her anxiety not to exasperate her enemy beyond the possibility of reconciliation, imposed limitations on the commanders, and thus the Portugal expedition under Drake and Norris in 1589 had ended in practical failure. Her Majesty, Raleigh wrote later on, reviewing the story of the past, did everything by halves, and would not trust her men of war. During the next six years the fighting strength of England was wasted in desultory attacks on Spanish commerce, and while the Queen hesitated, Philip, who had profited by his lessons and had grasped the necessity for moving only with strong squadrons, gained time to renew the fabric of his navy and prepare a second invasion. There was, however, no lack of warning. The efforts of Spain were consistently and openly directed to securing a base of operations nearer to the Channel, and the recrudescence of a rebellious spirit in Ireland offered an ominous parallel to the conditions which had preceded her former disastrous attempt. The disgrace of Drake, and the subsequent banishment of Raleigh from Court, had at a most unfortunate moment removed from the Council of the Queen two of the most powerful advocates of *Thorough*, and meanwhile the menace grew till it became too obvious to disregard. At length Drake, though hampered by a command shared with the veteran Hawkins, now enfeebled by years and infirmities, was allowed to put into execution his long-cherished plan for a descent on Panama, the most important outpost of Spanish colonial empire, and the key to her Pacific trade. By the diversion thus effected in seas remote from home, valuable time was gained. Spain was inevitably compelled to despatch a fleet in pursuit, while the protection of her western convoys and the watch at sea for the returning expedition fully occupied the rest of her available strength. Meanwhile in England preparations were being rapidly advanced for some maritime enterprise on a large scale, the object of which was kept a close secret. The contemplated attack on the Spanish coast was no new plan, but one which had been urged again and again since Drake's triumphant raid on Cadiz had paralysed the aggressive power of the enemy. Once more, however, the success of the issue was endangered by a divided command and personal considerations, for with the brilliant but hot-blooded Essex, whose military reputation could as yet

K

scarcely justify supreme command, was associated the cautious and experienced Lord High Admiral, in whom the Queen had implicit confidence. The withdrawal of Sir Francis Vere and his seasoned veterans from the Netherlands increased the misgiving which these naval preparations excited on the continent, but plausible excuses were readily found for abnormal activity. The growing disaffection in Ireland offered a colourable pretext for the recall of the troops, while the necessity of holding the maritime highways open for the return of Drake and Hawkins sufficed to account for the mobilisation of the fleet. More than all, the Queen's hesitation to give direct orders for a descent on the Spanish coast justified the failure of Philip to anticipate the action which ensued. In the midst of these preparations two disastrous episodes brought home to every man in England the extreme gravity of the situation. Vague rumours respecting the expedition to Panama received alarming confirmation. For the first time in his life Drake had encountered failure, and the veteran father of the fleet was dead. Then at the end of March the Archduke Albert, who had succeeded to the command of the Spanish forces in the Netherlands, made his brilliant dash on Calais. The danger was extreme. Henry the Fourth of France had been outwitted, and a Dutch squadron, mobilised to act in concert with the British fleet, failed to force an entrance and carry food to the beleaguered garrison. Calais, however, might yet have been saved had not the Queen and Henry lost time in haggling over the conditions of co-operation. Essex, despatched in haste to Dover with all available troops, fretted his heart out in justifiable indignation at

the conflicting orders which tied his hands; while the
Lord High Admiral, bringing round the ships at this
critical moment to embark the land forces, found that
he had been superseded by the young favourite as sole
commander, and despatched his resignation in a letter of
indignant remonstrance. At length, on the 15th of April
the distracted Essex finally received authority to sail.
On that disastrous day the citadel of Calais fell, and a
Spanish garrison was definitely established on the
threshold of the menaced kingdom.

The relief was now no longer to be contemplated, and
the original plan of action was resumed. Means were
found to pacify the offended Lord High Admiral, who
was reconciled to Essex and restored to his original
position. Raleigh had not yet been forgiven, but in a
moment of national crisis his reputation for resource
and ability, and above all, the great influence he exercised over the seamen in the western counties were not
forgotten. Recruits for the army and the navy no
longer came in as they had done during the imminent
peril of 1588, and the lieutenant of Cornwall was not a
man whose services could be dispensed with when enterprises of great moment were in hand. Moreover, in
entrusting the chief command by sea and land to
the Lord High Admiral and Essex in joint commission, the Queen and her councillors had realised the
danger that an old head and a young one might not
always see with the same eyes. Five of the most experienced military and naval leaders in England were
therefore selected to advise the Generals-in-Chief and
act as a Council of War. Raleigh was appointed a
member of their Council, receiving the rank of Rear-

Admiral of the Fleet, and with him Lord Thomas Howard, who as his senior held the rank of Vice-Admiral. Their functions were purely naval. The military members of the board were Sir Francis Vere, Lord Marshal of the Army; Sir George Carew, Lieutenant of the Ordnance; and Sir Conyers Clifford, Serjeant-Major, a position which may be compared to that of the Adjutant-General to-day. Mr. Anthony Ashley, who was knighted during the expedition, was Secretary to the Council.

The immediate danger at Calais made it more than ever probable that a descent on the Spanish coast would be countermanded, but in the meantime the scattered forces which had been equipped in readiness, including the Dutch squadron, moved on towards their rendez-vous at Plymouth, while Lord Thomas Howard and Raleigh remained behind in the Thames organising the transports and store-ships. Then further pretext for hesitation was afforded by the news which rang with a sinister boding through the land and gave new courage to the mariners of Spain. Drake was dead. Far away off Puertobello, "beneath some great wave," the terrible sea-captain was resting in his ocean-shroud. His great scheme had ended in failure; the remnants of his leaderless squadron no longer preoccupied the attention of the enemy, and the hand put up for defence was free to strike again. Essex perceived the necessity for immediate action, but while the irresolution of the Court increased, circumstances also tended to protract delay. It was May before the Lord High Admiral, detained by contrary weather, could reach Plymouth. Lord Thomas Howard, who had pushed on with such of the London ships as had completed their commissions, followed close on his heels; but Raleigh was still unable to get the rear-guard to sea, and lay distracted in the Thames. Cecil, urged by the generals to hasten his departure, received a despairing reply. He could not raise the crews to man the ships. "As fast as we press men one day they run away another and say they will not serve. The pursuivant found me in a country village a mile from Gravesend, hunting after runaway mariners, and dragging in the mire from alehouse to alehouse." Raleigh's detractors were, on this as on every other occasion, ready to discredit his motives; but Essex appreciated the untiring zeal which he ever displayed in a patriotic cause, and wrote to him in terms which are pleasant to record in view of the past and future relations of these two brilliant rivals. "I will not entreat you to make haste," he protested, "but I will wish and pray a good wind for you. And when you are come, I will make you see I desire to do you as much honour, and give you as great contentment as I can. For this is the action and the time in which you and I shall be both taught to know and love one another." He joined the fleet on the 21st of May, and at length on the 3rd of June the expedition got clear of Plymouth Sound.

Many contemporary records of the action at Cadiz have been preserved. The accepted official version was based by Cecil on a report from the Lord High Admiral, and published with the sanction of the Archbishop of Canterbury, as censor of the press, to the exclusion for the time being of all others. Most of the chief officers employed, however, penned their own accounts of the affair, and of these Raleigh's is certainly the best known to fame. If the authorship of the anonymous account, which has been assumed with good reason to be that drawn up for Essex by his secretary, Mr. Henry Cuffe, cannot be positively determined, there exist, nevertheless, two other documents, one of which was certainly, and the other with all probability, prepared by Essex himself in answer to hostile criticisms on the campaign. There are also the commentaries of Sir Francis Vere, the notice published in the naval tracts of Sir William Monson, and a very detailed report drawn up by Dr. Marbecke, the Queen's physician, who accompanied the expedition.   Not the least interesting record of the campaign is one which has just been published for the first time by the Navy Records Society, from the pen of Sir William Slingsby (or Slyngisbie), who served on Carew's staff, and whose narrative is distinguished by an impartiality not to be found in other writers, for the most part partisans either of Raleigh or of Essex.

The numbers of the fleet are variously estimated with the want of accuracy characteristic of the time, but whether the smallest estimate, of one hundred and ten, or the largest, of one hundred and fifty, be accepted, the greater proportion of these ships were, it is clear, victuallers, transports, or small craft.   The men-of-war, including pinnaces, did not exceed fifty, of which seventeen or eighteen only were Queen's ships.   The Dutch squadron consisted of eighteen men-of-war. Slingsby mentions that a number of unattached barques followed upon adventures of their own.   The troops were supposed to constitute an entire army corps, but it is more than doubtful whether ten thousand men could have been landed.   The British fleet was divided into four squadrons, each complete in itself with its complement of victuallers and transports. The Lord High Admiral led the first squadron in the famous *Ark Royal*, once the *Ark Raleigh*, with Sir Robert Southwell in the *Lion* as his divisional Vice-Admiral. Two other Queen's ships, a pinnace, three merchant men-of-war, and fourteen other merchant vessels as transports or victuallers, with five sail of hoys or fly-boats completed the division. The constitution of the other divisions was similar. The Earl of Essex led the second squadron in the *Due Repulse*, with Sir Francis Vere as his Vice-Admiral in the *Rainbow*. Lord Thomas Howard, Vice-Admiral of the combined fleet, led the third in the *Merhonour*, with Captain Robert Dudley (Leicester's son) in the *Nonpareil* as his second in command ; while Sir Walter Raleigh, Rear-Admiral of the fleet led the fourth in the *Warspite*, with Sir George Carew in the *Mary Rose* as his Vice-Admiral. The Dutch squadron formed a fifth division under Admiral John van Dyvenvoord, with Captains Gerhantsen and Lensen as Vice and Rear-Admirals.

Up to the last the destination of the expedition had been kept secret, and they sailed very wide of the land in order to avert suspicion. Light pinnaces acting as scouts intercepted any passing craft which might carry intelligence of their movements to the enemy, and fortunate captures enabled them to escape observation till they rounded Cape St. Vincent, whence they were sighted at last. But their object had now been secured. Cadiz had made no preparations for defence, and most of the commanding officers were absent from their post. It was once more the unfortunate Duke of Medina Sidonia who, as Captain-General of the Andalusian coast, was to bear the burden of responsibility for a new disaster. Although he was not yet recovered from an attack of fever which had kept him for a month on a sickbed, he displayed remarkable energy so soon as the alarm was given, and took all available precautions for the defence of the harbour. The strength of the ships in Cadiz consisted, according to Raleigh, of seventeen galleys, four Spanish galleons, known as the Apostles, the *S.S. Philip, Matthew, Thomas,* and *Andrew,* "two great galleons of Lisbon; three frigates of war, accustomed to transport the treasure; two argosies, very strong in artillery; the Admiral, Vice-Admiral, and Rear-Admiral of Nueva Espana; with forty other great ships bound for New Mexico and other places." As is usual in contemporary accounts no two statements of the strength of the enemy's force agree, but an official Spanish despatch from the President of the Contratacion (or Chamber of Commerce) to Philip enumerates four Spanish and two Portuguese galleons, three treasure frigates, returned from the Indies after Drake's disaster, three powerful ships of the Levant, and a fleet of twenty galleys.

In order to understand the varying phases of the action at Cadiz, it is necessary to realise the characteristic features of the harbour. Conceive a bay roughly taking the form of a bent bow, broken by many irregularities and excrescences, with the chord of its arc some fifteen nautical miles in length. Adjusted to the southern portion of this crescent, and occupying nearly a third of its whole area, is the island of Leon, separated from the mainland by a narrow river-like channel, and connected at one point by the bridge of Suazo. From

the north-western shoulder of the island a long straight
slender spit of land stretches north by west, spanning
the crescent like the string of the bow for approximately
another third of its whole length.   At its extreme
point, which widens into a rocky plateau, is the city of
Cadiz. The northern horn of the crescent is Point Rota.
By vessels rounding Cape Rota the outline of the arc
is seen to project seaward towards Cadiz, forming a
headland upon which stood the castle of Sta. Catalina.
Behind this headland lies Port St. Mary. Once more
about the centre of the crescent, where the handle of
the bow should be, a bold promontory runs westwards
towards the landspit on which Cadiz is situated,
terminating in Matagorda point; and exactly opposite
from the landspit itself, a small headland fortified by the
Castle of Puntal juts out to meet Matagorda. Between
these two points the navigable channel is not a mile in
breadth. The island of Leon is the southern limit of
the second basin thus formed, landlocked on every side
save where it is entered by the Puntal channel, though
vessels of light draft can use the passage between the
island and the mainland. To the east of this great
basin are Port Royal and Caracca.

The lightness of the wind made the final advance of
the English slow, and on the morning of the 18th they
lay some twelve leagues off the entrance of the outer
harbour. At a council held that morning it was decided
that Essex should attempt the city, while the Lord High
Admiral and Lord Thomas Howard attacked the fleet.
Sir Alexander Clifford with a small squadron was to
operate against the galleys, and Raleigh was told off to
the inshore station to prevent the escape of shipping

coastwise. He departed to his station, and during his
absence the whole plan was remodelled. It was then
decided that Essex should endeavour to secure a landing
on the outer side of the city towards the open sea, while
Howard was to land on the inner side to the south,
somewhere on the long promontory which joins Cadiz
to the island of Leon, thus preventing the arrival of
succours from the mainland. In the meantime Raleigh
and the Dutch squadron were to contain the enemy's ships
in the harbour. On Sunday morning, the 20th of June,
the fleet advanced with a freshening breeze to within
cannon range of the city batteries, and then unaccount-
ably, as it seemed to those in Cadiz, tacked off to sea
again. Some unexplained difficulty in carrying out
the plan of action had arisen, which Mr. Corbett, an
exhaustive student of this campaign, attributes to a
miscalculation of the distance they had had to cover.
A further discussion ensued between the principal
officers, in which Raleigh, still absent on the duties
assigned him, did not take part. Essex was in favour
of assaulting the harbour with the advantage of the
wind, which was obviously the right course; but Howard
hesitated to throw his ships into action until the fire of
the forts had been silenced by a land attack, and Essex,
yielding to the advice of his senior, began to disembark
the storming parties.

Raleigh, who had been delayed in his cruise along the
coast by the pursuit of some corn-ships endeavouring to
slip from the mouth of the Guadalquivir into the shelter
of Cadiz, rejoined the fleet at this juncture, and found
the work of disembarkation far advanced. A heavy sea
was running and the long boat of the *Rainbow* had been

swamped with the loss of fifteen lives. The surf was breaking ominously over the rocks which shut in the shelving beach of the Caleta, the creek where Essex was to effect a landing in the face of the forces drawn up to dispute it. He perceived at once that the plan was foredoomed to failure, and recorded an emphatic protest. Essex was disposed to agree, but scrupled to re-open the discussion of a plan upon which Howard had insisted. At length, however, he yielded to Raleigh's entreaties, and sanctioned his endeavouring to urge a reconsideration of the Lord High Admiral's decision and an immediate assault on the ships. The freshening wind was a convincing argument, and Howard was, with some difficulty persuaded. Raleigh rowed back with the good news, and, as he neared the *Repulse*, he shouted out in his excitement the one word *Entramos !* Essex, fretfully striding his poop, caught the joyful message on the wind, and in a fever of enthusiasm flung his plumed hat into the sea in the direction of the harbour mouth. This was Raleigh's first great service; a second was to follow. The work of reshipping the troops and boats consumed many hours, and before the fleet could weigh, the afternoon was already so far advanced that it was obvious that they must either make a night attack or defer the action until the following morning. Essex would have preferred to emulate the example of Drake, but Howard advocated postponing the advance till daybreak. To have sailed in at nightfall with a divided command and no plan of action, with a large flotilla of transports in the tail, would have involved a risk, which only the genius of Drake could have justified. Raleigh supported Howard, and their more cautious counsel

prevailed.   As evening fell the fleet anchored once more
before the broad entrance to the outer basin, between
Cadiz and the headland on which stood the castle of
Sta. Catalina.   At a Council of War held that night
the plan of attack was developed.   Raleigh's suit to
lead the van was approved.   The ships assigned to him
for this purpose, whose names have for the most part
since become famous in the glorious annals of the navy,
were, besides the *Warspite*, the *Mary Rose*, the *Lion*, the
Rainbow, the *Swiftsure*, the *Dreadnought*, and the *Nonpareil*,
with twelve London ships.   Fly-boats for boarding were
to follow.   Howard and Essex were to lead the main
body of the fleet with the great ships less adapted for
manœuvring in shallow waters.   Lord Thomas Howard,
however, who had not been present at the opening of the
Council protested against the precedence accorded to
Raleigh, and proposed to take over the small and handy
Nonpareil from Mr. Dudley, as his own ship, the *Merhonour*,
was among the largest in the fleet.   Such a claim could
not be contested, and the leadership of the van was
entrusted to the two admirals.   Raleigh himself thus
recorded the arrangement : " For mine own part, as I was
willing to give honour to my Lord Thomas, having both
precedency in the army, and being a gentleman whom I
much honoured, so yet I was resolved to give and not
take example for this service, holding mine own reputation dearest, and remembering my great duty to Her
Majesty.   With the first peep of day, therefore, I
weighed anchor, and bare with the Spanish fleet, taking
the start of all ours a good distance."

The Spanish flotilla had already withdrawn into the
inner basin, and as the English advanced, the galleons

and frigates which had been lying under the lee of Cadiz retired and took up their berth athwart the Puntal channel, leaving the city, and St. Mary Port opposite, to the defence of the land forces and batteries. The galleys still lay under the city wall, with their prows bent against the English as they entered, seconding the artillery of the forts. "To show scorn to all which," says Raleigh, "I only answered first the fort and afterward the galleys, to each piece a blur with my trumpet; disdaining to shoot one piece at any or all of those esteemed dreadful monsters." Other vessels following, however, beat upon them so heavily that they took to their oars and joined the fleet in the strait, filling up the gaps between the galleons.

Raleigh himself pressed on, as fast as the light wind permitted, towards the Puntal channel, where the galleons and other fighting craft of the enemy appeared to bridge across the whole of the narrow space. He directed his attention more especially to the *St. Philip* and the *St. Andrew*, with which, mindful of the *Revenge*, he had an account to settle. Having received definite orders not to lay his ships alongside and board, but to await for that purpose the arrival of the promised fly-boats, he anchored by the galleons and opened fire with Lord Thomas Howard, Southwell, Carew, and Clifford in support. His tactics at this period of the fight have given rise to some controversy. Sir Anthony Standen, no partisan of Raleigh, bears witness to the efficacy of his artillery fire. Sir William Monson, on the other hand, criticises the position taken up by him, maintaining that he anchored at too great a distance from the Spaniards; but he mentions that in a subsequent discussion Raleigh contended that his dispositions were governed by the depth of the water. Slyngsby bears this out by recording that the ships came " so near the Spanish fleet as the channel would give them leave," and elsewhere it is stated that he had to wait for the flood tide. It may well be assumed that though there was depth enough for the galleons to withdraw one by one through the Puntal channel, there was now too little water to enable the English to deploy into line at close quarters. In any case Howard shares the responsibility for the movement. Later, when Essex came up in the *Swiftsure*, they all moved farther in, but the artillery duel had been going on for three hours, and the state of the tide may by that time have allowed more room to manœuvre. It is possible also that Raleigh, who had little experience of naval warfare, had yet to gain his knowledge of range and gunfire. That his courage cannot be called in question his whole career, not less than his conduct in the subsequent phases of the action, abundantly proves; and if there is any justification for the criticisms of so bitter a partisan as Monson, which the small losses on the English side seem to some extent to justify, it was not long before he amply atoned for any want of judgment that he may have shown in taking up his first position. The further development of the battle may be told in his own words.

Now after we had beaten, as two butts, one upon another almost three hours (assuring your honour that the volleys of cannon and culverin came as thick as if it had been a skirmish of musketeers), and finding myself in danger to be sunk in the place, I went to my lord general in my skiff, to desire him that he would enforce the promised fly-boats to come up, that I might board ; for as I rid, I could not endure so great a battery any long time.   My lord general was then coming up himself; to whom I declared that if the fly-boats came not I would board with the Queen's ship,—for it was the same loss to burn or sink, for I must endure the one.   The earl finding that it was not in his power to command fear, told me that whatsoever I did, he would second me in person upon his honour.   My lord admiral, having also a disposition to come up at first, but the river was so choked as he could not pass with the *Ark*, came up in person into the *Nonpareil* with my lord Thomas.

While I was thus speaking with the earl, the marshal, who thought it some touch to his great esteemed valour, to ride behind me so many hours, got up ahead my ship ; which my lord Thomas perceiving, headed him again, myself being but a quarter of an hour absent.   At my return, finding myself from being the first to be but the third, I presently let ship anchor, and thrust in between my lord Thomas and the marshal, and went up further ahead than all them before, and thrust myself athwart the channel, so as I was sure none would outstart me again for that day.   My lord general Essex, thinking his ship's side stronger than the rest, thrust the *Dreadnought* aside, and came next the *Warspite* on the left hand, ahead all that rank but my lord Thomas. The marshal, while we had no leisure to look behind us, secretly fastened a rope on my ship's side towards him, to draw himself up equally with me ; but some of my company advertising me thereof, I caused it to be cut off, and so he fell back into his place ; whom I guarded, all but his very prow, from the sight of the enemy.

Now if it please you to remember, that having no hope of my fly-boats to board, and that the Earl and my lord Thomas both promised to second me, I laid out a warp by the side of the *Philip* to shake hands with her (for with the wind we could not get aboard), which, when she and the rest perceived, finding also that the *Repulse* (seeing mine) began to do the like, and the rear-admiral my lord Thomas, they all let slip, and came aground, tumbling into the sea heaps of soldiers, so thick as if coals had been poured out of a sack

in many ports at once, some drowned and some sticking in
the mud.   The *Philip* and the *St. Thomas* burnt themselves;
the *St. Matthew* and the *St. Andrew* were recovered by our
boats ere they could get out to fire them.[1]   The spectacle
was very lamentable on their side ; for many drowned themselves ; many, half-burnt, leaped into the water ; very many
hanging by the ropes' ends by the ships' sides, under the
water even to the lips ; many swimming with grievous
wounds, stricken under water, and put out of their pains ;
and withal so huge a fire, and such tearing of the ordnance
in the great *Philip*, and the rest, when the fire came to
them, as, if any man had a desire to see hell itself, it was
there most lively figured.   Ourselves spared the lives of all
after the victory ; but the Flemings, who did little or nothing
in the fight, used merciless slaughter, till they were by myself, and afterward by my lord admiral beaten off.

No sooner had the defence of the inner basin col-
lapsed than Essex gave orders for the troops to get into
the boats, and himself rowed off to find the spot best
suited for a landing on the spit which connects Cadiz
with the island of Leon.   Only a small proportion of the
forces destined for disembarkation were at present
within reach, but circumstances favoured a bold attack.
The unfortunate Medina Sidonia had witnessed the
disaster of the galleons, and given orders for the laying
up of the *flota* in Port Royal and Carracca Creek, under
cover of such defence as the galleys could provide.   He
was making his way to the Suazo bridge to hurry up
reinforcements, when Vere obtained sanction for the
brilliant feat of arms which secured the city gates to the
English before Howard arrived with a second division of
troops.   Essex had relied upon the Lord High Admiral
to follow up the success achieved at sea, and to pursue

[1] In a note by Raleigh in his own copy of *Les Lauriers de Nassau,*
he claims to have taken both these galleons himself.

the *flota*, at the mercy of the victorious fleet, into the
recesses of the inner basin; but Howard interpreted his
duty otherwise, and hastened with all available forces
to the support of his colleague.   Once more the danger
and confusion inseparable from a divided command
received significant illustration.   Every officer of importance and authority followed the more immediate
prospect of glory and plunder offered by the sack of
Cadiz, and the fleet was left without direction or
control.   Raleigh himself, though he had received
a severe wound, "interlaced and deformed with
splinters," in the latter part of the action, swayed
by the general movement, was carried ashore on his
men's shoulders, and rode into the town on a horse
sent him by the Lord High Admiral.   But the pain of
his wound and the danger of being further injured in
the press of disorganised troopers was so great that he
soon withdrew, the more readily when he realised that
there was no admiral left with the fleet, and but few
seamen on board the ships.   He, however, saw enough
to enable him to write to Cecil a generous letter in
cordial commendation of Essex, who, he said, "hath
behaved himself both valiantly and advisedly in the
highest degree; without pride, without cruelties; and
hath gotten great favour and much love of all."   At
daybreak next morning he sent his nephew, John Gilbert,
with a message to the generals, begging them to order
the fleet to follow up the Indian *flota*, which was beyond
the power of help.   But all was in hopeless confusion
ashore, and his urgent appeal received no answer.   Perhaps the propositions submitted by the merchants of
Cadiz and Seville for the ransom of these ships had

L

already been laid before the generals. In any case negotiations with this object were opened in the course of the morning, and, while the action of the fleet was suspended, Medina's officers adopted the heroic resolution of burning the *flota* with its priceless freight, estimated at twelve million ducats. Only the galleys, or rather a certain number of them escaped, slipping out by the Suazo channel after the English, detailed to hold the bridge, had withdrawn. The material disaster to Spain was only rivalled by the moral blow to her prestige, which rendered the fight at Cadiz one of the most memorable in our annals, and from this victory may, perhaps, be dated the decline of her influence as a world-power.

The question of the permanent occupation of Cadiz was now discussed. Essex strenuously advocated its retention, and was anxious to remain behind as governor. The Lord Admiral, however, who understood his royal mistress, refused to return to England without him, and a majority of the council were adverse to the proposal, on the plea that the provisions still unconsumed would not suffice to maintain a garrison until relief could be sent from England. Half-measures were the order of the day, and Essex was forced reluctantly to renounce his ambition. The castles and forts were then razed to the ground, everything of interest or value which could be placed in the transports was carried away, and hostages for the ransom of the prisoners distributed among the ships. Their subsequent treatment somewhat detracts from the credit of the victors, who in other respects behaved with a restraint which gained for them the commendation of the Spaniards themselves.

The two great ships the *St. Matthew* and *St. Andrew* were brought away as prizes, but the rich Indies fleet had been lost through grave mismanagement and the want of co-ordination between the sea and land services. With regard to the spoils secured Raleigh wrote :

The town of Cales was very rich in merchandise, plate and money ; many rich prisoners (were) given to the land commanders, so as that sort are very rich. Some had prisoners for sixteen thousand ducats ; some for twenty thousand ; some for ten thousand ; and besides great houses of merchandise. What the generals have gotten, I know least : they protest it is little ; for mine own part I have gotten a lame leg, and a deformed ; for the rest either I spake too late, or it was otherwise resolved. I have not wanted good words, and exceeding kind and regardful usage ; but I have possession of nothing but poverty and pain. If God had spared me that blow I had possessed myself of some house.

The statement is disingenuous, for the report of the royal commissioners on the spoils of Cadiz shows him to have held plunder valued at not far short of £2000, which he was allowed to retain. In matters of business he undoubtedly displayed a somewhat grasping and acquisitive character, but it must also be conceded that the greater part of the fortune which he had at one time accumulated was spent in the public service. One valuable asset was brought back to England, the fruits of a descent upon Faro, which was ineffectual as a military operation. This was the library of Bishop Osorius, of Sylves and Algarva, which was claimed for Essex, but afterwards presented to the University of Oxford, where it formed an important nucleus for the great Bodleian Library then in process of formation. It

is conceivable that the presentation may in some degree
have been due to Raleigh's influence, inasmuch as he
was himself, even in the days of his failing fortunes, a
liberal contributor to the famous institution initiated by
Sir Thomas Bodley.

The last phase of the campaign gave rise to long and
bitter disputes. After the descent on Faro a junction
was effected off Lisbon, whence the fleet was to proceed
to the Azores, to intercept the returning Spanish
convoys, in accordance with the original scheme of the
expedition. The weather, however, proved contrary,
and the squadrons were driven northward and dispersed
over a wide area. So soon as they could resume touch,
another council was held, at which Raleigh opposed any
further operations in the Azores at the present season,
and the scheme was rejected on account of the shortness of supplies. Essex was, nevertheless, prepared to
go himself with a small squadron, provisioned with such
stores as the rest of the fleet could spare. Monson
suggests that the spoils of Cadiz made the majority of
the commanders anxious to return home, and, never to be
trusted when criticising Raleigh, attributes his opposition
to jealousy of Essex. Raleigh may be credited with
higher motives. He had shown himself to be cautious
in sea service, especially when great issues were at stake.
He had experienced the dangers of the present divided
command, and had assisted in averting disaster by
bringing the views of the two generals into tardy
harmony at a critical moment. He perceived the
fleet, in which there was much sickness, to be a little
out of hand, and after the experience of Lord
Thomas Howard at the Azores, he was justified in

disapproving the despatch of a weak force to operate there. If a strong fleet was unable to proceed for the reasons which had rendered the retention of Cadiz impossible, Raleigh had good reason to advocate the abandonment of the enterprise altogether. The utmost which Essex could persuade his colleagues to attempt was a descent upon Corunna and Ferrol, where he found not a ship to destroy. The Queen who, as usual, was deeply interested in the partition of the spoils, and indignant that they had not been greater, found fault with her faithful old servant, the Lord High Admiral, for not having supported the proposal of Essex to sail to the Azores. In his reply to certain criticisms on the campaign Essex attributes the more conspicuous omissions to dissensions in his council, and in two places mentions Raleigh by name as sharing the responsibility. He must, however, have convinced himself that Raleigh's opinions expressed at the Council were given in good faith and not without justification, for soon after their return from Cadiz they were for a time on terms of friendly intimacy. Not only did Essex not oppose his eventual restoration to Court, but he summoned him to the Council of War which met in the ensuing autumn, and, on the renewal of his own command at sea, once more secured his former Vice-Admiral as a colleague.

From Ferrol the squadrons hurried home. There was a lack of dignity in the anxiety of the rival commanders to be the first to report the proceedings of the fleet, and claim, each for himself, a maximum of the credit. If the views of the various leaders on the due apportionment of merit in this action resembled those of the Athenian admirals after the battle of Salamis, the verdict of his countrymen on Raleigh's services has been similar to that of the Athenians in the case of Themistocles. The figure of the magnificent courtier, in his plumed and jewelled bravery on the poop of the *Warspite*, defying the artillery of the forts and the ordnance of the galleys with a blast from his silver trumpet, or thrusting his ship athwart the Puntal channel in generous emulation for the post of danger, appealed to the popular imagination; and, though Essex bore no public testimony to his deserts, there is ample evidence that by the public at large he was regarded as the hero of the fight at Cadiz. His friend and admirer, Sir George Carew, bore witness in a letter to Robert Cecil that "that which he did in the sea service could not be bettered"; and Sir Anthony Standen, an officer and partisan of Essex, wrote to Burghley in the following terms:—"Sir Walter Raleigh did, in my judgment, no man better; and his artillery most effect: I never knew the gentleman until this time, and I am sorry for it, for there are in him excellent things besides his valour; and the observation he hath in this voyage used with my lord of Essex hath made me love him."

CHAPTER IX

1597

THE action at Cadiz roused the aged bigot at Madrid to one last display of energy, and neither the exhaustion of his treasury, the mutinous attitude of his nobility, the despair of the ruined merchants, nor even the pacific counsels of the papal nuncio could alter his determination to wipe out this dire disgrace. The convoys had reached home in safety. With the galleons returned from foreign service, and vessels seized by embargo to act as transports, a new Armada was prepared in Lisbon and San Lucar, and the command entrusted to a Lepanto veteran, Martin de Padilla, Adelantado of Castille. At the same time the policy of half-measures pursued at home had gradually brought about a situation which justified grave anxiety. The Spaniards were firmly established in Calais and in Brittany. Ireland was threatened with another rebellion, and Spanish officers were reported to have landed there to organise revolt. The long duration of the war had caused acute distress, and even the city of London pleaded inability to continue supplying those large contingents hitherto so generously equipped. Military organisation was practically non-existent, and the navy was in no condition, after the strain which it had lately undergone, to resume the offensive. At such a crisis it was to Essex, whose influence in overcoming the Queen's vacillation had been revealed in the late emergency, that all men looked as to the man of the hour, and for a while he rose to the height of the occasion with a soberness and strength which justified his popularity. When in the first days of November news arrived that the Spanish fleet was actually concentrating in Ferrol, a Council of War was summoned to meet under his auspices, which included all the most experienced captains, such as Vere, Clifford, Norris, Borough, Willoughby, Carew, and Raleigh.

Raleigh's opinion that the contemplated invasion would not be attempted until the following summer was soundly supported by logical and convincing arguments; but he had not reckoned with Philip's insensate impatience, and gave him credit for prudence which he did not possess. Events proved that the forecast of Essex, who, holding that the enemy would come on without delay, was supported by a majority of the Council, correctly interpreted the movement to Ferrol. It was decided that Plymouth, the Isle of Wight, and Southampton should be strongly garrisoned, while the fleet was to be employed in giving the enemy check, so as to allow time for the land forces to concentrate at any menaced spot. But once more the elements and Philip's crazy infatuation, in despatching an unready fleet to sea to cope with Atlantic storms, relieved the country from the need for further preparations. A gale wrecked seven galleons and twenty-five other

vessels on the rocks of Finisterre, and the remnant of
the broken Armada was helpless for further aggression.
Still the old King's courage was not broken, and, though
he was forced to repudiate his loans, a new armament
was equipped during the winter at Ferrol with such
energy as a bankrupt exchequer could enforce. Proposals submitted by Essex and Cumberland for an
attack on Ferrol were rejected. The danger was not
yet sufficiently urgent, and the inland counties were
murmuring at the obligation to contribute to the fleet.
Essex took the rejection of his scheme very ill; and
he had other causes for discontent in the promotion
of Robert Cecil, in whom he instinctively divined an
antagonist, to the Secretaryship of State, in place
of his own candidate, Sir Thomas Bodley, and in
the Queen's refusal to bestow the Wardenship of
the Cinque Ports on his friend Sir Robert Sidney.
Raleigh, who saw no hope for action till he was pacified,
endeavoured to bring about a reconciliation with Cecil.
It was, however, only when the Queen herself gratified
the Earl's long-cherished desire by making him Master
of the Ordnance that his ill-humour passed. Raleigh's
efforts then bore fruit, and in April he met Essex and
Cecil in daily conference. On the 1st of June Cecil
brought him to the palace, where the Queen received
him graciously, and gave him authority to resume his
duties as Captain of the Guard. In the evening he
rode with the Queen, and ever after went boldly to
the Privy Chamber as of old.

In the meantime he had neglected no precautions for
the defence of his lieutenancy in the west of England,
which seemed destined to bear the brunt of the antici-

pated invasion. The following letter, which has only recently come to light, is of interest in illustrating the history of this period, as it shows that warrants were issued to private gentlemen to arm and train their tenants, and place their houses in a state to resist attack.

To my loving friend John Rashleigh, of the town of Fowey, Esquire.[1]

Whereas you have of your own great charge made a place of defence in your house at Fowey, and furnished the same with ordnance and munition for the better repulsing of the enemy upon any attempt by them to be made by sea against the said town, which place hath been seen and very well allowed of by my Deputy Lieutenant. I have therefore thought it requisite for Her Majesty's service to require you that you continue your care therein, and not to suffer the same to be impaired or disfurnished. And for the better effecting thereof, I do hereby assign and authorise you, your servants, and families, together with such twelve of your tenants dwelling in the said town, or next about, as yourself shall make choice of, to be always attendant to the said place of defence, and for that intent I hereby do discharge you and them from all watching, warding, training, mustering, and other martial services whatsoever. And that it shall be lawful for you to furnish, arm, provide, and train the persons above, and at all times, and to employ them in this service from time to time as occasion shall be offered, and as to your discretion shall seem convenient. In which doing this my writing shall be your sufficient warrant given under my hand and seal, the xiiiith (fourteenth) of April 1597.

Signed,　W. RALEGH.

---

[1] This letter, which is not included in the collection of Edwards, and which, so far as the author knows, is now published for the first time, has been placed at his disposal by Mr. Jonathan Rashleigh of Menabilly, to whom certain property of the kindred family of Raleigh has passed by direct descent. The letter is written in the hand of a secretary, but the signature is in Sir Walter's own writing, and his seal is affixed.

Preparations for an attack on the Spanish coasts were now once more prosecuted. Raleigh was entrusted with the victualling of six thousand men for three months; and Essex, in virtue of his new office, devoted his indomitable energy to putting some system into the military organisation of the country. By the middle of June a fleet, consisting of seventeen royal ships with their due contingent of pinnaces, transports, and store-ships, got to sea under the chief command of Essex, with Lord Thomas Howard as Vice-Admiral, and Raleigh as Rear-Admiral, while the fourth squadron of twenty-two Dutchmen was led by Dyvenvoord. Five thousand soldiers were on board under Vere as Lord Marshal, who, to his indignation, was nominally subordinated to a Lieutenant-General in young Lord Mountjoy, the latest favourite of a Queen still fancy free. At Cadiz Vere and Raleigh had parted not on the best of terms. While the fleet lay off the Kentish coast Essex caused them to meet and shake hands, which they did right willingly, having had nothing between them "which might blemish reputations."

Essex had instructions to attack the fleet preparing at Ferrol, unless the Adelantado had already got to sea, in which case he was to operate against him at his discretion. Having secured the command of the sea, he had authority to proceed to the Azores and intercept the Spanish convoys. Unfortunately the watchful eye of old John Hawkins was wanting now, and the ships were full of defects and miserably manned. After battling for a week with an Atlantic storm Raleigh in the *Warspite*, believing the fleet had already put back, returned to Plymouth. Essex held out a few days longer and reached Falmouth with the *Merhonour* sinking under him. Only the old professional sailor Lord Thomas rode out the gale, and made Corunna before he rejoined the flag. Bad luck pursued Essex. His ships became infected with sickness, and the gale showed no signs of abating. At length a new flagship, the *Lion*, was ready to receive him. He disembarked all the troops with the exception of a thousand Netherland veterans, and got away with the wind on the 17th of August.

It seemed clear that at so advanced a season the Adelantado would not hazard any serious attempt at invasion that year; nevertheless the Queen had insisted on the movement against Ferrol, which was now to be limited to a fire-ship attack, and with this object the first rendezvous was fixed at Finisterre. A gale drove the fleet into the Bay of Biscay, and they had much ado to beat out again. The *St. Matthew*, one of the Cadiz prizes, was disabled, and only carried into a French port by the undaunted courage of Carew. Essex, who had again transferred his flag to the *Repulse*, was delayed by a dangerous leak, and in doubling Cape Prior Raleigh's mainyard snapped, forcing him to drive before the wind and pass on to the second rendezvous at Lisbon. The *Dreadnought* stood by him in his difficulties, which were increased by the failure of his mainmast, and a number of other vessels followed him. An attack on Ferrol with the reduced squadron was impracticable, and Spanish captures confirmed the report that the Armada would not sail that year. Raleigh, on the other hand, was told off Lisbon that the Adelantado had actually got away to the Azores, and managed to convey this improbable information to Essex, who eagerly swallowed it, and ordered the Rear-Admiral to join him at the islands. On the 15th of September the two Admirals met at Flores and dined together. Satisfactory explanations of his reasons for parting company were given by Raleigh, and Essex, who was in reality relieved to have so good an excuse for running direct to the Azores, treated him with every consideration, in spite of the endeavours of his enemies to create friction.

A pinnace homeward bound from the Indies brought a further misleading report that the treasure fleet, even if it sailed that year, would in any case avoid the islands, and Essex unfortunately developed his plan of action with his usual precipitancy on the assumption that the information was correct. The various islands of the central group were assigned to different squadrons, and they were to distrain for supplies to enable them to hold the sea. The strongly fortified roadstead of Terceira was not to be attempted at present. Essex and Raleigh were to co-operate in seizing the roadstead of Fayal, the second position of strength. Mountjoy and Blount were despatched east to St. Michaels. Lord Thomas Howard was to watch the approaches to Terceira, while the Dutch squadron undertook Pico. Raleigh, the last to arrive at Flores, was short of water, and had commenced filling his casks when he received orders to follow Essex without delay to Fayal, but the impetuous General was already out of sight by the time he got to sea. When on the following day he anchored in the roadstead the co-operating squadron was nowhere to be seen. He waited impatiently, and only on the third day called a Council to discuss the situation, at which the partisans of Essex strongly opposed landing until the missing ships arrived. He waited yet another day, and was then compelled by a shift of the wind to change his position and lie under the lee of a headland which screened him from the town. This brought him in view of a convenient watering-place, and as there was still no sign of the missing General, he determined to complete the operations which had been interrupted at Fayal, landing a company to guard the water party. The Spanish troops, however, seeing his preparations, marched down to hold the springs. With two hundred and sixty seamen and volunteers, he rowed ashore in the face of an enemy twice as numerous and protected by entrenchments. The seamen wavered under their heavy fire, but Raleigh, bidding those follow him who were not afraid, rallied their courage, and clambering over broken rocks led a brilliant dash on the entrenchments, which the Spaniards abandoned. Action was now engaged, and it was impossible to draw back or prolong the delay without discredit. The boats returned to the ships for a complement of veteran troops, which brought up the force to some five hundred men. The road to the town of Orta, some five miles distant, was guarded by two forts, which enfiladed the line of march. Raleigh, with forty gentlemen volunteers, led them past the fort on the headland without waiting for his armour. But the fire was hot and the troops ran for cover. Then buckling on his cuirass, he set out with Sir Arthur Gorges, the historian of this action, and a small company to reconnoitre the road, under a searching fire from the fort. Gorges was wounded in the leg, and Sir Walter himself had several bullets through his clothes, but the reconnaissance was suc-

cessful. A safe line of advance was discovered, and both
the town and the second fort were evacuated on their
approach. Only the fort on the headland remained to
be dealt with. Early the next morning Essex, who,
retaining both Mountjoy and Howard, had gone in pursuit of an imaginary treasure ship, entered the roadstead. His mortification was extreme. Single-handed
his rival had made himself master of Fayal, and the
honours of the fight were his alone. In the bitterness
of a disappointment for which he had only himself to
blame, it was not difficult for his jealous partisans to
persuade him that Raleigh had broken orders and
rendered himself liable to the extreme penalty of disobedience. The officers who had landed were placed
under arrest, and the Rear-Admiral was summoned to
the *Repulse* to give an account of his action. His
defence was clear and complete. The article of war
under which he was called in question laid down that
no captain of a ship or company, if separated from the
fleet, should land without orders from the General or
some principal commander under pain of death. He
claimed, however, to be a principal commander, upon
whom, in succession to Essex and Howard, the whole
command would by royal letters patent devolve. As
such he was not subject to the article in question.
Moreover, he had orders to complete his water at Fayal,
and it was this operation which had brought on a
general action. He protested against the arrest of his
officers, and claimed to be alone responsible. Essex
appeared to be satisfied with this explanation, and went
ashore to visit Raleigh in his quarters. Lord Thomas
Howard intervened in a spirit of conciliation, and

persuaded Raleigh to offer a formal excuse, which Essex
honourably accepted. The incident was closed, but it
had given Raleigh an insight into the real sentiments
of Essex towards himself which he was not likely to
forget, and no mention of the capture of Fayal was
recorded to his credit in the public despatches. Meanwhile the other fort had been evacuated, and nothing
now remained but to carry off the ordnance and such
plunder as the town afforded.

The general plan of action had not been followed. Only the Dutch squadron, after laying waste
the island of Pico, was at its appointed destination
guarding the western approaches. Essex now led his
combined fleet to Graciosa and thence to St. Michaels,
which he announced his intention of taking before
returning home. Some confusion arose in the trans-
mission of orders, and four ships, among which was
Monson's, got away to the west instead of the south-
east. Scarcely had Essex sailed when Monson found
himself in sight of the plate-fleet, escorted by eight
Spanish galleons. All through the night he made the
concerted signals, but no friendly sail bore up, and it
was only in the morning that the *Garland* found him,
followed by the *Mary Rose* and *Dreadnought*, and seconded
his efforts to bring the enemy's rearguard to action.
The Spaniards refused battle and held on their course
till they had carried the convoy safely under the guns
of Terceira. Incredible mismanagement had snatched
the prize from the Englishmen's grasp. The successive
invasion of islands which they could not hold was of
little practical value. The Angra road of Terceira, with
its powerful defences, was the real key of the situation,

and this Essex had excluded from his scheme of operation, as too strong for the small force at his disposal.
The capture of the fortified roadstead of Fayal was a
comprehensible step : the dispersion of the fleet among
the islands, with a view to rapid concentration, should
the plate - fleet be sighted, was also an intelligible
proposal ; but the orders given to the united squadrons
to proceed to St. Michaels could not be defended.
Monson, in his account of the expedition, attributes
all the blame to the inexperience of the Commander-
in-Chief, and to his weakness in yielding to the representations of divers gentlemen who, "coming principally for land service, found themselves tired by
the tediousness of the sea." Monson himself did
his best to retrieve the disaster, and attacked the
Spaniards in the very mouth of the harbour. But an
attempt to cut out some disabled ships was repelled by
overwhelming forces, and there was nothing left for the
four British ships to do but impotently to await the
return of the fleet. Before that took place, on the last
day of September, the treasure had been landed and
stored, and the galleons were drawn up in an impreg-
nable position under the shelter of the forts. In his
despair Essex was now ready to undertake what he had
deemed impossible, even before the arrival of the Spanish
reinforcements. Howard and Raleigh were willing to
second the attempt with their seamen, but the plan was
found to be impracticable, and it was decided to await
the next movement of the enemy at St. Michaels. On
his way, however, Essex had succeeded in capturing
a rich Havana ship of four hundred tons, whose cargo,
consisting of gold, silver, pearls, and spices, went far to

M

pay for the cost of the expedition. Raleigh had the generosity to express his satisfaction that there would now be "no repining against this poor lord for the expenses of the voyage."

Ill luck pursued them to St. Michaels, where Raleigh was left to make a demonstration off Punta Delgada, while Essex and Howard sought a more sheltered landing-place at Villa Franca. A big East India carrack was observed standing in for the bay. Her capture seemed inevitable, when one of the Dutch ships gave the alarm by prematurely opening fire, and she altered her course and ran ashore. The crew escaped in boats, and the splendid prize, laden with spices, was burned to the water's edge, perfuming all the coast, before Raleigh and his men could reach her through the heavy sea in their barges. The march overland from Villa Franca to the capital was found to be too long and arduous, and Raleigh was ordered to rejoin the rest of the fleet, which had meanwhile been restocked. Too much time had been lost, and the stormy season was already at hand when, on the 9th of October, they sailed for home in the most direct line each ship could make.

That very day the last Armada had sailed for the channel. The Adelantado, driven to sea against his better judgment by Philip's importunity, had orders to establish a base at Falmouth. Thence the fleet was to return and embark contingents from Lisbon. With a large number of English ships detained in the Azores, with rebellion in Ireland, and a Spanish occupation of Calais and Brittany, the scheme offered no insuperable difficulties. But the Adelantado had sailed too late, and the English could count on the autumn gales as a

constant ally. The Channel defence squadron and the
land forces were mobilised, thanks in great measure to
the reforms inaugurated by Essex, with a rapidity on
which Philip had not reckoned; and the fleet returning
from the Azores in ignorance of the Spanish move and
unhampered by strategic obligations, made a quick
journey home, in spite of the tempestuous weather,
which was once more to disperse the forces of the
invader. The journey was, however, not without incident. The *Warspite*, which throughout had not proved
too seaworthy, was in collision soon after the start,
and became so leaky that she was with difficulty kept
afloat. John Davis, who was acting as navigating
officer to Essex, failed, in spite of all his experience, to
recognise the banks of Scilly, and passed north of the
Land's End in spite of the protest of Raleigh's sailing-
master, heading straight for the Welsh coast. The
signal guns of the *Warspite*, however, arrested Essex
before it was too late, and he tacked about. ·Raleigh
himself, who had been unable to water or provision at
St. Michaels, anchored in the last extremity at St.
Ives, whence he made his way overland to Plymouth,
and found that Mountjoy had already arrived with
four galleons. Essex followed shortly afterwards, and
posting up to London, received full powers to provide
for the national defence, in a letter from the Queen,
which made no allusion to his recent failure beyond a
caution to "weigh well the value of intelligence before
taking irrevocable action." Raleigh, in the meantime,
was organising the forces of his western lieutenancy,
while Howard took charge of the fleet. The progress
of the Adelantado remained a mystery, until a captured

Spanish fly-boat gave information that the Armada had been scattered by the easterly gales at a point some ten leagues from the Lizard. A few stragglers held on to Falmouth, and were actually sighted there; others took refuge, and were captured, in the ports of the Bristol Channel. Ineffectually the mighty fleet had melted away before the rage of the elements, and ship after ship, without waiting for orders, ran back before the wind to Spain. Thus for the third and last time came to nought Philip's stubborn effort to put back the hand of time and arrest the progress of our national destiny. This disaster, and the ensuing recrudescence of activity on the part of the English privateers, taught him on his death-bed the lesson which his life had left unlearned; and in his last advice to his successor he urged him to come to terms with that stubborn race of heretics who had proved too strong for him, and to accord them the license to travel and trade in the Indies, the refusal of which had transferred to England the sceptre of the sea.

The following year was big with great events. If Henry the Fourth of France, by the peace of Verviers, was pledged to withdraw his half-hearted support, the Netherlands renewed their treaty with the Queen. Philip and his life-long adversary, the veteran Burghley, were both removed from the scene. The exhaustion of Spain and the vigour of the Protestant Powers marked a new distribution of forces, which tended to the restoration of peace. There was to be one more alarm of invasion, and one more summons to the flag, if indeed the mobilisation of 1599 was not in reality rather a precautionary measure occasioned by the menace of domestic disturbances. In any case, Lord Thomas Howard, with Raleigh as Vice-Admiral, organised the naval forces with a promptitude and energy which discounted the plans of the enemy. The threatened attack was never made, and the fleet was paid off without having fired a shot against the "Invisible Armada." This was Raleigh's last naval experience. Throughout his career he was rather a soldier than a sailor by profession, and he never enjoyed the opportunities afforded by an independent command. In one at least of the two expeditions to the Spanish coast, in which he led a squadron, his judgment contributed in no small degree to the success of the enterprise. His title to fame does not rest on his achievement as an admiral, but in a man so various and so versatile his sea service is at least respectable, and it afforded him brilliant occasions for the display of that conspicuous gallantry in which he was surpassed by none of his great contemporaries. Henceforth new names appear in the annals of the sea, and the giants of old withdraw from the quarter-decks of the galleons.

CHAPTER X

THE failure of the campaign in the Azores had been viewed with remarkable indulgence at Court. But Essex was out of conceit with himself, and gave way to the ill-humour which he never concealed from the Queen when his imperious will was thwarted or a rival received preferment. The growing influence of Cecil, in whom, notwithstanding their intimacy, he recognised an antagonist, was as distasteful to him as the advancement of the "sycophant" Cobham; but what he for the moment most resented was the bestowal of an earldom on the Lord High Admiral. As a holder of one of the four great offices of state the new Earl of Nottingham could now claim precedence over all other earls, of whatever date of creation. Alleging the plea of ill-health he withdrew from Court with his offended dignity, suffering the real cause of his irritation to be advertised by the group of flatterers who had identified themselves with his fortunes. After a first outburst of anger at his pretensions the Queen was quick to relent, and Raleigh, who since his restoration to favour had displayed his usual address in securing his position, was employed to effect a reconciliation.

166

His ingenious suggestion was adopted. Essex was created Earl Marshal, and becoming thus the incumbent of another of the four great offices, recovered the precedence of his rank. But the favourite was only appeased at the expense of Nottingham, who had enjoyed his temporary triumph, and now himself retired from the Court in turn. The growing familiarity of Raleigh, Essex, and Cecil was once more the subject of comment; and when the last-named left for France in February, 1598, to watch the negotiations between Henry and Spain, some sort of compact appears to have been drawn up by the triumvirate, in accordance with which Essex pledged himself during Cecil's absence not to urge councils which might contravene his policy or press for appointments which he could not approve. His attitude, however, towards the Spanish negotiations tended once more to create friction at Court, which other episodes rendered acute. His defence of the young Earl of Southampton, the friend and patron of Shakespeare, who had committed the unpardonable crime of matrimony, was hardly forgiven, when the Queen's refusal to entertain his candidate, Sir George Carew, as Ormonde's successor in Ireland, led to the memorable scene in Council at which Elizabeth, provoked by a gesture of impatience, dismissed him with a box on the ear. To the wild words which he is said to have used on this occasion Raleigh attributed his final downfall, and from this time both he and Cecil abandoned any further hope of an understanding. The death of Burghley had brought on the struggle for supremacy which was to prove fatal to Essex, and the preferment of Cecil made them irreconcilable enemies.

His ambition, thwarted in the immediate present, saw possibilities in the future. The burning question of the succession filled all men's thoughts. King James of Scotland, who was endeavouring to form a party in England to support him in the day of issue, opened secret communications with Essex, as he also did in Ireland with the rebel Tyrone, with whom the former, as Lord Deputy, was shortly to attempt a composition. It is probable that Cecil had early knowledge of these intrigues, and realised that there would be no place for himself or for Raleigh in the councils of a king who believed he owed the reversion of the throne to Essex. If there is no evidence of a definite breach with Raleigh at this time, there is evidence of the bitterness with which Essex regarded the renewal of his ascendency over their royal mistress. The fact is they had been, consciously or unconsciously, life-long antagonists. To a noble of the sixteenth century the successful Raleigh appeared in the light of a dangerous adventurer, whose ostentatious equipages savoured of the parvenu. Sir Walter, on the other hand, proud as Lucifer, and conscious that he came of as good a stock as any in England, resented the appreciation he could not ignore; and his resentment was not the less deep because his self-control enabled him to bear with temper much that he regarded as insolence. In their various encounters Raleigh had not unfrequently shown himself the better gentleman. The year after his arrival at Court Essex had unmasked his feelings in a letter to an intimate friend. During a royal progress to Theobalds the Queen, while staying at North Hall in Hertfordshire, had given some real or imaginary cause for offence by

ignoring the presence of his sister, the wife of Sir
Thomas Perrot, who in early days had quarrelled with
Raleigh. He had told the Queen that her real reason
for offering this disgrace to himself and his sister "was
only to please that knave Raleigh." The Queen's
remonstrance, he added, "did so trouble me that, as
near as I could, I did describe unto her what he had
been and what he was. I was loth to be near about
her, when I knew . . . such a wretch as Raleigh highly
esteemed of her."

In the following year, a few weeks after the defeat of
the Armada, the Council intervened to prevent a duel
between the rivals, all reference to which has been
buried in silence. Then followed their unexpected
meeting during the expedition to Portugal, when a
fresh occasion of conflict arose through the support
given by Essex to his partisan, Sir Roger Williams, in
his attempt to embargo Raleigh's share of prize
money, and on Sir Walter's temporary withdrawal from
Court, Essex remained all-powerful with the Queen
until he incurred her anger by his marriage with
Frances Walsingham. In the hour of his disgrace
Raleigh once more became the indispensable courtier at
the Queen's right hand, till he in turn, by a similar
indiscretion, fell under displeasure, and Essex resumed
the place to which he held it presumption in another to
aspire. It was long before Raleigh found forgiveness,
and once he had ceased to be formidable as a rival the
great qualities, which even his worst enemies admitted,
could not be ignored by a man of frankly generous
character like Essex, who had grown older and wiser
since their first encounter ten years earlier. He there-

fore welcomed his former rival's participation in the
Cadiz enterprise with that open-hearted warmth which
was natural to him when left to his own impulses.
The results of the expedition were, however, little
calculated to promote harmony between these two restless natures, whose only bond of union was their
common eagerness to prosecute the war with Spain.
The Islands' voyage only served to widen the breach.
The little success achieved redounded exclusively to the
credit of Sir Walter, who would have been more than
human if he had forgiven the scene on the quarter-deck
of the *Repulse*. Restored to favour and daily consulted
on questions of foreign and domestic policy, while
Essex himself was wilfully exhausting the patience of a
most indulgent mistress, Raleigh became the object of
his cordial detestation, which he was petty enough to
exhibit by a most unfortunate attempt to humiliate his
rival. He had learned that, at a tournament to be held
on the Queen's birthday, Raleigh, who was now in his
forty-seventh year and somewhat beyond the age for
such rough sports, nevertheless intended to appear, and
that his train would be distinguished by orange-coloured
plumes. He accordingly mustered a large company, said
to have numbered some two thousand horsemen, decorated
in similar fashion, and himself, attired in an orange suit
with closed vizor, entered the lists at their head, thus
reducing Raleigh's little band to the semblance of a
section of his own following. The device served him
ill, for he made so poor a show in the tilting that he
found it discreet to change his dress and reappear
unmasked in a livery of green. His identity was,
however, detected, and Bacon has preserved the ironical

reply made to a spectator who inquired why the orange knight had changed his colours, "Surely because it may be reported that there was one in green who ran worse than he in orange-colour."

The appointment of a new governor to Ireland, where the rebellion, which had gathered strength under Tyrone, demanded a ruler of experience, gave rise to much discussion. It has been maintained that the appointment was actually offered to Raleigh and was by him refused; but it is scarcely credible that he would have declined so great an office, however distasteful a return to "that lost land" might have been to his inclinations, nor is it probable that Essex would have accepted a position which had been rejected by his rival. Mountjoy's nomination was seriously considered, but was opposed by Essex on the grounds of his want of experience and a devotion to study which prejudiced his activity. The pacification of the Continent offered few opportunities to an ambitious soldier, and the prospect of military operations in Ireland may have first induced Essex to covet the governorship. It is also reasonable to assume that both Cecil and Raleigh were forward in urging his appointment to the grave of reputations. In any case he consented at last to fill the thankless post himself, and he had no sooner left to take command of the largest army which had ever been mustered in Ireland, than he realised that in accepting office he was playing into the hands of his enemies, as he candidly admitted in his desponding and passionate letters to the Queen. His partisans took care that his wrongs should be in all men's ears. His open-handed generosity, his courage and his magnificence, had ever made him a popular idol, and he now came to be regarded as the victim of self-seeking intriguers who had triumphed over his disinterested patriotism. There must have been some extraordinary fascination, some indefinable ascendency in Essex, which won for him the constant affection of the populace, the devotion of his personal adherents, and almost persuaded no less a man than Mountjoy to contemplate the crime of treason for friendship's sake.

In Ireland he assumed a royal state, and proclaimed an era of amnesty and restitution. A humaner policy in that distracted land may well have been the more judicious course, but it was adopted before he had time to form any real estimate of the situation, and it was certainly inconsistent with his instructions. His repeated truces with Tyrone, followed by perpetual demands for reinforcements and subventions, gave colour to the suspicion that his policy was less inspired by motives of benevolence than by the ambition to guarantee his own independence and overawe his enemies. To Raleigh, as to most of his contemporaries, composition with rebellion was inconceivable, and it was his inspiration which Essex detected in the severe letters of censure which his proceedings evoked from the Queen. The compact resulting from his interview with Tyrone was the culmination of a policy which fulfilled the anticipations of those who had foreseen that his administration of Ireland would inevitably lead to his ruin. In the summer of 1599 a sudden mobilisation of all the available forces in England was ordered. A fleet under Lord Thomas Howard and Sir Walter put to sea with extraordinary rapidity ; a guard of six thousand men was told off for the protection of the Queen's person ; and for a fortnight chains were stretched across the streets of London, and lights maintained all night. No former menace of the Adelantado's armadas had ever produced such a panic, and a general suspicion was aroused that such preparations were less inspired by the dread of foreign invasion than by news which had reached the Queen's advisers of some desperate project conceived by the Lord Deputy. Sir Christopher Blount, on the scaffold, in answer to a question of Raleigh's, unhesitatingly replied that Essex had in Dublin discovered to him his intention "to transport a choice part of the army in Ireland into England, and to land them in Wales, at Milford, or thereabouts," and having thus secured his communications, to gather together such other forces as would enable him to march on London. Blount himself had urged him rather "to go over himself with a good train, and make sure of the Court," and such was the course which Essex pursued, without waiting for the authorisation of Queen or Council. He found the Queen at Nonsuch, and bursting unannounced and unceremoniously into the private apartments, was committed as a prisoner to the Lord Keeper's custody. The story of his treason, of which the final act was but an episode, is in many points obscure ; but it is possible from the confessions of his fellow-conspirators to reconstitute a good deal of the preliminary history, which indicates clearly that the real object in view was the removal of Cecil, Raleigh, and others of the Queen's advisers. The subject can only be dealt with here in so far as it has been held to compromise the character of Raleigh, and in order to defend him from the charge of being privy to the death of

Essex. That Raleigh desired to render him innocuous, that after much provocation he failed in the generosity he had displayed in previous encounters, is neither doubtful nor surprising ; that he was active in procuring the Earl's final condemnation is a charge which there is no evidence to sustain.

It appears from contemporary correspondence that public indignation was aroused by the detention of the Earl, who had been committed to honourable captivity at York House, on the 1st of October, 1599, without any form of trial, and at a Court of Star Chamber held on the 28th of November it was agreed to declare the causes of his imprisonment. Cecil was the means of conveying to the Queen a letter of submission, which saved him from being brought before that dreaded tribunal. In March he was permitted to occupy his own house, and on the 5th of June he appeared before a special commission, appointed to examine into the administration of Ireland, and to try the charge of disobeying the royal command. The sentence of the commissioners, in which it was made clear that had he been brought before the Star Chamber perpetual imprisonment in the Tower must have followed, was that he should exercise no public office, and continue a prisoner at the Queen's pleasure in his own house. Cecil, who was studious not to appear as in active antagonism to so popular a personality, is reported at this time to have been constant in good offices to his prisoner, who was released on the 26th of August.

During a great part of 1600 Raleigh was absent from Court. In March and April he was at Sherborne. In May he accompanied Cobham on a secret mission to Prince Maurice, who was endeavouring to relieve Ostend, to which the Archduke had laid siege. On his return, apparently in July, he was appointed Governor of Jersey, whither he proceeded in the early autumn, and before the end of the year he was back again at Sherborne. To this period, and probably to the early months of 1600, must be ascribed a much-debated letter to Cecil, preserved among the Hatfield papers. It is signed with the initials W. R. only, and bears no date, but it is endorsed *Sir Walter Raleigh* in Cecil's own writing, and 1601 has been added by a later hand. The assignment to 1601 is obviously an error. After the open rebellion of Essex at the beginning of that year, there would have been no occasion for Cecil to invite an opinion on the opportuneness of magnanimity, and Sir Walter was in London during the outbreak and the trial. The matter of the letter clearly points to a time when the question of trial before the Star Chamber hung in the balance, and when Cecil had assumed an overt attitude of conciliation. It was probably written from Sherborne, where Will Cecil, who was being brought up with young Walter Raleigh, would be before the writer's eyes. The text is as follows.

Sir—I am not wise enough to give you advice ; but if you take it for a good counsel to relent towards this tyrant, you will repent it when it shall be too late. His malice is fixed, and will not evaporate by any our mild courses. For he will ascribe the alteration to her Majesty's pusillanimity, and not to your good nature ; knowing that you work but upon her humour, and not out of any love towards him. The less you make him the less he shall be able to harm you and yours. And if her Majesty's favour fail him, he will again decline to a common person.

For after-revenges, fear them not ; for your own father that was esteemed to be the contriver of Norfolk's ruin, yet

his son followeth your father's son, and loveth him. Humours
of men succeed not, but grow by occasions of time and power.
Somerset made no revenge on the Duke of Northumberland's
heirs.   Northumberland, that now is, thinks not of Hatton's
issue.   Kelloway lives, that murdered the brother of Horsey ;
and Horsey let him go by all his lifetime.

I could name you a thousand of those ; and therefore
after-fears are but prophecies—or rather conjectures—from
causes remote. Look to the present and you do wisely. His
son shall be the youngest earl of England but one, and, if his
father be now kept down, Will Cecil shall be able to keep as
many men at his heels as he, and more too.   He may also
match in a better house than his ; and so that fear is not
worth the fearing. But if the father continue, he will be able
to break the branches, and pull up the tree, root and all.
Lose not your advantage ; if you do, I read your destiny.—
Yours to the end,   W. R.

(*Added in the margin*).   Let the Q. hold Bothwell, while
she hath him.   He will ever be the canker of her estate and
safety.   Princes are lost by security, and preserved by pre-
vention.   I have seen the last of her good days, and all ours,
after his liberty.

Admirers of Raleigh's genius cannot but wish this
letter unwritten. He had received ample provocation,
and could not ignore the danger to himself involved in
the restoration to fortune of one whom he had little cause
to love.   The partisans of the Earl ascribed all his mis-
carriages to the machinations of Raleigh, who bore the
brunt of the popular indignation, while the adroit Cecil,
for the most part, managed to escape criticism.   The
letter indeed contains nothing to justify the interpretation
of those who have read it as an attempt to dissuade Cecil
from recommending a pardon after the condemnation of
Essex.   The whole phraseology indicates that it was trial
before the Star Chamber, with its inevitable consequences
of imprisonment in the Tower, which Raleigh was advo-

cating, and the very reference to his son as destined
to be the youngest earl in England, however we may
interpret a careless phrase, is evidence that there was no
question of attainder at the time this letter·was penned.
Yet it remains an ungenerous letter, and one would wish
Raleigh to have erred on the side of generosity, the
more so as this lapse from better judgment was only
temporary, and he afterwards bitterly regretted his
hostility.

During the Earl's long confinement, his friends, concerned for his safety, had reopened the correspondence
with King James; and even Mountjoy, under the
influence of an ardent passion for his sister, had been
tempted to contemplate treasonable courses, while he
believed his friend to be in actual danger.   He was,
however, quick to repent, and though the attempt was
made to seduce him from loyalty in Ireland, where he
had succeeded Essex as Lord Deputy, he declined to
lend himself to any intrigue.   Towards the end of the
year (1600) a letter was drafted to King James inviting
him to send the Earl of Mar to London by the 1st of
February following, ostensibly on an embassy to the
Queen, but in reality to concert action with Essex and
his party.   In the instructions prepared in anticipation
of his arrival, certain individuals are indicated whose
"counsels and endeavours tend to the advancement of
the Infanta of Spain to the succession of this crown."
They are in the west, Sir Walter Raleigh, supreme
in Cornwall and Jersey, and thus able to ensure
the Spanish landing; Lord Cobham in the east,
controlling the Cinque Ports; Sir George Carew in
Ireland; the Lord Treasurer and the Lord Admiral,

N

both of them "being principally loved by the principal secretary, Sir Robert Cecil, who, for the further strengthening of himself, hath established his own brother, Lord Burghleigh, in the government of the north parts." Thus it was that Essex, with whom Raleigh had fought the Spaniard in so many campaigns, instilled into the mind of James that subtle poison which was never eradicated, and was the first to formulate the monstrous charge on which he was tried and condemned, and for which at last he died.

As the critical moment drew near when Essex was definitely to show his hand, but little secret was made of his intentions. The Government were fully warned of the coming rebellion, and had taken all necessary measures of precaution. On the 7th of February he refused to obey a summons to the Council. The following day the storm burst. In the morning Raleigh endeavoured to convey a friendly warning to an old friend, Sir Ferdinando Gorges, by inviting him to a meeting. Gorges agreed, with the consent of Essex, to meet him in a boat on the river. He thanked him for his advice but said it came too late. Afterwards, at his examination, he stated that Sir Christopher Blount had endeavoured to persuade him to kill or to seize Sir Walter, against whom the movement was "particular," at this interview. He refused to be a party to such treachery. Blount, however, fired four shots at him from a boat as he returned from the interview, and on the scaffold begged forgiveness for his ill intent. On that memorable Sunday when Essex with his band of disaffected gentlemen raised the standard of revolt, spreading the monstrous cry that the crown of England

was sold to the Spaniard, Raleigh was not brought
directly into contact with the rioters. It was only
when Essex, proclaimed a traitor, had withdrawn after
scenes of violence into the house he had made defensible,
that he was employed under the Lord High Admiral to
invest it. At his preliminary examination Essex gave
as his reason for not attending the Council that Raleigh
and Cobham had prepared an ambush for him, but he
was unable to offer any evidence to support the slanderous
accusation, which Blount admitted was "a word cast out
to colour other matters." At the trial on the 19th of
February Raleigh was examined as a witness, and gave
his account of the interview with Gorges, which the
latter confirmed in spite of the protestations of the Earl.
Six days later Essex, brilliant, impetuous, lovable, but
intolerant of rivalry and implacable in defeat, was led
to the block in the thirty-fourth year of his stormy
life. Raleigh attended the execution in his capacity as
Captain of the Guard, but he withdrew, as the prisoner
approached the scaffold, into the armoury of the Tower.
The infamous Stukeley did not scruple afterwards to
circulate calumnious stories of his demeanour during the
execution. Such charges need no contradiction; they
are too obviously the invention of a mean-spirited nature
seeking to palliate the blackness of his own treachery.

CHAPTER XI

IT was long before the tragic end of Essex was forgiven by the people. The Queen's popularity waned from the hour of his death, which so affected her strength and spirits that her alternate humours of depression and irritability made it difficult for her advisers to approach her on matters of business. She does not, however, appear to have shown any resentment against his political antagonists, and Raleigh's influence enabled him, in return for due consideration, to procure the pardon of two of the conspirators, Littleton and Baynham. Such payments were the acknowledged perquisites of courtiers, and not accounted dishonourable. He had been little at Court during the previous year, but he now resumed his ceremonial duties and accompanied the Queen on her last royal progress. She had anticipated a visit from Henry the Fourth, who was actually at Calais, and with this object went as far as Dover. Henry did not come, but he sent an envoy to greet the Queen in the person of the famous Rosni, Duke of Sully, an old acquaintance of Raleigh. Sully in his memoirs recounts the manner of their meeting. He was under the impression that his arrival at Dover was unknown;

but he had scarcely entered his room before some one approached him from behind, and touching him on the shoulder, exclaimed, "I arrest you as my prisoner in the Queen's name." Rosni, turning, recognised his old friend, who immediately conducted him to the royal presence. Later, when Elizabeth repaired to Windsor, Raleigh paid a hurried visit to Sherborne, whence he forwarded information collected from West-country skippers as to the movements of Spanish armaments, which were once more occupying the attention of ministers. In September he was back in time to take charge of the mission of the Duke of Biron, sent to announce the marriage of Henry to Marie de Medici. He showed his guests the monuments at Westminster, entertained them at the Bear-garden, and laboured "like a mole" to complete the arrangements for their journey to Basing, where the Queen was staying with the Marquis of Winchester. He then returned to the West to keep his watch on the Adelantado's fleet, which, as he rightly foretold, was destined for the invasion of Ireland. On the 13th of October he was able to announce the landing of a powerful force which lay intrenched outside the town of Kinsale, whence they had been twice beaten off by the garrison before the arrival of Mountjoy and Carew. These were years of feverish activity. His colonial schemes had never slumbered, and he maintained his privateering squadrons constantly at sea. He engaged in joint ventures with Cobham and with Cecil, who was, early in 1603, morbidly anxious that his name should not appear as a member of the firm. He was busy with plans for reform in Jersey, where he had been recently appointed governor, under a patent which conveyed to him the manor of St. Germains, but at the same time, by a characteristic stroke of the pen, reserved £300 of the governor's salary for the Queen's disposal. Brief as was his term of office,—only two visits to the island can be established with certainty—his name was long remembered there with gratitude. He established a system of land-registration, and he abolished the compulsory service of the inhabitants of the Mont Orgueil district in the *corps du garde*. He is also said to have initiated a trade, which afterwards became very profitable, between Newfoundland and Jersey. His Wardenship of the Stannaries also gave him constant work and complicated issues to decide. He was still in possession of his Irish estates, which he did not part with until December, 1602. He was planting and digging lakes at Sherborne, where moreover he had continual troubles with the bailiff he had himself appointed, whose claims to certain prerogatives in virtue of his office led to a number of lawsuits. This John Meeres, whose wife was a kinswoman of Essex, and who appears to have been carried away by partisan spirit, was afterwards appointed commissioner to carry out the forfeitures ensuing from Raleigh's attainder.

Besides these manifold and absorbing interests and the duties of his office at Court, he devoted himself with zeal to his Parliamentary work when his presence in London during session rendered it possible. His enlightened opposition to the persecution of sectarians, and to the compulsory provisions of a bill for enforcing attendance at church has already been mentioned. More remarkable, however, is his exposition of the principle of *laissez faire*, in a speech on the Act for

Sewing Hemp, and in favour of repealing the Statute of Tillage. On the former proposal he said, among much that is worth quoting : "For my part I do not like this constraining of men to manure or use their ground at our wills ; but rather let every man use his ground to that which it is most fit for, and therein use his own discretion. For halsers, cables, cordage, and the like, we have plentifully enough from foreign nations." And speaking to the latter measure, he used these striking words : "I think the best course is to set corn at liberty, and leave every man free, which is the desire of a true Englishman." These liberal views did not, however, prevent him from energetically defending his privileges as Warden of the Stannaries, when a general protest was raised against monopolies. The patent for the pre-emption of tin, which he held as representative of the Dukes of Cornwall, had not, he maintained, been disadvantageous to the miners, whose weekly earnings had doubled since his incumbency. Nevertheless, if all exceptional privileges were revoked, he was ready to see his own cancelled also.

The relations between Cecil and Raleigh had been intimate for many years. Their correspondence is as often domestic as official, and the letters abound in playful messages from Lady Raleigh, whose faith in Cecil's friendship was never shaken to the last. How genuine was Raleigh's regard for him is nowhere better revealed than in the letter which he addressed to him in 1597 on the death of his wife, a sister of Lord Cobham. It is impossible to read this letter, which has almost a touch of classic inspiration in its manly simplicity, without realising both the sincerity of the

affection which inspired it and the writer's conviction of
the nobility of character of the friend whom he was
endeavouring to console.   Cecil's motherless child spent
much of his boyhood at Sherborne, where his father
visited him; and frequent messages reassured him as
to young Will Cecil's health and spirits.   Cecil was a
partner in many of Raleigh's privateering ventures, and
he contributed to the cost of the Guiana enterprise.   A
long community of interests, culminating at last in their
common antagonism to Essex, appeared to confirm this
solidarity; and until the latter disappeared from the
scene they remained in close and confidential intercourse.
Then imperceptibly Cecil's regard for his old associate
began to cool, although Raleigh does not seem to have
been aware of any change in his sentiments.   Already,
in June, 1601, he had written to Carew complaining of
the "mutinies of those I do love," and lamenting that
the better man was swayed by the less worthy, namely,
Cobham.   The inception of this coolness is not easy to
trace, but it is evident that after the death of Essex he
never again took Raleigh into council or confidence.   A
crisis was at hand.   It was obvious that the Queen's
life could not be greatly prolonged, and it was equally
evident that King James of Scotland would have the
suffrages of the English people.   This was as well understood by Raleigh as by Cecil.   Both of them had
incurred the mistrust of the heir presumptive, and to
both of them it became imperative to lay out their plans
for the future.   It is probable that Raleigh, who perhaps
did not aspire to the highest office, desired Cecil's confidence at this juncture, and he certainly made one effort
to gain it.   But the confidence which Cecil withheld

from him he bestowed elsewhere, in a quarter incompatible with friendship for his old associate. Outwardly their relations continued to be cordial, and Raleigh seems to have been quite unconscious of Cecil's growing alienation, but inevitably there grew up a new cleavage of interests and influences. As the Queen's vigorous mind began to decay, she grew less careful in reserving her intercourse to those whom her penetrating instinct had approved as worthy. Such men as Southampton, with the countenance of Essex, and Cobham, in spite of his opposition, had come to occupy positions to which their merits were by no means commensurate. Cobham owed to family connections and great wealth his first rise to eminence and his position as a favourite. But even to his contemporaries the "sycophant" was really an object of contempt, and one of the many enigmas in the life of Raleigh is presented by his association with so poor a creature. He was himself now at the zenith of his prosperity. It is true he had not achieved his ambition of entering the Privy Council, and so long as he advocated continuance of the war with Spain, the Queen, whose desire for peace grew more intense with years and infirmities, was easily persuaded not to add another voice to the opposition. As Captain of the Guard, however, he had even greater facilities for tendering advice than a seat in the Council afforded. To Cecil, who had always credited him with soaring ambition, he may well have appeared in the light of a possible rival. From the opportunities of the coming crisis an adroit and adaptable intriguer might conceivably secure for himself a position intolerable to one of the old nobility, who looked upon government as their

exclusive privilege, and irksome to the hereditary legis-
lator who had hitherto had little experience of the
saving grace of opposition.   Throughout his career
Raleigh had shown a singular incapacity to inspire confidence in his contemporaries, and they would not
neglect an opportunity of impressing Cecil with the
dangerous elements in his formidable personality. That
mistrustful nature, incapable of sentiment, began in
good time to provide for all future contingencies.

The embassy of Lord Mar and Mr. Edward Bruce,
despatched in accordance with the suggestion of Essex,
only reached London after his execution on the 25th of
February. The abortive attempt at rebellion and its
prompt suppression had materially altered the situation,
but James appears to have been persuaded that, in
spite of the failure of his martyr, as he termed him,
there was still every prospect of a rising against the
Queen's authority, which the envoy might turn to his advantage. The unwarrantable assurance of the language
they were instructed to hold, not unaccompanied by
threats of the attitude he might assume if his advances
were rejected, shows how little James understood the
English. Lord Mar, however, proved an able diplomatist,
and realising that the wild charges of Spanish intrigue
which Essex had flung at the heads of his adversaries
were a monstrous fiction, did his master the good service
of not acting on his instructions. He determined to
sound Cecil on certain points, and found him disposed
to favour an exchange of views for which it was easy to
assign a plausible pretext. It was agreed that the King
should henceforward refrain from any attempt to secure
parliamentary or other recognition of his reversion of

the crown, and that he should enter into direct secret communication with Cecil, using a preconcerted code of cipher to indicate certain individuals. King James himself was to figure as the number 30, and Cecil as 10. The ambassador's return was followed immediately by the inauguration of that private correspondence, the fortunate preservation of which throws so much light on the history of this period. In the first of these letters the King, expressing his satisfaction at Cecil's plain and honourable dealing, requests him to accept as their intermediary "his long-approved and trusty" Lord Henry Howard, the number 3 of the correspondence. To this letter Cecil replied at length, explaining the grounds of his opposition to Essex and justifying his own conduct in entering into the secret correspondence. He sets forth the state of the Queen's health, and reassuring him as to her intentions, urges patience and inaction on the part of James in view of certain weaknesses in the mind of Her Majesty. He endeavours to secure a monopoly of the King's confidence by warning him that "all that it was possible for art and industry to effect, against the person of a successor, in the mind of a possessor, hath been in the highest proportion laboured by many against you." As yet he specifies no names. He accepts Lord Henry Howard, whom he describes as "my friend"—the qualifying "worthy" being struck out upon revision. In the second of these verbose epistles from the pedantic monarch, Cecil is addressed as "right trusty and well-beloved"; in the third he has already become "my dearest 10." There exist in all seven letters from the King, and six from Cecil. The correspondence of the

intermediary is far more voluminous.   Lord Henry
Howard, afterwards Earl of Northampton, a son of the
poet Surrey and a brother of the Duke of Norfolk, both
of whom had died upon the scaffold, was commended to
James by the traditions of his house, and won his affection
by the assiduous flattery which was palatable to the
monarch's extraordinary vanity.   His secret correspondence with the King reveals his malignant hatred
of Sir Walter, and to the gratification of this hatred and
the ruin of his personal enemies he constantly devoted
his undoubted abilities.   From his inspiration of the
murder of Overbury we may gauge his scruples in contriving the downfall of an enemy.   His sentiments can
scarcely have been unknown to Cecil when he accepted
Howard as a medium of communication.   As negotiations
progressed they were made clear in unmistakable terms,
and if it be not possible to adduce direct evidence that
the Secretary was privy to his intrigues, it is quite
impossible that he can have ignored the baseless charges
insinuated in the secret correspondence to poison the
mind of King James.   In Cecil's own letters there is
but one direct allusion to Raleigh by name, but that is
one of the highest importance in estimating the part he
played in subsequent events, if read in connection with
what had occurred in the meantime.   In November the
Earl of Lennox came to London on an embassy from
King James.   Raleigh was then attending the Queen's
last Parliament.   His correspondence with Cecil had
been continuous through the summer and autumn, and
abounds in little evidences of intimacy ; nor is there, up
to this date, any direct evidence that Cecil's sentiments
towards him had undergone any change.   Lennox had

an interview with Cobham, and subsequently with Raleigh. Some knowledge of what passed at those interviews is derived from Howard's reports. He informed the Secretary that Cobham's motive was to gain an advantage over Cecil himself and establish relations with Lennox, who was somewhat antagonistic to Mar and Bruce. To Lord Mar, in Scotland, he meanwhile represented Cecil as having temporised with Cobham, and as having refused to declare himself on the succession. Raleigh, he wrote, after seeing Lennox had gone to Cecil, and admitted that the Earl had invited him to private conference. He had, however, protested he was "too deeply beholden to his own mistress to seek favour elsewhere that should diminish his sole respect to his own sovereign." Cecil replied, "You did well, and as I myself would have made answer, if the like offer had been made to me." The King had also commenced a correspondence with Lady Kildare, the daughter of the Lord High Admiral, now married to Cobham, and with the Earl of Northumberland. The former Howard diligently laboured to discredit; the latter he represented as a mere puppet in the hands of Raleigh and Cobham. Their alliance he thus gracefully disposed of: "Hell cannot afford such a like triplicity that denies the Trinity." Cecil's privity to the correspondence is revealed by a passage in this letter, in which he begs Lord Mar in replying not to allude to consultations at Durham House, because the Secretary, who would see his reply, had given him no authority to report them.

The negotiations with Lennox probably served to quicken Cecil's sense of the danger to which he might

be exposed if Raleigh and Cobham were taken into
council and learned the secret of his understanding with
King James, the more so as he had little trust in their
caution and reticence. It may also be presumed that
Lord Henry Howard had poured into his ears such
poison as he could render plausible to so discerning a
listener, and it was doubtless in consequence of such
insinuations that he unburdened himself to Sir George
Carew, writing, "our two old friends do use me unkindly,"
and adding, "all my revenge shall be to heap coals of
fire on their heads." There is, however, no symptom of
such a forbearing spirit in the letter which he had
addressed to James in February, 1602, the third letter
of the secret correspondence. After recording his satisfaction at the King's attitude, which made him feel secure
that if their communications ever came to light the Queen
would detect nothing in them but what tended to her
repose and safety, he expresses apprehension that his
own sincerity might fall under suspicion, if the "treasure
of a prince's secret" should be discovered by the indiscre-
tions of certain individuals incautiously admitted to the
monarch's confidence. Lest there should be any doubt as
to whom he is referring, he particularises as follows :

> If I did not some time cast a stone into the mouths of
> these gaping crabs, when they are in their prodigal humour of
> discourses, they would not stick to confess daily how con-
> trary it is to their nature to resolve to be under your
> sovereignty ; though they confess (Raleigh especially) that
> (*rebus sic stantibus*) natural policy forceth them to keep on
> foot such a trade against the great day of mart. In all
> which light and sudden humours of his, though I do in no
> way check him, because he shall not think I reject his free-
> dom or his affection, but always (*sub sigillo confessionis*) use

contestation with him, that I neither had nor ever would *in individuo* contemplate future idea, nor ever hoped for more than justice in time of change, yet, under pretext of extraordinary care of his well-doing, I have seemed to dissuade him from engaging himself too far, even for himself, much more therefore to forbear to assume for me, or my present intentions.

Let me therefore presume thus far upon your Majesty's favour, that whatsoever he shall take upon him to say for me . . . you will no more believe it . . . be it never so much in my commendation, than that his own conscience thought it needful for him to undertake to keep me from any humour of imanity, when, I thank God, my greatest adversaries and my own soul have ever acquitted me from that of all other vices.   Would God I were as free from offence towards God, in seeking for private affection to support a person whom most religious men do hold anathema.

. . . I will therefore leave the best and worst of him, and other things, to 3 [Lord Henry Howard's] relation, in whose discretion and affection you may *dormire securus*.

Cecil's long service to his country, his great industry, and his sterling common-sense have predisposed his countrymen to view his attitude towards Raleigh with indulgence, and no less an authority than Mr. Gardiner, in referring to the one passage in these letters in which Sir Walter is mentioned by name, only observes that it is not complimentary, but that it is very different from Howard's constant abuse.   Read in connection with the rest of the secret correspondence, it seems to call for harsher criticism.   Cecil knew that Raleigh had with himself been included in the charge of favouring the claims of the Infanta, and was equally prejudiced in the eyes of the King by his opposition to Essex.   In rehabilitating himself he adroitly secured a monopoly of the King's confidence.   Not only did he not reach out a hand to help his old friend and associate in the crisis, for which he had all in readiness, but he represented Raleigh as with Cobham hating the King at heart, and only hypocritically maintaining a parade of appearances to safeguard himself in "the great day of mart." The significance of the allusion to his supposed unorthodoxy, addressed to the sanctimonious James, is palpable. He endeavoured to undo any credit which Raleigh might have gained through the reports of Lennox or Northumberland, and finally, in leaving "the best and worst of him" to the tender mercies of Lord Henry Howard, whose discretion he could guarantee, he endorsed the calumnies which the malignity of his worst enemy could invent. And this was done at a time when he was maintaining every outward appearance of cordiality, drawing his share of profits from their joint privateering adventures, and leaving his only son in Lady Raleigh's care at Sherborne. How different was the attitude of Northumberland, who wrote about the same time to James, that though he might be of a faction contrary to some of the King's supporters,

I must needs affirm Raleigh's ever allowance of your right, and although I know him insolent, extremely heated, a man that desires to seem to be able to sway all men's fancies, all men's courses, and a man that out of himself, when your time shall come, will never be able to do you much good nor harm, yet must I needs confess what I know, that there is excellent good parts of nature in him, a man whose love is disadvantageous to me in some sort, which I cherish rather out of constancy than policy, and one whom I wish your Majesty not to lose, because I would not that one hair of a man's head should be against you that might be for you.

One other document must be briefly reviewed. It is a memorandum or part of a letter without date, address, or signature. One copy, beginning and ending with an incomplete sentence, and having the appearance of a rough draft, is among the Cotton manuscripts in the British Museum. Another version, longer and more complete, but so corrupt in text as to be unintelligible in places, is published in the Oxford edition of Raleigh's works, where it is described as from the Burghley Papers. No trace, however, of the document can be found at Hatfield. It contains a long and elaborate exposition of a subtle scheme submitted by the writer for discrediting Raleigh and Cobham with the Queen. The identity of the writer with Lord Henry Howard seems to be placed beyond question by a reference to his only brother, the Duke of Norfolk, and internal evidence leaves little doubt that it was intended for Cecil's eyes. A reference in the Cotton manuscript to King James, under the symbol of 30, shows that it was meant for one of the few individuals in possession of the confidential cipher, and the contents make it clear that it was not written either for the King or for his ambassadors. The suggestion that the person addressed should "hold back correspondence with neighbour States" could not well be made to any one but the Secretary of State, and the general lines of the scheme laid down are such as could only have been followed by a Minister having in his hands the threads of policy. There are, it is true, two references to Mr. Secretary in the third person, but this might be a mere rhetorical form, and in the second case it might perfectly well be the Scottish Secretary who is indicated. If, however, there is little doubt that this

O

letter or memorandum was intended for Cecil, there is, on the other hand, no evidence that it was actually submitted to him, nor that he adopted its conclusions. It is significant that it should have been at some time or other among the Burghley Papers, and it is at least a curious coincidence that Cobham did actually involve himself in just such questionable negotiations, and fell into just such errors of judgment as are prescribed for him.

It is suggested that the Queen's mind must first be prepared. Her Majesty must be enlightened as to the cause of Cobham's and Raleigh's discontent, namely, their failure to secure high office, and persuaded that they really lay the blame on her, while affecting to complain of Ministers. She must be made to understand the peril in which princes stand who countenance persons odious to the multitude. "She must be told what canons are concluded in the chapter of Durham, where Raleigh's wife is president," whose vindictive spirit has been aroused by the frustration of Ħer hopes to be readmitted to the Court.

The way that Cobham hath elected to endear himself is by peace with Spain—so must you embark this gallant Cobham, by your wit and industry, in some course the Spanish way ; as either may reveal his weakness or snare his ambition.—Be not unwilling, both. before occasion of any further employment, to engage him in the traffic with suspected Ministers, and upon the first occasion of false treaty to make him the Minister.—The Queen did never yet love man, that failed in a project of importance put into his hand, as in this there is great odds will fall out.

He urges his correspondent, if the necessities of the case required it, to hold back correspondence with

neighbour States, "respecting more the oath to serve
with fidelity than the custom of the Court or of the
time," and warns him not to let friendship plead for
Raleigh or Cobham.   "The best course were in all
respects, to be rid of them.   Fortune's almsmen and
instruments of giddiness in a tickle time, must be undertaken before they can be prophets, to know their
strength, like colts; for it may be that by the benefit
of wind and tide, they may make better speed than we
expected."   He then contrasts Raleigh's methods with
Cobham's, and submits that while appearing to work on
antagonistic lines their real object is to be on the right
side in any eventuality.   Cobham displays the rough
hands of Esau in vigorous execution, Raleigh the soft
eye of Jacob in covering hypocrisy.   Cobham inveighs
against the Scottish hopes, Raleigh applauds their expec-
tations.   Cobham complains of the small account which
is made of noblemen, Raleigh proclaims them all to be
fools.   Cobham rails at Cecil's friends, Raleigh excuses
them.   Cobham is the "block almighty that gives
oracles," Raleigh "the cogging spirit that still prompteth
it."   Finally, in view of the charges upon which Raleigh
was condemned and eventually executed, the following
cryptic passage is full of significance.   "The main
foundation of their future building in a diverse element,
is grounded upon peace with Spain, and combination
with the North; out of these two respects, there may be
ways invented to dissolve them, before they ascend
into those high regions, that should send them back
like meteors, with combustion or crudity."

There is much more in the letter, but the pith
of the matter is the intrigue thus submitted for

Cecil's approval. If there is no direct evidence that it actually came under his notice or that he was influenced by its contents, it serves at any rate to reveal the disposition of the confidant whose discretion he had guaranteed to King James. Nor can we forget that in the following year the French Ambassador reported to his King that Cecil had procured Raleigh's disgrace. On the other hand, it must be admitted that but little is known of Raleigh's attitude and conduct during the last years of the Queen's reign. Cobham had certainly been engaged in intrigues which were susceptible of a very unfortunate interpretation. Raleigh was in close and intimate relations with him, and there may have been more than we are aware of to justify Cecil's suspicions, and reasonable ground for the complaint which he made in his letter to Carew. That he had determined Raleigh's career should end with the Queen's death there can be little doubt; and seeing that the steps which he took to achieve his end, combined with Raleigh's own imprudence, eventually brought his old friend to the scaffold, it is charitable to assume that the consequences of his resolution were more serious than he had himself anticipated. At best he must be accused of a singular lack of generosity, and it is not surprising that some of those who have investigated the many enigmas of Raleigh's chequered life should have framed a far graver charge against him.

CHAPTER XII

1603

"MY seat hath been the seat of Kings; and I will have no rascal to succeed me! Trouble me no more. He who comes after me must be a King. I will have none but our cousin of Scotland." Such was the last characteristic utterance of the dying Queen. On the 24th of May, the day after she had given her tardy sanction to a succession which had long been recognised as inevitable, she expired, and with her death, save for a brief epilogue, the curtain falls upon the scene of Raleigh's life as a man of action. The news reached him in the west of England, whence he immediately set out for London. On the 5th of April James started on his progress south, and Cecil, who had lost no time in proclaiming the new King, joined the Court at York. He took immediate steps to prevent Cobham and Raleigh from obtaining access to their Sovereign, by an order directing all public officers to remain at their posts during the royal progress. Cobham, however, had already started, and Raleigh, pleading as an excuse the necessity for His Majesty's authorisation to enable him to carry on the

government of Cornwall, hastened to meet the King.
His reception was far from cordial, if Aubrey's gossiping
account may be credited, for James, on hearing his
name announced, greeted him with an offensive pun :
"On my soul, I have heard rawly of thee." Aubrey
suggests that the King was uneasy in his presence,
feeling that magnetic "awfulness and ascendency" of
the man, who was one that a prince "would rather be
afraid of than ashamed of." In any case James signed
the letters of authorisation without delay, and in reporting the matter to Cecil, who was not present, his
secretary ventured the opinion that, during this brief
visit, he had taken no great root.

A feeling of mutual antipathy was unavoidable
between two natures so radically dissimilar as those of
Raleigh and the King. But it is nevertheless probable
that, had not the mind of James been deeply prejudiced
against him before their meeting, Sir Walter's adroitness
and shrewd understanding of men would have enabled
him to dissemble his real sentiments, and that he would
have found means to secure the countenance of a
naturally good-natured monarch. There was, however,
nothing in common between them. Even the pompous
erudition which James was so fond of displaying was
not the fruit of arduous studies, such as those to which
Raleigh had devoted hours stolen from sleep, and had
matured by intercourse with spirits keen as his own.
His learning, superficial rather than profound, tended
only to make him a pedant, and, as his tongue was too
large for his mouth, so his discourse was too voluminous
for its matter. His presence was undignified; his
awkward gait and ungainly movements, his wide-rolling

eyes, which continually wandered from the person he
was addressing, were characteristic indications of his
unstable and suspicious character.   His friends were
chosen from those who flattered his inordinate vanity,
and they retained his favour longest who understood
that his self-complacent humour, petulantly obstinate
when opposed, could easily be won by deference.   To
such a nature the masterful personality of Raleigh was
as antipathetic as was the policy with which he had
been identified.   The leader who had stood at the head
of the war party was inevitably an object of mistrust
to a king who genuinely desired to play the part of a
conciliator, and whose natural craving for repose re-
coiled from action and enterprise.   The dialectician,
who had been called an atheist, was inevitably repellent
to the student of theology, who aspired to be the
defender of the faith in fact as well as in title.   The
man of genius, whose unbending fibre had never allowed
him to suffer fools gladly, was inevitably prejudiced in
the eyes of a monarch who could neither endure contradiction nor perceive merit in an antagonist.   Raleigh
can hardly have failed to realise from the manner of
his reception that his prospects in public life were over,
and such a realisation would make less inherently improbable the story told by Aubrey of his enigmatic
speech to James when the King expressed his conviction
that, had necessity arisen, he could have made good his
claims by force of arms.   "Would to God," said Sir
Walter, "that it had been put to the test."   "Why do
you wish that?" inquired the King.   "Because," he
replied, "you would have known your friends from
your foes."

There was, however, no immediate breach, and when, a fortnight later, he was replaced by Sir Thomas Erskine as Captain of the Guard, an apparent compensation was offered by the restoration to the governorship of Jersey of the portion of salary reserved by the late Queen. The suspension of his patent of wines was only part of a general measure abolishing monopolies. He accepted the inevitable with becoming resignation, and it is not easy to credit the authenticity of a letter which he was reported to have addressed to the King expressing resentment against Cecil for the loss of his offices, and throwing on the Secretary the responsibility for the condemnation of Essex and the execution of the Queen of Scots. He was too shrewd to advance so preposterous a charge, nor does it appear probable that he at this time entertained any hostility towards the old friend, to whose good offices he was shortly to appeal. A further rebuff was to follow. Bishop Tobias Matthew of Durham advanced the claims of his see to Durham Place, and Raleigh received peremptory orders to vacate the house he had occupied for twenty years. If Cecil, who had contemplated some such action before the Queen's death, was not responsible for Matthew's suit, it was he, at any rate, who eventually benefited by it. For the Bishop during his brief tenure managed to convey some portion of the property to his son, who sold it to Cecil. The next incumbent granted him a lease of other portions, and on the Strand frontage of his old friend's residence he constructed a market or bazaar, which, under the name of the New Exchange, soon became both popular and profitable.

At the house of his uncle, Carew of Beddington,

where he next met the King, Sir Walter imprudently appeared before the pacific monarch in the character of an advocate for the continuance of the war, offering to raise two thousand men at his own charges for the invasion of the Spanish dominions. A similar policy was set forth with clearness and moderation in his *Discourse touching a War with Spain and of the Protecting of the Netherlands.* Such proposals found no patient listener in James, who was at this time disquieted by the knowledge that Sully, the Ambassador of the French King, was endeavouring to unite such unattached and dissatisfied politicians as Northumberland, Southampton, and Sir Griffin Markham, the impoverished chief of a great Catholic family, in a party hostile to any exclusive pacification between England and Spain. Sully had also approached Raleigh and Cobham, without any definite results. Unwelcome as he must have realised his presence to be, Sir Walter nevertheless continued to attend the Court, and was at Windsor when the first arrests were made in connection with the Surprising Treason.

The plot of the priests, the Surprising Treason, or treason of the Bye, as it was called in distinction to the treason of the Main, arose out of the intrigues of William Watson, a secular priest, who was first led into dangerous courses by his hatred of the Jesuits. He had assumed, on the strength of an interview accorded him before the accession, that he had secured the King's countenance for all Catholics who could prove their loyalty, and he accordingly exerted his influence in favour of the Scotch succession. The exaction of the fines for recusancy dispelled his illusions, and drove him into the ranks of the discontented. With Francis

Clarke, another priest of similar opinions, he entered
into secret negotiations with Markham, with George
Brooke, the dissolute younger brother of Cobham, and
Anthony Copley, an adventurer and former pensioner of
the Pope, who became eventually, if he was not actually
employed as such, the detective agent on whose information the arrest of the conspirators was made. At a
conference held at Markham's seat of Beskwood a
desperate plan was conceived for enforcing the redress
of Catholic grievances, involving nothing less than the
seizure of the person of the King, who was to be
honourably confined in the Tower, simultaneously
secured by a *coup de main*, until he had given the
required assurance of toleration. The method of procedure was the organisation of a monster petition. The
petitioners, who were to assemble in London in thousands
at a given date, were to be bound by oath to use all
lawful means to restore the Catholic faith ; and it was
anticipated that at the critical moment they would
easily be persuaded to follow their leaders in the more
vigorous action contemplated. The promoters then
separated to rally the Catholic gentry. Through the
instrumentality of Brooke, himself a Protestant, the
young Lord Grey de Wilton, indignant at the favour
shown at Court to certain of his own personal antagonists, was drawn into conference with Markham and
Watson, in spite of his own marked puritanical views,
and for a time at any rate countenanced a plot,
which he had no valid excuse for supporting. The
seizure was to have taken place at Greenwich on the
24th of June, but a change in the King's plans made
the conspirators choose Hanworth instead, where he

would rest on his way to Windsor. Watson, however, had realised that, should the scheme succeed, their new ally Lord Grey, by far the most influential of his confederates, would be able to turn to account whatever advantages were gained, a prospect far from pleasing to the priestly element. He concluded that his cause would be better served if the Catholics played the part of defending their sovereign from a Puritan intrigue, and therefore disclosed to his followers the intentions of Grey, from whose clutches the King was to be rescued by a counter attack, and then lodged in the Tower for safety. The 24th of June arrived. Although a great many Catholics had assembled to sign the petition, their numbers were inadequate for so dangerous an enterprise, and the King went his way in peace. Grey had quarrelled with Markham, and declined to have any further dealings with the confederates, who, finding that the Government were in possession of their secrets, fled from the scene of action. Copley had made confidences to the arch-priest Blackwell, and Blackwell had transmitted all the information available to the Jesuits as well as to the Bishop of London, who at once communicated with Cecil. Copley himself, was the first to be arrested, and in the course of a few weeks all the other leaders were secured. Unconsciously Watson had been of infinite service to the Jesuits his enemies, and the ultimate object of a conspiracy, of which he was himself the victim, was gained ; for James, now persuaded that the majority of the party had been staunchly loyal, received their deputation and consented not only to remit the fines for recusancy, but to throw open the highest offices in the kingdom to Catholics.

It may be well, before endeavouring to unravel the tangled web of circumstance in which Raleigh now found himself enmeshed, to clear the ground by establishing what had been his previous relations with two personalities who figure in the capital charge against him.   The first is Lady Arabella Stuart, the great-granddaughter of Margaret, sister of Henry the Eighth and cousin of King James.   She was one of the many candidates whose possible succession to the throne had been discussed.   Brought as an orphan child to Court, Sir Walter saw her for the first time the year before the Armada sailed.   Elizabeth proposed to marry her to the young King of Scots, but James did not need the sanction of marriage to justify his appropriation of her paternal estates in Scotland.   The reasons for her confinement in the Tower in 1603 can only be conjectured, but in the previous year she had provoked the Queen's lively displeasure by a projected union with William Seymour, the future Duke of Somerset. Cobham, well aware that he had incurred the dislike of King James by his persistent enmity to Essex, had found an opportunity of seeing Lady Arabella some time before the Queen's death, and among the many schemes which his inconstant intellect revolved, the possibility of setting her up as a rival claimant to the throne had presented itself.   He, however, abandoned the idea after his interview, and told Cecil that he had resolved never to hazard his estate on her account. She was, no doubt, the unconscious puppet of many schemers, but there is nothing to connect Raleigh's name with her unhappy story, save the one recorded meeting with the girl of twelve years in 1587, and his own incidental statement that he had never liked her.

The second is the Count of Arenberg, minister of the Archduke Charles, now sovereign prince of the Spanish Netherlands and husband of the Infanta Isabella, whose shadowy claim to the succession of Elizabeth was a pretext for the cry of Essex that the throne of England was sold to the Spaniard. Cobham had already been in correspondence with Arenberg before the late Queen's death, in the interests of peace, and was invited by him, towards the end of 1602, to repair to the Netherlands. After the accession of James, Arenberg, who had probably not realised how entirely Cobham's position had been compromised, wrote to him again, and the letter was referred to Cecil and the King, who for the moment only observed that Cobham was busier about the matter than he need be. Unconsciously he was taking upon himself the dangerous part for which Lord Henry Howard had cast him, embarking "in some course the Spanish way" and trafficking with suspected ministers. Arenberg in another letter indicated a confidential agent, La Fayla, through whom and another foreign intermediary, La Renzi, further correspondence was carried on. At this period Cobham and Raleigh were in constant communication, though only the latter still frequented the Court. They had intercourse on "matters of private estate," but they differed radically on the burning question of peace or war. Cobham hoped to retrieve his position by becoming an indispensable factor in the peace negotiations, and anticipating that he would be entrusted by Arenberg with large sums to distribute to councillors and politicians, held out a prospect of sharing the spoil to Raleigh, who was obviously a man to be gained, if possible, to the cause. In June, 1603, Arenberg himself came upon an embassy to London, and was escorted by Lord Henry Howard, who was no doubt able to obtain from him certain lights as to his previous negotiations with Cobham. It was afterwards alleged that the proposal of a subvention to Raleigh was on this occasion renewed. He denied it at the trial, and at some time or other overtures were certainly made to him, though he professed not to have regarded them seriously, and to have endeavoured to dissuade Cobham from the foolish course of offering bribes to Cecil and Mar. It would be interesting to learn by whom the negotiations were initiated which ended, as researches in the archives at Simancas have proved, in making Cecil for the rest of his life a pensioner of Spain.

Copley's examination left no doubt as to the complicity of Brooke. His relationship to Cobham inspired the suspicion that the latter was cognisant of the plot, and it came out that Markham had requested Brooke to obtain, through his brother, as Lord Warden of the Cinque Ports, a passport to enable him to leave England. In an abstract of Watson's admissions drawn up by Sir William Waad, there is a wild story of "something spoken" by Brooke concerning Raleigh's surprising the King's fleet, which is discounted by the qualification, "what it was I cannot possibly call to mind." There is also similar hearsay evidence of a speech attributed to Cobham in the presence of Raleigh and Grey, as to the "depriving of His Majesty, and all his royal issue, both of crown, life, and all at once"; an

alleged utterance suspiciously resembling the proposed
destruction of the "fox and his cubs" used by the
Attorney-General with deadly effect at Raleigh's trial,
for which baseless invention Brooke prayed for pardon
before receiving the communion on the morning of
his execution. Such evidence sufficed to create a presumption of Cobham's privity to the conspiracy, and almost
immediately after Brooke's arrest on the 14th of July
he was interrogated by the Council as to his knowledge
of the priest's treason. In the meantime Sir Walter
had also been invited to furnish explanations. He was
walking on the castle terrace at Windsor one morning,
waiting to ride abroad with the King, when unexpectedly
Cecil approached and invited him to remain behind.
The date on which this took place is not recorded, and
the minutes of his examination, to which there is no
reference in the Council registers, appear to have been
suppressed; but it must have taken place immediately
after Copley's examination on the 12th, and before that
of Cobham. We have two distinct and essentially
different versions of what passed, one given by Raleigh
himself at his trial, the other on the same occasion by
Cecil. Raleigh stated that he was questioned at
Windsor touching the Surprising Treason, plotting with
the Lady Arabella, and practices with Lord Cobham.
He admitted that he had followed up intimations given
under examination by a letter to Cecil, urging the
apprehension of La Renzi. Cecil's reply to the foreman
of the jury, who inquired about the relative chronology
of Raleigh's letter and Cobham's accusation, is far from
clear, but the following words are unambiguous: "I
think he was not then examined touching any matters

concerning my Lord Cobham, for only the surprising treason was then in suspect." The presumption to be derived from Raleigh's statement is that his letter to Cecil was merely intended to throw further light on matters of which Brooke had already talked. He wrote to Cobham that he had cleared him, and this he may well have believed, holding that the correspondence with Arenberg involved nothing which could be called in question, and only referred to negotiations for the peace, to which he personally was opposed. The letter in question, to which great importance was attached at the trial, was entrusted for delivery to his old retainer Keymis, and confirms his testimony that at Windsor he was interrogated as to practices with Cobham. The fact also that he drew attention to the correspondence, carried on through La Renzi, shows that he had no suspicion that a charge of treason was involved, which could be brought home to himself; nor is it reasonable to suppose, if he were conscious of having countenanced a treasonable intrigue, that he would have inculpated an accomplice who could retaliate by disclosing their association.

Little information tending to incriminate either Raleigh or himself was elicited by the first cross-examinations of Cobham; but on the 20th of July he admitted having discussed with Arenberg the advisability of procuring five hundred thousand crowns from Spain, and added that no steps were to be taken about distributing this money among the discontented till he had spoken with Sir Walter. The letter to Cecil about La Renzi was then shown him, and, assuming that Raleigh had denounced him, he broke out into passionate invective, affirming that it was solely at his instigation that he had entered upon these courses. On leaving the Council chamber he repented of the wrong he had done and, before he came to the foot of the stairs, he had retracted his fatal assertion. But the effect of his reckless utterance was irretrievable. Without it no charge could have been framed against Raleigh, who on the strength of it was immediately committed to the Tower.

Blow after blow had fallen in rapid succession on his proud and lonely spirit. One by one the offices which he had filled so adequately had been taken from him. Long since he must have realised that Cecil had abandoned him; and now the only one of the new King's ministers to whom he might have looked for intercession, had himself summoned him to the Council. His capacity for concentrating on his person the hatred of his contemporaries was brought home to him with convincing bitterness. He could hardly call one man of influence in England his friend. He was conscious of many errors in the past, and his pride rebelled against the prospect of enduring the merciless analysis of legal procedure as then practised in the courts. A justifiable mistrust of the application of the law of treason made his committal to the Tower appear already tantamount to a conviction. He could not hope that his son would, like the heir of Essex, be spared the disabilities entailed by a father's attainder. His health broke down under the strain of anxiety, and it is not strange if at such a moment the masterful mind gave way to despair. His unbending nature had as yet not learned how to submit, and in the bitterness of his heart he determined on a course which at least would spare his wife and child

P

the consequences of his disgrace. A letter of farewell addressed to Lady Raleigh from the Tower is a true expression of his distracted mind, and reveals the deliberate intention he had formed of taking his life. It is too long to quote in its entirety, but the following are the most characteristic passages :

Receive from thy unfortunate husband these his last lines ; these the last words that ever thou shalt receive from him. That I can live never to see thee and my child more !—I cannot. I have desired God and disputed with my reason, but nature and compassion hath the victory. That I can live to think how you are both left a spoil to my enemies, and that my name shall be a dishonour to my child,—I cannot. I cannot endure the memory thereof. Unfortunate woman, unfortunate child, comfort yourselves, trust God, and be contented with your poor estate. I would have bettered it, if I had enjoyed a few years.

For myself, I am left of all men that have done good to many. All my good turns forgotten ; all my errors revived and expounded to all extremity of ill. All my services, hazards, and expenses for my country—plantings, discoveries, fights, councils, and whatsoever else—malice hath now covered over. I am now made an enemy and traitor by the word of an unworthy man. He hath proclaimed me to be a partaker of his vain imaginations, notwithstanding the whole course of my life hath approved the contrary, as my death shall approve it.

But, my wife, forgive thou all, as I do. Live humble, for thou hast but a time also. God forgive my Lord Harry,[1] for he was my heavy enemy. And for my Lord Cecil, I thought he would never forsake me in extremity. I would not have done it him, God knows. But do not thou know it, for he must be master of thy child and may have com-

---

[1] Lord Henry Howard.

passion of him.   Be not dismayed that I died in despair of
God's mercies.   Strive not to dispute it.   But assure thyself
that God hath not left me, nor Satan tempted me.   Hope
and despair live not together.   I know it is forbidden to
destroy ourselves ; but I trust it is forbidden in this sort,—
that we destroy not ourselves despairing of God's mercy.
The mercy of God is immeasurable ; the cogitations of men
comprehend it not.[1]

The attempt upon his life is briefly referred to in the
correspondence of Beaumont, the French Ambassador,
as well as in a despatch of the Venetian Secretary ;
and further details are found in a letter from Cecil
to the King's Ambassador in Paris, in which he states
that he was himself present in the Tower, engaged
in examining some of the prisoners, when Sir Walter
tried to kill himself.   He went to him and " found him
in some agony,—seeming to be unable to endure his
misfortunes, and protesting innocency, with carelessness
of life."   The self-inflicted wound was, however, not
serious, and was, as appears from a letter of Sir John
Peyton, the Lieutenant of the Tower, nearly healed by
the 30th of July.

It is regrettable that the minutes of evidence taken
from the prisoners have in so many cases been lost or
suppressed.   No record of Cobham's examination on the
20th of July can be found in the State Papers, and it is
only from Cecil's correspondence that we know of another
examination in which he cleared Sir Walter on most
points.   In August and October he was again cross-
questioned, without any results, so far as the further
incrimination of Raleigh was concerned, and on the 24th

---

[1] In this letter there is a reference to an illegitimate daughter,
whom he commends to the kindness and charity of his wife.

of the last month he expressed to Sir George Harvey, who had succeeded Peyton at the Tower, his anxiety to exculpate him. This laudable desire was thwarted by Harvey, who confessed the fact to Cecil after the trial was over, as an extenuating plea against the punishment of his own son when he was committed to prison for having assisted in an exchange of intelligence between the prisoners. Raleigh had succeeded in sending a letter to Cobham, entreating him to do him justice, and, by the connivance of young Harvey, a reply in which Cobham admitted the wrong he had done him was passed under the door of his cell. The terms of this reply did not altogether satisfy Sir Walter, and Cobham then wrote him a second and ampler letter, which he had with him in his pocket in Court. The day before the trial Cobham wrote to the Lords repudiating his retractation. What influences had in the meantime been brought to bear upon him can only be conjectured. Not even after Raleigh's condemnation could this miserable creature abide by one consistent statement. Just before his own trial he repeated his charges, but at the trial itself he denied that Sir Walter had been privy to his purpose to go to Spain, and maintained that the proposal to distribute money among the discontented was a conceit of his own, never communicated to any. He had the unfortunate reputation of "uttering things easily." No doubt during their intercourse in the last years of the late Queen's reign, many political combinations had been discussed by them, which were never intended to pass beyond the limits of speculative controversy. Cobham, who seems to have been incapable of weighing his own words, was probably equally incapable of distinguishing between the theoretic and the deliberate in the utterances of his associate.   Irresponsible phrases lingered vaguely in his ill-compacted brain, and for a moment seemed to justify an accusation, which upon reflection he realised was baseless.   It is hardly conceivable that English judges should have attached weight to the evidence of a witness who repudiated his own statements so soon as he had made them.   But the law of treason in its narrowest interpretation required at least one witness, and no other witness was available.   Raleigh, who knew his character, begged repeatedly to be confronted with his accuser.   His appeal was consistently rejected, and on Cobham's unconfirmed and often retracted charge alone, so far as we can learn from the records of his trial, he was, to the eternal disgrace of British justice, found guilty and condemned.

CHAPTER XIII

THE honourable presumption of English law that a man
is innocent until he has been proved guilty did not
obtain in the sixteenth century; and in the King's
patent transferring the government of Jersey to Sir John
Peyton in August it was already declared that Raleigh's
office had been forfeited on account of his grievous
"treason intended against us." The contrary principle
received ample illustration during his trial. The
indictment, dated the 21st of September and prepared
from the various examinations, was to the effect that he
had compassed with Cobham and Brooke to deprive the
King of his crown, to subvert the government, to alter
the true religion, and to levy war against the King; that
he had discussed with Cobham rebellion against the King
and the means of raising Arabella Stuart to the throne;
that Cobham was to procure, through Arenberg, six
hundred thousand crowns from Spain, and enlist the
Spanish King's support in favour of Arabella, who was
to undertake to maintain a firm peace with Spain, to
tolerate Papistry, and to be guided by the King of

Spain, the Archduke of Austria, and the Duke of Savoy in contracting marriage; that Raleigh had delivered to Cobham a book traitorously devised against the King's title, and finally that he was to receive eight or ten thousand crowns out of the money provided by Arenberg. The gravity and multiplicity of the charges must have surprised even the prisoner, conscious though he was of the wide latitude allowed to constructive treason.

The hearing was delayed for nearly two months. Plague was virulent in London, and the Tower itself became infected. The Court of King's Bench was to assemble for the next term at Winchester, and thither, accordingly, the prisoners were transferred. Sir William Waad accompanied Raleigh in his own coach, and it was found necessary to take precautions for his protection from the fury of the mob. He had never in the days of his zenith flattered the rank breath of popular esteem, and now in the hour of disgrace he bore their outrage with the same haughty indifference. The trial took place on the 17th of November before Sir John Popham, Chief Justice of England, Chief Justice Anderson, and two puisne justices, Gawdy and Warburton, with whom were associated as special judges, by commission of oyer and terminer, the very group of Privy Councillors who had prepared the case on which the indictment was framed, the Lords Suffolk, Mountjoy, Wotton, and Cecil, Lord Henry Howard, Sir John Stanhope, and Sir William Waad. Their presence on the bench does not appear to have been in any way repugnant to the feeling of the time. The Lord Chief Justice himself had assisted in the examination of Cobham, and in the course of the trial constituted himself a witness for the prosecution.

If the presence of Cecil among their number is to be
regretted, the appointment of Lord Henry Howard to
sit in judgment on the man he had consistently traduced
is not the least of the blots which stain the memory of
King James. The committal by the Privy Council had
already decided his fate, but the public trial served to
devolve upon a jury the responsibility for his condemnation. The prisoner was allowed no counsel, and had to
face alone the charges prepared by the most skilful of
professional lawyers. Sir Edward Coke, assisted by
Sergeants Hele and Phillips, prosecuted. The violent
malignity of his forensic methods, stimulated on this
occasion by his habitual obsequiousness to the dispensers
of patronage, and his relationship to Cecil, whose sister
he had married, have earned for this distinguished
lawyer an unenviable notoriety. To the indictment
Sir Walter pleaded *not guilty*, and he refrained from
challenging the names of any of the jurymen. He only
begged, as his memory was weakened by illness, to be
allowed to answer the various points as they were
successively brought forward. Coke opposed the plea,
on the ground that the King's evidence ought not, by
dismemberment, to lose its grace and vigour. The Chief
Justice, however, overruled the objection. Sergeant
Hele opened the proceedings with a rough summary of
the indictment. Coke followed, and began by describing
the conspiracy of the Bye, submitting, when Sir Walter
reminded the jury that he was not charged with complicity in the priests' treason, that all these plots were
connected, like Samson's foxes, by their tails, though
their heads were no doubt distinct. Then, after a somewhat irrelevant historical sketch of notable treasons, he

went on to anticipate any objection on the part of the accused to the inadequacy of the evidence, by arguing that it was not necessary to produce two witnesses to treason.   There was, however, he contended, in the present case more weighty evidence than that of a second witness, for, "when a man, by his accusation of another, shall, by the same accusation, also condemn himself, and make himself liable to the same punishment, this is by our law more forcible than many witnesses, and is as the inquest of twelve men."   The cogency of this argument might logically have been invoked to establish the guilt of Cobham ; it is difficult to perceive its application to the case of Raleigh.   Treason, he maintained, had four progressive stages ; its conception in the heart, its participation in the mouth, its application in the hand, and lastly its consummation.   The first was present here in its widest extension, for these traitors had said there would be "no safety till the fox and his cubs were taken away," and turning on the accused with a rhetorical gesture he exclaimed,"To whom, Sir Walter, did you bear malice ?   To the royal children ?"   Raleigh protested his inability to understand the purport of this tirade.   He had nothing to do with the conspiracy of the priests.   If the Attorney would prove any one of the charges raised, he would confess himself a traitor. "Nay, I will prove all," Coke retorted.   "Thou art a monster ; thou hast an English face, but a Spanish heart." It was thus that the Attorney-General addressed the man of Cadiz and the Azores, whose self-imposed life's work had been to give the Queen "a better Indies than the King of Spain hath any."   He went on to sketch the negotiation with Arenberg with an ingenious subtlety of narrative, designed to insinuate that Raleigh was the prime mover and Cobham only an executive agent. Raleigh broke in with an appeal to his judges : "Let me answer, it concerns my life !" But Popham supported Coke's "Thou shalt not," with the ruling that the Attorney was dealing with the general charge, and only when all the evidence had been laid, would he be allowed to reply to each particular. Coke had, however, lost his temper, and cautioned the accused not to provoke him. Cobham, he said, was neither a politician nor a swordsman ; the invention of these schemes belonged to a politician, their execution to a swordsman. Raleigh was both, but such was his Machiavellian calculation that he would talk with none but Cobham, for he was convinced one witness could never condemn him.

He then referred to Cobham's retractation, communicated in a correspondence between the two prisoners in the Tower, which he eloquently characterised as the most horrible practice that ever came up out of the bottomless' pit of the lowest hell. Describing the attempt of Cobham to antedate a letter to the Governor of Dover in order to facilitate a repudiation of the intent to go abroad for treasonable purposes, he suggested that this artifice was devised after he had had intelligence with Raleigh in the Tower, and shouted down the latter's indignant protest with : "All that he did was by thy instigation, thou viper ; for I *thou* thee, thou traitor !"

Cobham's examination, taken down on the 20th of July, was next read. He confessed to conferences with Arenberg with a view to obtaining a sum of money and a safe-conduct from the King of Spain. He had also intended to go to Flanders to confer with the Archduke,

and return by Jersey to discuss with Sir Walter the
distribution of the money among the discontented in
England.   At this point in the examination the letter,
written by Raleigh to Cecil after his own examination
at Windsor, had been shown to Cobham, whereupon,
said the report, he broke out in violent denunciations of
Raleigh, calling him villain and traitor, and asserting
that all he had done had been instigated by him.
These words the Attorney caused to be read a second
time.   Raleigh, moreover, had spoken of plots and in-
vasions, but his memory was not clear as to details,
and Cobham expressed the fear that, once in Jersey, he
would betray him to the King.

Sir Walter was now allowed to address the Court.
He had been, he said, examined at Windsor on three
points, the Surprising Treason, plotting in favour of
Arabella, and practices with Cobham.   To none of these
was he privy.   It was true he had suspected Cobham
of dealings with Arenberg.   When questioned on this
point a little later by the Attorney, he explained that he
had believed their intelligence was only such as might
be warranted.   He knew of the intercourse with La
Renzi, of which he gave intimation to Cecil.   Cobham,
on seeing his letter, had used bitter words, but forthwith
repented and admitted he had done him wrong.   Was
it reasonable, he asked the Court, to think him so mad
as to enter into a conspiracy with Cobham to the
advantage of Spain, at a moment when the realm, united
with Scotland, was stronger than ever before?   Was any
one better acquainted with the weakness and poverty of
Spain than himself, who had thrice fought the Spaniard
on the sea, at a cost of forty thousand marks of his own

treasure. The pride of Spain was indeed so abated, to
such straits was Philip driven for money, he could never
have been so free with his crowns to Cobham. Nay, he
himself had just submitted a treatise to the King setting
forth conclusive arguments against a peace with Spain.
His intercourse with Cobham was limited to matters of
private estate, on which he constantly lent him advice.
As for knowledge of his conspiracies, he protested
before Almighty God he was as clear as whoever there
present was freest.

The minutes of another examination of Cobham were
now read. They are not to be found in the State Papers,
and the reports of the trial are not consistent as to their
contents. It appears, however, that Cobham had at
first declined to sign his testimony, but agreed to do so
if the Lord Chief Justice declared it necessary. Popham
hereupon informed the Court that he had advised
Cobham to subscribe his name, which the latter after
some hesitation did. He gratuitously added that
Cobham's countenance and action at the time went far
to satisfy him that the confession was true. Raleigh
here submitted that, if charges against him were to be
extracted from Cobham's confessions, they should be
supported by reasonable evidence. Cobham was well
known to have a habit of abusing his friends and
repenting of it. One of the jury then asked for information as to the relative dates of Raleigh's letter to
Cecil and of Cobham's accusation. Cecil undertook to
reply, though professing his compunction on account of
his former attachment to Raleigh. His reply certainly
confused the issue. The first disclosures came, he said,
from Copley, but they concerned the Surprising Treason,

which, he understood from Brooke, had been communicated to Cobham.   Raleigh gave him a clue by
indicating La Renzi, but was not then to the best of
his knowledge interrogated on any matter concerning
Cobham, for only the Surprising Treason was then
suspected.   His hearers would naturally jump to the
conclusion that Raleigh's letter was a spontaneous
declaration incriminating Cobham.   To Raleigh's plea
that the accusation was made in a moment of heat, Coke
replied that Cobham had twice called for the letter, and
reflected before he denounced him as a traitor; and then,
with an assurance remarkable in one who should have
been a master of the laws of evidence, he announced
that it would be plainly established that Cobham had
said to Brooke two months earlier : " You come upon the
Bye.   Sir Walter and I are upon the Main to take the
King and his cubs."

Raleigh now claimed to be confronted with his
accuser, urging with much force the plea that one
witness was, by the law of the land as by the word
of God, inadequate to condemn, yet declaring himself ready, if Cobham would maintain the accusation
to his face, to confess himself guilty.   Popham replied
that the statute of Edward the Sixth, on which he
based his contention, had been revoked by a later
statute of Mary, which only required two witnesses
in certain specific treasons, and Warburton found it
apposite to remind him that many horse-thieves would
get off free if they could not be condemned without
witnesses.   An appeal to equity fared no better.
Equity, he was told, must proceed from the King; from
the Court he could only have justice.   Cecil pressed

the judges to declare how the law stood with regard to the confrontation, for which the prisoner so earnestly pleaded. He was himself aware that the whole charge rested on Cobham's unsupported statement, and must for his own peace of mind have desired its corroboration in open court. The Lord Chief Justice, however, refused to entertain the appeal, on the grounds that "there must not be such a gulf opened for the destruction of the King."

Coke proceeded with the evidence advanced by the prosecution. Part of a letter written on the 29th of July by Cobham to the Council was read, in which he confessed having applied to Arenberg for a passport from the King of Spain, and for four or five hundred thousand crowns to be used as occasion offered. He quoted extracts from confessions of Copley, Watson, and Brooke, mere hearsay repetitions of statements that Raleigh and Cobham stood for the Spanish faction. Raleigh's admission that Cobham had offered him ten thousand crowns was put in, together with his reply, "When I see the money I will make you an answer." From which Coke deduced the following conclusions : Raleigh was to have a portion of the money destined for discontented persons ; Raleigh was a discontented person ; therefore he was a traitor. Well might the prisoner exclaim, "Mr. Attorney, you have seemed to say much, but in truth nothing that applies to me." After once more suggestively referring to the "fox and his cubs," and apostrophising the prisoner as a "spider of Hell," he endeavoured to show that Brooke believed his brother to have been inspired by Raleigh, and, following up this clue, he accused him of having supplied Cobham with a treasonable book.

This absurd charge was easily disposed of by the prisoner. The book was published twenty-six years earlier, in justification of the action taken against the Queen of Scots; he had copies of all such books that came out at the time, and this particular one was from Burghley's library. He had not given it to Cobham, who had taken it from his table; for himself he had neither read it nor commended it. Not less irrelevant was the citation of gossip repeated by a sea-going pilot, to the effect that at Lisbon he had heard a Portuguese gentleman say the King would never be crowned, for his throat would first be cut by Don Cobham and Don Raleigh.

Portions of Cobham's evidence, dealing with the letter conveyed by Keymis, were next read. Sir Walter's letter stated that he had cleared him of all charges, and that Lord Henry Howard had said he was "fit to be on the action," because he was discontented. Keymis had added verbally that his master bade him be of good comfort, for one witness could not condemn him. Raleigh interposed, saying that Keymis had added these words on his own initiative. This has been stigmatised by Mr. Gardiner as an unlucky falsehood, which damaged the value of Raleigh's protestations in the estimation of his hearers. It is, however, readily conceivable that Keymis, who was too honest a man to have invented the message, may have interpreted a reflection of Sir Walter's which bore on his own case, as a communication to be made to Cobham, or the latter may have assumed that the reflection, repeated to him spontaneously by Keymis to cheer him, was a direct message from Raleigh. The point could easily have

been settled by calling for evidence from Keymis, but
the presence of a witness whom Waad had menaced
with the rack might have been awkward, and indeed
no witnesses were called before the Court. Once more
Raleigh begged to be confronted with his only accuser,
and Cecil is reported to have proposed an adjournment,
in order that the King's pleasure might be taken. The
judges remained unmoved, and Coke, preparing for the
surprise he was about to offer, inquired of the prisoner,
"If my Lord Cobham will say you are the only
instigator of him to proceed in the treasons, dare you
put yourself on this?" The reply was: "If he will
speak it, before God and the King, that I ever knew
of Arabella's matter for the money out of Spain, or of
the Surprising Treason, I put myself on it. God's will
and the King's be done with me!" These were precisely
the points which Coke had laboriously attempted to
establish by circumstantial evidence, supplemented by
the effrontery with which he assured the jury that he
never knew a clearer treason, and that the King's safety
and Sir Walter's acquittal could not agree.

At this stage he introduced a new feature into the
case. A note from Raleigh had been thrown into
Cobham's window in the Tower attached to an apple,—
"Adam's apple whereby the Devil did deceive him!"
Thereupon Cobham had, he admitted, made a retractation,
but afterwards he could not rest until he had reaffirmed
his accusation.[1] He then caused to be read the follow-

---

[1] In one of the reports of the trial Raleigh is made to say that
he "never had intelligence with Cobham *since he came to the
Tower.*" It is obvious that the italicised words are interpolated.
There were other witnesses besides Cobham to an exchange of
communications. Raleigh himself had in his pocket, and was

ing letter written by Cobham to the Lords of the
Council only the previous day :

I have thought it fit in duty to my Sovereign, and in
discharge of my conscience, to set this down to your Lordships, wherein I protest upon my soul, to write nothing but
what is true.   For I am not ignorant of my present condition,
and now to dissemble with God is no time.

Sir Walter Raleigh, four nights before my coming from
the Tower, writ to me desiring me to set it down under my
hand,—and send to him an acknowledgement under my
hand, that I had wronged him ; and that I should herein
renounce what I had formerly accused him of.   I since
have thought how he went about only to clear himself by
betraying of me.   Whereupon I have resolved to set down
the truth, and under my hand to retract what he cunningly
got from me ; craving humble pardon of His Majesty and
your Lordships for my double dealing.

His first letter I made no answer to.   The next day he
wrote me another, praying me, for God's cause, as I pitied
him, his wife and children, that I would answer him in the
points set down ; putting me in hope that the proceedings
against me would be stayed.

With the like truth I will proceed to tell you my
dealings towards Count Ar(enberg) to get him a pension of
£1500 *per annum* for intelligence ; and he would always
tell and advertise what was intended against Spain ; for the
Low Countries ; or with France.   And coming from Greenwich one night, he acquainted me what was agreed upon
betwixt the King and the Low Countrymen, that I should
impart it to Count Ar.   But upon this motion for £1500
per annum I never dealt with Count Ar.   Now, as by this
may appear to your Lordships, he hath been the original
cause of my ruin.   For, but by his instigation, I had never

---

about to produce in Court, the letter which Cobham had sent him
in the Tower.   Besides, Coke's rejoinder would, if these words were
to stand, be quite irrelevant: "Go to, I will lay you on your
back for the confidentest traitor that ever came to a bar.   Why
should you take eight thousand crowns ?"

Q

dealt with Count Ar. And so hath he been the only cause
of my discontentment : I never coming from the Count but
still he filled and possessed me with new causes of discon-
tentments. To conclude : in his last letter he advised
me that I should not be overtaken by confessing to any
particular. For the King would better allow my constant
denial than my after-appealing. For my after-accusing
would but add matter to my former offence.

"O damnable atheist !" was the Attorney's forcible
comment as he continued his harangue, and asked the
prisoner what he said to this letter. Raleigh, who was
for a moment overwhelmed, could only reply, "I say
that Cobham is a base, dishonourable poor soul." This
new letter was a painful surprise to him, though there
was nothing in it amounting even to a confession of
treason by Cobham himself. Foreign pensions for
purposes accounted warrantable were often offered to
courtiers and accepted by them. But he had never
anticipated the repudiation at the eleventh hour of
the solemn retractation given to him in writing,
and he could not fail to perceive that this letter lent a
plausibility to much of the irrelevant testimony which
had been produced. Recovering himself, he drew from
his pocket Cobham's letter to himself, and explained the
circumstances under which it had reached him in the
Tower. It was the second letter replacing the first,
which was not to his content. Cecil was invited to
read it, as he was familiar with the writing. It ran as
follows :

Now that the arraignment draws near ; not knowing
which should be first, I or you ; to clear my conscience,
satisfy the world, and free myself from the cry of your blood,
I protest upon my soul, and before God and his angels, I

never had conference with you in any treason ; nor was ever moved by you to the things I heretofore accused you of. And, for anything I know, you are as innocent and as clear from any treasons against the King as is any subject living. Therefore I wash my hands and pronounce, " Purus sum a sanguine hujus." And so God deal with me and have mercy on my soul, as this is true.

Raleigh's comment was brief and to the point. The letter to the Lords was but a voluntary confession, the letter to himself under oath, accompanied by the most earnest protestations a Christian man could make : " Therefore believe which of these hath most force." Nothing would have been easier than to produce Cobham and interrogate him on oath in the presence of the prisoner as to which of these letters represented the truth. But such a gulf might not be opened for the destruction of the King. In view, however, of the glaring contradiction between the terms of the two documents it was felt necessary to assure the jury that the final letter was not extracted under any promise of pardon. The jury then withdrew to deliberate, and in less than a quarter of an hour returned with a verdict of *Guilty.*

The prisoner was asked if he had anything to urge in stay of judgment. He replied : " My Lords, the jury have found me guilty. *They must do as they are directed.* I can say nothing why judgment should not proceed. You see whereof Cobham hath accused me. You remember his protestation that I was never guilty. I desire the King should know the wrong I have been done to of the Attorney since I came hither. I desire the Lords to remember three things to the King ; I was accused to be a practiser with Spain. I never knew that my Lord Cobham meant to go thither. I will ask no

mercy at the King's hands if he will affirm it. Secondly,
I never knew of the practices with Arabella. Thirdly, I
never knew of my Lord Cobham's practice with Arenberg, nor of the Surprising Treason."

The coarse brutality of tone assumed by the Chief
Justice in passing sentence goes far to justify the tale
that he had taken purses in the days of his youth. He
reminded Raleigh that he had been taxed by the world
with blasphemous opinions and, dragging into publicity
the name of the illustrious Hariot, adjured him not to
be persuaded by "that devil" that there was no eternity
in heaven, for so thinking he would find eternity in hell-
fire. He then gave the repulsive sentence which condemned the hero of Cadiz and the apostle of England's
colonial empire to be drawn on a hurdle to the place of
execution, to be hanged and cut down alive, to have his
heart plucked out, and the head severed from the body,
which should be divided into four quarters, and disposed
of at the King's pleasure. The condemned man obtained
permission to say a few words to certain of the Lords.
He craved their intercession that his death might not be
ignominious, and that, if pardon were refused, Cobham
might die first, for, he said, "he can face neither death
nor me without acknowledging his falsehood."

The question of Raleigh's guilt or innocence is one
wholly independent of the iniquity of his condemnation.
Guilty he may or may not have been, but lawyers and
historians are practically unanimous as to his legal
innocence, and in the larger tribunal of public opinion
his sentence was immediately reversed. His calm and
dignified manner, contrasting with the obsequious and
unseemly violence of Bench and Attorney, made a deep

impression on the numerous spectators, who told throughout the country the story of a trial which brought
nothing but discredit on English legal procedure.   His
temper, courage, and judgment, under provocation which
excited the pity and anger of the audience, justified the
opinion of Dudley Carleton, who wrote that, "save it
went with the hazard of his life, it was the happiest day
that ever he spent," and that "never was a man so hated
and so popular in so short a time."   If a careful study
of the records suggests the suspicion that Raleigh did
not state all that he knew, that he kept back certain
information, which might be adversely interpreted, until
he found the Court had knowledge which compelled the
admission, the supposition cannot justify his condemnation on the evidence adduced.   There were points in his
answers which may have prejudiced his hearers as to his
veracity.   The standard of veracity was not high in
those days in men of Raleigh's calibre.   He had at the
outset adopted the precedent of denying all knowledge
of Cobham's proceedings, and such a denial was not consistent with his subsequent admission that he had been
offered a bribe for forwarding the peace.   Afterwards
he explained that he believed he had succeeded in
diverting Cobham from those humours.   Of Cobham's
guilt there could be little doubt, and apart from his own
admissions, it was known to the examiners who sat as
judges that he had written to Arabella Stuart, informing
her that he had enlisted the support of the Spanish King
to her title.   There was also evidence connected with
the Arenberg negotiations which the respect due to a
foreign envoy made it difficult to produce in Court, but
there was nothing worth a moment's consideration as

evidence to establish Raleigh's complicity, save the
accusations of Cobham himself, who made and repudiated
charges with the same facility with which Lord Henry
Howard changed his religion.   The foreign envoy, who
if Raleigh was guilty, was his fellow-conspirator, was
suffered shortly afterwards to return and continue the
peace negotiations, and finally departed with a handsome
testimonial from James to his prudence and integrity.
The verdict of posterity has fully confirmed the contemporary estimate of the judgment of the Court at
Winchester, in which the accusers sat as arbiters, and
one of these very judges is reported on his death-bed to
have admitted that never had the justice of England
been so depressed and injured as in the condemnation
of Raleigh.

CHAPTER XIV

1603–1615

THROUGHOUT the wretched farce of his trial Raleigh had
stood manfully at bay, enduring with quiet dignity the
affronts of his enemies and the desertion of his friends.
Now, when all was over, the strain and tension of the
long struggle was once more succeeded by profound
depression, and we find him with a sudden change of
demeanour suing in language of humiliation for a life
which he had never hesitated to risk in honourable
service. If some excuse for the extravagance of his tone
may be found in the hyperbole which the custom of the
day prescribed for addresses to the throne, the character
of the man himself will suggest, to those who study it
with sympathy, some further extenuation for his undignified plea. His strenuous heart, still conscious of power,
his tireless brain, revolving life's incommensurate accom-
plishment and cherishing great dreams yet unrealised,
could not tamely accept the final sentence of extinction.
His vital energy rebelled against the pride which should
have sealed his lips. Conscious that he had done nothing
which merited death, he believed his innocence would

some day be established, and even in the shadow of a prison there was scope for intellectual activity. He might envy if he could not echo the nobler utterance of Grey : " *Non omnibus eadem decora,*—the house of the Wiltons have spent many lives in their prince's service, and Grey cannot beg for his." To Raleigh's sanguine temperament hope could not fail while life remained, and to his hope he desperately clung. He craved the intercession of the Lords of the Council to procure at least one year's respite. To the King he wrote : "Save me, therefore, most merciful Prince, that I may owe your Majesty my life itself, than which there cannot be a greater debt. Lend it me, at least, my Sovereign Lord, that I may pay it again for your service when your Majesty shall please." And he reminded Cecil of their former friendship, worn out, he feared, by change of time and his own errors. But this weakness was not of long duration, and as he penned what he believed to be his last farewell to the noble woman, whose love had filled his life, he enjoined her to recover the letters in which, for her sake and his son's, he had sued for a life which he now disdained himself for begging. This letter, which is undated, but which was evidently written on what he believed to be the eve of his execution, speaks to us across the centuries with the pathos which belongs to all true emotions, and reveals the best and brightest side of Raleigh's character at a moment when there was no need for concealment, no interest to serve, no place more for hope or ambition.

You shall receive, dear wife, my last words in these my last lines. My love I send you, that you may keep it when I am dead ; and my counsel, that you may remember it when

I am no more. I would not with my last will present you with sorrows, dear Bess. Let them go to the grave with me, and be buried with me in the dust. And, seeing it is not the will of God that ever I shall see you in this life, bear my destruction gently, and with a heart like yourself.

First, I send you all the thanks my heart can conceive, or my pen express, for your many troubles and cares taken for me, which—though they have not taken effect as you wished —yet my debt is to you never the less ; but pay it I never shall in this world.

Secondly, I beseech you, for the love you bare me living, that you do not hide yourself many days, but by your travail seek to help your miserable fortunes, and the right of your poor child. Your mourning cannot avail me that am but dust.

You shall understand that my lands were conveyed to my child *bonâ fide*. The writings were drawn at midsummer was twelvemonths, as divers can witness. My honest cousin Brett can testify so much, and Dalberie, too, can remember somewhat therein. And I trust my blood will quench their malice that desire my slaughter ; and that they will not also seek to kill you and yours with extreme poverty. To what friend to direct thee I know not, for all mine have left me in the true time of trial ; and I plainly perceive that my death was determined from the first day. Most sorry I am (as God knoweth) that, being thus surprised with death, I can leave you no better estate. I meant you all mine office of wines, or that I could purchase by selling it ; half my stuff, and jewels, but some few for my boy. But God hath prevented all my determinations ; the great God that worketh all in all. If you can live free from want, care for no more ; for the rest is but vanity. Love God, and begin betimes to repose yourself on Him ; therein you shall find true and lasting riches, and endless comfort. For the rest, when you have travelled and wearied your thoughts on all sorts of worldly cogitations, you shall sit down by Sorrow in the end. Teach your son also to serve and fear God while he is young, that the fear of God may grow up in him. Then will God be a husband unto you, and a father unto him ; a husband and a father which can never be taken from you.

Bayly oweth me two hundred pounds, and Adrian [1] six hundred pounds. In Jersey, also, I have much owing me. The arrearages of the wines will pay my debts. And, howsoever, for my soul's health, I beseech you pay all poor men. When I am gone no doubt you shall be sought unto by many, for the world thinks that I was very rich; but take heed of the pretences of men and of their affections; for they last but in honest and worthy men. And no greater misery can befall you in this life than to become a prey, and after to be despised. I speak it (God knows) not to dissuade you from marriage—for that will be best for you—both in respect of God and of the world. As for me, I am no more yours, nor you mine. Death hath cut us asunder; and God hath divided me from the world, and you from me.

Remember your poor child for his father's sake, that chose you and loved you in his happiest times. Get those letters (if it be possible) which I writ to the Lords, wherein I sued for my life, but God knoweth that it was for you and yours that I desired it, but it is true that I disdain myself for begging it. And know it (dear wife) that your son is the child of a true man, and who, in his own respect, despiseth Death, and all his misshapen and ugly forms.

I cannot write much. God knows how hardly I stole this time, when all sleep; and it is time to separate my thoughts from this world. Beg my dead body, which living was denied you; and either lay it at Sherbourne if the land continue, or in Exeter church, by my father and mother. I can write no more. Time and Death call me away.

The everlasting, infinite, powerful, and inscrutable God that is goodness itself, mercy itself, the true life and light, keep you and yours, and have mercy on me, and teach me to forgive my persecutors and false accusers; and send us to meet in His glorious kingdom. My true wife, farewell. Bless my poor boy; pray for me. My true God hold you both in His arms.

Written with the dying hand of sometime thy husband, but now (alas) overthrown.

Your's that was; but now not my own,

W. RALEIGH.

[1] Adrian Gilbert.

But time and death were not yet calling him away, and, as though the dignity of British justice had not been sufficiently humiliated, another act of this tragic comedy was still to be played out on the scaffold itself. The two priests, Clarke and Watson, the prime movers in the Surprising Treason, were executed on the 29th of November with all the hideous details laid down in their barbarous sentence, and on the 5th of December George Brooke suffered the extreme penalty. In his dying declaration, according to the evidence of Dudley Carleton, who was present, he spoke of his offences as less heinous than they had appeared to be, and protested his confidence that the God of truth would thereafter bring to light matters which would make for his justification. It would seem, from a letter addressed to Cecil, referring vaguely to a promise to cancel past injuries, that he had had reason to hope for his intercession. The much-talked-of reference to the destruction of the fox and his cubs, which had by subtle insinuation been imputed to Raleigh, was, he contritely confessed, the invention of his own malicious imagination. His last utterances were enigmatic, but they caused a flutter of alarm at Court, and tended to impress public opinion still more profoundly with the unsatisfactory character of the trials. The headsman's cry of "God save the King" found no response in the crowd.

The 10th of December was fixed for the execution of Grey, Cobham, and Markham. Raleigh, from whom the Bishop of Winchester had failed to extract a confession, was, it seems, to be brought to the scaffold three days later. The Queen was pleading for his life, and the

King had some not unnatural scruples about signing the warrant. Meantime there was a possibility that the last utterances of his fellow-prisoners might provide further justification for his sentence. From the window of the room in Winchester Castle where he was confined he saw Markham led out to die, and it is not easy to believe in the smiling face with which the French Ambassador reported he watched the solemn proceedings. Markham showed great fortitude, but he protested that he had been encouraged by vain hopes of mercy, and had not prepared himself for death. At the last moment the sheriff, Sir Benjamin Tichborne, stayed the executioner. Reprieve had arrived just in time, and turning to the prisoner, he said, "You say you are ill-prepared to die; you shall have two hours' respite." Markham was then led away, and Grey was brought, in ignorance of what had passed, to take his place. His bearing was manly and cheerful; he declared himself ready to atone for his great fault, because his eye had been dim to discern the peril which menaced the King, and his last thought was for the honour of his house, which he trusted this one fault would not be held to stain. The sheriff suffered him to conclude his prayers and take leave of life, and then announced that by the King's command the order of execution had been changed; Cobham was to die first. Grey was then led away and Cobham was conducted to the scaffold. In marked contrast to his craven demeanour at his trial, he now displayed a stout indifference to his fate, which led certain of the spectators to surmise that he was really aware his life was not at stake. He prayed at great length, and took occasion to assert once more the truth of all he had deposed against Sir Walter. He was then informed that he was to be confronted with some other prisoners, and remained on the scaffold until Grey and Markham were brought back. Meanwhile Raleigh, whose warrant was destined to remain unsigned, and who therefore could not even here be confronted with his accuser, watched the scene in perplexed bewilderment from his window. The sheriff asked whether the three prisoners admitted their guilt, and upon receiving affirmative replies, announced the mercy of the King. Then at length the crowd broke into genuine and prolonged applause, and the curtain fell upon this undignified scene, for which James must bear the sole responsibility. On the 16th of December Raleigh was removed to the Tower.

He addressed a becoming and not undignified letter of thanks to the Sovereign who had vouchsafed to spare him, and to "stop his ears to the urging of private hatred and public law." To Cecil he wrote as to a friend who had saved his life, in humbleness of heart that he had ever doubted that friend's constancy and devotion. "Nothing," he protested, "now could ever outweigh the memory of your Lordship's true respects had of me; respects tried by the touch; tried by the fire; true witnesses, in true times; and then only, when only available." So he was able to write under the influence of the reaction, holding life, to him infinitely precious, once more within his grasp. Cecil's intervention at this crisis went further, and was of great avail in preserving to his estate some remnant of his shattered fortunes. The Governorship of Jersey and the Lieutenantcy of Cornwall had both been taken from him.

His patent for the license of wines, which was not
terminated with the suppression of monopolies, was
transferred to Nottingham, as appears from a letter
of Lady Raleigh, applying for the arrears accumulated
during the period of suspension. It is possible that
Cecil exerted his influence to prevent the Lord
High Admiral from putting forward a counter-claim,
but it was in preserving Sherborne for a time at any
rate to the family that his interposition was most
useful. Many suitors had already importuned the King
for the reversion of the Dorsetshire property, and immediately after the conclusion of the trial commissioners
set to work cutting down the woods, and selling the
stock which Raleigh had laboured with his usual
thoroughness to improve. The Secretary procured a
stay of execution. The Sherborne estate, first transferred to Raleigh on a ninety-nine years' lease, had
subsequently been granted him in fee-simple. While
still a lease-holder he had conveyed the property to
trustees for his son. After the grant in fee-simple he
seems to have made another conveyance to his son,
with reversion to his brother in default of direct heirs,
but the history of these dispositions is obscure. In 1602
he received a challenge from Sir Amyas Preston, the
hero of La Guayra, who had failed to join him in the
expedition to Guiana. This challenge, probably arising
from the partisanship of Preston for Essex, Raleigh
in the end declined to accept, for reasons which
were considered adequate according to the standards
of the time; but the threatened danger to his life
caused him to execute in haste a new conveyance to
himself, with remainder to his son Walter, or his heirs,

and in default of issue to his brother, Sir Carew Raleigh. There was a technical flaw in the conveyance, apparently some accidental omission by the clerk who engrossed the document, but for the present it held good. His own life interest alone was thus forfeited by his attainder, and Sherborne, together with other manors in Dorset and Somerset, were assigned by the Crown to trustees to hold for Lady Raleigh and her son. He was apparently aware that the form of conveyance was open to contention, for he had not been long in the Tower before he begged Cecil to obtain an opinion from the Lord Chief Justice and the King's attorney as to its validity. The opinion of the authorities consulted confirms the view that some important formula had been omitted by the copying clerk, and on this omission must be based such justification as could be invoked for the confiscation of the estate, which was eventually bestowed on the King's favourite, Carr. Some pretence of compensation was made to Lady Raleigh and her children by the assignment of £8000 as purchase money for Sherborne and its dependencies, with an annuity of £400 a year in lieu of her jointure. Of the capital sum only a portion was ever paid, and this was consumed in the last fatal expedition to Guiana; on the remainder interest was irregularly found by the Exchequer. Raleigh at length reluctantly and perforce consented to the transfer of the property, and the conveyance was declared void in 1609. The capital value of the annuity and the sum actually paid represented a very inadequate price for the magnificent estate to which he was so deeply attached; and the real spirit of the transaction is aptly illustrated in the well-known tradition of the King's reply to Lady

Raleigh, when on her knees she begged him to save Sherborne for her children, only to be repulsed with the all-sufficient answer, "I maun ha' it for Carr." The favourite did not, however, remain long in possession, for the King, who had bestowed the estate, repurchased it for a sum of £20,000, in order to give it to Prince Henry. It has been surmised that the Prince, who had a romantic admiration for his father's illustrious prisoner, sought to acquire Sherborne in order eventually to restore it to Raleigh. His premature death prevented the realisation of this design, and it reverted to the King, who once more transferred it to Somerset, on receiving back the purchase-money. On Somerset's attainder it was granted to Sir John Digby, afterwards Earl of Bristol, as a reward for his having undertaken at his own charges the burden of an embassy to Spain. Nevertheless some misgiving appears to have existed as to the legality of these transactions, for years afterwards, when in a new reign Carew Raleigh petitioned Parliament for his restoration in blood, he was told by Charles that the first step must be his absolute renunciation of all right to his father's property.

Hard as were the conditions meted out to him, Raleigh appears to have suffered less severely than his fellow-prisoners, with the exception of Copley whose services were rewarded by early liberation. Sir Griffin Markham was also released on condition that he left the country, which he did in such abject circumstances that on landing in Flanders he was compelled to pawn his silver sword-hilt in order to obtain food. Eventually, however, he found employment as a soldier of fortune in the armies of the Archduke Albert. Grey and Cobham, whose vast estates were confiscated, were maintained by a small bounty from the Crown. Grey died in captivity. Cobham, who survived Raleigh by a few months, was eventually, in 1617, allowed to leave the Tower and visit Bath for his health. At the end he appears to have been in great straits, and to have ignominiously closed his miserable existence in the house of a poor woman, formerly his servant, in the Minories. Sir Anthony Welldon, in his *Court and Character of King James*, tells an improbable story of a re-examination of Cobham, carried out in consequence of a request from the Queen, after which Cecil is reported to have informed the King that "my Lord Cobham hath made good all that he ever wrote or said." He records the sordid end of Raleigh's evil genius: "He died lousy, for want of apparel and linen; and had starved, had not a trencher-scraper, sometime his servant in Court, relieved him with scraps, in whose house he died." It is not possible to believe that the judgment which contemporaries and historians have agreed to pass on this miserable creature has been unjust.

The monotony of prison routine was in many ways made light for Sir Walter; so much so indeed that he did not at first realise that more than a temporary restraint could be placed upon his liberty. He hoped to be allowed to enjoy a partial freedom on parole, and, within a year of his conviction prayed for permission to pay his customary visit to Bath. The grim gate seemed not to have closed behind him for ever, when he found himself temporarily transferred to the Fleet in the early months of 1604. A bull-baiting entertainment in honour of the King had been organised at the

R

Tower, and the royal visit implied an amnesty to offenders confined there, which could not be extended to the more important prisoners of State. When he returned the precincts were once more infected by plague. His wife and son, who had been allowed to join him, moved during the prevalence of the epidemic to lodgings in the neighbourhood, where it is probable that Carew Raleigh, the son of his captivity, was born. He was allowed to receive friends, and among those who most frequented his society was his old associate, Thomas Hariot the metaphysician. Before long Sergeant Hoskyns and the Earl of Northumberland, Raleigh's generous advocate with the King, accused of complicity in the Gunpowder Plot, joined the symposium in the Tower. The lieutenant, Sir George Harvey, found entertainment in his conversation, and not unfrequently dined with him. He moreover gave up to his prisoner's use his own garden, whence Sir Walter enjoyed a pleasant outlook over the green glacis of the fortress. The Bloody Tower, where he had first been lodged while awaiting trial, continued to be his residence. From the terrace he could watch the busy river, running down to freedom and the sea, the forbidden highway to those distant worlds, beyond his contracted horizon, where his unfettered spirit still schemed to found a goodly heritage for his countrymen. In the garden he was allowed to convert "a little henhouse" into a chemical laboratory, and there he at first spent most of his time absorbed in those researches for which his half-brother, Adrian Gilbert, had first given him the taste, developed during long hours of enforced leisure on shipboard. He is even said to have discovered the art, afterwards lost again for a long period, of distilling fresh water from salt. A portion of his time was also doubtless devoted to the education of his son Walter, who may have been ten years old when the gates of the Tower closed on his father. Some four years later he matriculated at Corpus Christi College, Oxford, where he studied under the tutelage of Dr. Daniel Fairclough, and showed good natural abilities and some disposition for music. He took his degree in 1610, and then returned to London, where there is reason to believe his further instruction was superintended by no less a guide and philosopher than the illustrious Ben Jonson, of whose association with the Raleighs the gossips have recorded racy anecdotes. It is told how on one occasion the poet, who had a weakness for good cheer, was conveyed, overcome with the fumes of canary, in a clothes-basket, at the instance of his graceless charge, into the presence of Sir Walter, who did not fail to improve the occasion by a suitable lecture. Pupil and master alike had the misfortune to kill a man in a brawl, and as young Walter's victim was a retainer of the Lord Treasurer, it became necessary that he should quit the country in haste. It seems probable that Ben Jonson, who in 1614 was for a short time Raleigh's fellow-prisoner in the Tower, accompanied him to the Continent.

As months went by the pride and arrogance of manner which had made Raleigh so unpopular were forgotten, and men considered rather the great services he had rendered and the contrast of his former fortunes with his broken life. At the hour at which it was his habit to take his daily exercise, crowds would gather

below the Tower garden to watch the solitary figure
pacing up and down, with a curious interest which time
softened to an indignant sympathy. Fathers would
bring their little sons to see the man who had sailed
beyond the sunset, and had borne the brunt of the great
duel with Spain, now almost the last of a little band of
heroes whose names were fast passing into the mythic
cycle. It was not strange that young Prince Henry, as
he too came to look at the gallant figure in the courtly
dress, which even in prison Raleigh still affected, should
sigh with a boy's generous resentment to think that his
father should keep such a splendid bird in a cage.

With the arrival of Sir William Waad, the examiner
in the investigations preceding his trial, who succeeded
Harvey as lieutenant in 1605, his liberties were curtailed.
Some frivolous charge of cognisance in the Gunpowder
Plot afforded the necessary pretext. Waad held it
unbecoming that Sir Walter should display himself in
the garden, and he drew up new regulations, directing
prisoners to withdraw to their quarters at the ringing
of the afternoon bell and forbidding their wives to
lodge in the Tower, much less to drive into the precincts
in their coaches. Lady Raleigh was, however, not
separated from her husband until 1610, when he was
charged with some new offence, the nature of which
remains a mystery, and was punished with three weeks'
close arrest. In 1606, in consequence of an unfavour-
able report of his health, he was allowed to occupy a
warmer lodging in the neighbourhood of his laboratory.

When he at length reluctantly realised that all
appeals for pardon were fruitless, he applied himself to
literature with that characteristic elasticity of mind

which had through life enabled him, if thwarted in one
direction, to divert his insatiable energy into some other
channel of ambition. Within the limits assigned to him
as a man of action it is not possible adequately to
consider him as a man of letters, and that aspect of his
many-sided nature must be reserved for separate treatment. Of his writings in prose three only were published
during his lifetime, *The Fight about the Isles of the Azores*
and *The Discovery of Guiana*, which have already been
discussed, and the great achievement of his captivity,
The History of the World. Any one of the three would
suffice to place him among the masters of English prose.
The authorship of some of the compositions attributed
to his pen has been called in question; many others
have probably disappeared, and among them a *Treatise
on the West Indies*, referred to in his *Discovery of Guiana*.
The Arts of Empire, published by Milton in 1658, *The
Maxims of State, The Discourse of Tenures which were before
the Conquest, The Discourse of War in General*, and the
economic treatise entitled *Observations touching Trade and
Commerce*, are probably the outcome of studies made in
collecting material for his great work, and the *Breviary
of The History of England*, if indeed it is by his pen,
which is very doubtful, may be regarded as a preliminary
exercise. *The Prerogative of Parliaments*, a dialogue addressed to the King, in which he brings the powers of
the Crown and the Legislature into happy concordance,
the two pamphlets on the proposed Savoy marriages,
and the admirable maritime treatises, written for the
enlightenment of his constant advocate, the young Prince
of Wales, necessarily belong also to the period of his
imprisonment. His versatile genius ranged from history

to religion and metaphysics, and from the fields of speculation explored in *The Sceptic* and *The Treatise on the Soul*,
he returned to the solid ground of practical philosophy
in his *Instructions to his Son and to Posterity.* It is not
possible to say at what precise period, though it was
undoubtedly after the last hope of pardon was abandoned, he conceived the noble ambition of spending the
remainder of a life, already far run out in other travails,
in writing as an introduction to *The History of England*
the story of the four great empires of the world. It
was no ordinary nature that long after fifty could still
contemplate an undertaking which in the seventeenth
century was esteemed a greater title to abiding fame
than all the achievements of his active years. The
history was published in 1614, but the title had been
registered three years earlier with the Stationers'
Company. Its success was immediate. Its profound
learning, which to modern readers may seem to over-
weight the narrative, compelled the reverent admiration of contemporaries. Only the King, whose invincible antipathy to Raleigh obscured his judgment,
would have none of a book which he stigmatised as
"too saucy in censuring the acts of princes." He even
went so far as to command that the first impression
should be called in, but a new edition appeared in 1617.
It need not surprise us that James was blind to the
merits of a work which Cromwell esteemed only second
to his Bible, or of a writer whose conceptions of history
and politics both Milton and Hampden held in
honour.

Raleigh's extreme carefulness as a historian led him
to seek confirmation from able scholars on all doubtful

points, and he acknowledges his indebtedness to learned friends in the preface. Dr. Robert Burhill, formerly his chaplain, assisted him in the interpretation of Hebrew, of which he admits his own ignorance. Hariot was his oracle on disputed questions of chronology or geography, and Hoskyns, the arbiter of style, is said to have revised the whole work for the press. Ben Jonson, who wrote the verses of the title-page, and no doubt offered scholarly criticism, boasted in his cups to Sir William Drummond, after Sir Walter's death, that he had himself made considerable contributions. On such slight evidence Isaac Disraeli, in his investigation of literary curiosities, vainly endeavoured to prove that *The History of the World* was only a compilation from erudite collaborators. From these reckless charges Raleigh's reputation as an author has been amply vindicated. It is sufficient to state that his work possesses the characteristic of all great histories, a unity of conception and method, which informs and vivifies the matter and excludes all presumption of literary association.

The History of the World contains not a few passages from the classics rendered with curious felicity into English verse, and in the closing hours of his life Raleigh's most solemn thoughts once more sought a poetic form. It is rare, however, for men whose lives are mixed with action to write much poetry after forty, and the majority of the verses which can with any degree of certainty be ascribed to his pen belong no doubt to a much earlier period of life. He cannot himself have attached great value to them, for, with the exception of an occasional piece inserted

in some other author's book, he did not have them
printed. In those days. every man of culture wrote
verses. Since the introduction of the Italian sonnet
metre and the *terza rima* into England by Surrey and
Wyatt, the Petrarchian mannerism and the cult of
form dominated the poetic literature of the day.
From such artificiality, from the over-elaboration of
conceit, Raleigh is no freer than his fellows, but there
is in the small sum total of his authentic work that
indefinable quality which distinguishes poetry from
verse. His longest achievement was the elegiac poem
called *Cynthia*, addressed to the Queen, of which only
the twenty-first and last book is extant.[1] If the other
cantos were as voluminous it must have rivalled *The
Odyssey* in the number of its lines. Probably the work
was incomplete, but portions of it were familiar to
Spenser, who admitted that he derived the name of
Belphœbe from Raleigh's excellent conceit of *Cynthia*.
It is not possible here to examine his title to the poems
which are popularly ascribed to him. Critics have
ventured to question his authorship of the famous *Silent
Lover*, and even of *The Soul's Errand*, also known as *The
Farewell* and *The Lie*, which in any case was not, as has
been pretended, composed by him the night before his
death, as it is known to have existed in manuscript
before 1596. Contemporary references, however, seem
to establish his claims to the latter beyond dispute. Of
The Pilgrimage and the lines written in the gate-house
at Westminster no critic can dispossess him, and his

[1] The Continuation to, or twenty-first book of, *Cynthia* was
apparently written after 1603 and during his captivity. See
Archdeacon Hannah's admirable edition of Raleigh in the Aldine
poets.

sonnet to Spenser has been registered in the roll of masterpieces.

Raleigh contemplated a second and even a third part of his *History of the World,* and collected notes for these further volumes. But in the concluding lines of the fifth and last book he makes it clear that the work would not be carried further, inasmuch, as, "besides many discouragements persuading my silence, it hath pleased God to take that glorious prince out of the world, to whom they were directed." The well-known story of his having burned the manuscript of the second part after convincing himself of the fallibility of all human judgment by his own incapacity to correctly appreciate an incident which occurred before his own eyes, may therefore be dismissed as apocryphal. His intercourse with the chivalrous young Prince, whose promising life was so prematurely cut short, had long formed the chief solace of his confinement, and had kept alive the spark of hope which permitted him not to despair. The Prince, who consulted him on many private affairs, had diligently collected all the evidence which might justify a reconsideration of his sentence, and it is said that not long before he caught the fatal fever which carried him off, he had induced his father to give him a reluctant promise that Sir Walter should be released the following Christmas.

The death of Salisbury some six months earlier had perhaps removed one of the obstacles to this end. In spite of the eloquent expressions of gratitude which Raleigh addressed to him on his reprieve, time had rather accentuated than softened their latent antagonism. To Raleigh it seemed inconceivable that an old associate and apparent friend should permanently abandon him to his fate. To Cecil it never occurred to run the risk of compromising his own position with the King by intervention on the prisoner's behalf. He was called upon in 1610 to examine Raleigh on account of some mysterious charge brought against him; and the sentence of close arrest which followed, together with Lady Raleigh's exclusion from the Tower, cannot have improved their relations. Raleigh consistently clung to the hope that he would eventually be released to lead one more expedition to Guiana, and although Cecil listened to his arguments with patience and apparent interest, their interviews led to no result, and disappointment only increased his bitterness. When at last the great opportunist died suddenly, on his way home from Bath, the survivor expressed his resentment more openly. He was even credited with the authorship of a coarse epitaph, unworthy of so refined a pen, in which Salisbury is satirised under the name of Hobbinol. Two years later his relentless enemy Northampton died, and soon after yet another of those whose names are inseparably connected with his fall—Lady Arabella Stuart—ended her career of misfortune in the Tower.

So twelve full years rolled by, transforming in their weary process the man of action into the student and philosopher, the hated courtier into a popular hero, the victim of a tyrannous oppression, who, in an era of national misgiving, appeared to his contemporaries alone to represent the old ideals for which a past generation had striven, and to sit in judgment on the degradation of the Court.

CHAPTER XV

THE SECOND EXPEDITION TO GUIANA

1617–1618

IT was only by a liberal use of his own money that Raleigh's release was finally brought about. The Queen had never ceased to plead his cause; the Prince of Wales had even, it is said, extracted from his father a reluctant promise of pardon; the King of Denmark had more than once attempted intercession. Still James remained obdurate, and any mention of the prisoner acted as an irritant to his natural good nature. But important changes had taken place in the influences behind the throne. Sir Ralph Winwood, the new Secretary of State, an avowed admirer of Raleigh, approved his anti-Spanish policy and the scheme for a new Guiana expedition which Cecil had tacitly discountenanced. It seemed not impossible to persuade the King, anxious above all for a peaceful reign, and hoping to secure it by a dynastic alliance with Spain, that the venture might rather serve than thwart his ambitions. Spain had hitherto received his advances coldly. A project which offered materially to increase his revenues might at the same time remind her that England was no negligible quantity. In reality his anti-Spanish advisers anticipated a definite rupture of relations from a revival of the policy of Elizabeth, entrusted for execution to the traditional enemy of Spain. Not less important than the change of ministers had been the change of favourites. With the disgrace of Carr, his partisans the Howards, who even after Nottingham's death remained hostile to Raleigh, became objects of mistrust to George Villiers, who had secured the reversion of the King's affections. The new favourite had impecunious relations. To two of these Raleigh presented £750 a-piece, as the price of their good offices, with the result that on the 30th of January, 1615, a warrant was issued for his release from the Tower in charge of a keeper. In March the Council authorised him to go abroad under supervision and prepare for his intended voyage, admonishing him, however, not to appear at Court. It was only two years later, a few weeks before his fleet left the Thames for Plymouth, that he was "fully and wholly" enlarged by Royal Warrant. The interval spent in completing his equipment was as sedulously employed, by those whose interest it was to thwart him, in countermining the enterprise of which they had ample warning.

Sir Walter spent his first hours of liberty in studying the changes which twelve years had effected in the streets and buildings of London. It is happily suggested by one of his biographers that he may well have directed his steps towards the great Abbey at Westminster. With what eager interest must the passers-by on the busy thoroughfare connecting the two cities have watched that long unfamiliar figure, still erect and tall, with something of the old look of confidence

returned to the careworn face, as he paused in front of
Cecil's new bazaar in Durham Place.   Not a few, we
may conjecture, followed at a respectful distance, when
he entered the Abbey doors and stood for a while,
deep in thought, before the new grave where, under a
massive canopy, the great Queen lay in effigy.

His long cramped energies found ample scope in the
preparation for his journey, and the keel of the *Destiny*,
of ominous name, was laid without delay.   All available
resources were devoted to the cause.   A portion of the
capital received for Sherborne, and lent to the Duchess
of Bedford, was called in, and Lady Raleigh parted
with a house and lands which she had inherited at
Mitcham.   In all he invested some £10,000, while
fellow-adventurers contributed about three times that
amount.   The rumoured wealth of the Guiana mines
had not met with universal acceptance, and the assay
of the specimen ores brought home had not been very
favourable ; but nothing shook his dauntless confidence,
and the fact that he invested in his preparations all
that remained of his own and his wife's shattered
fortunes is testimony to the sincerity of his faith.

The circumstances of his release could not fail to
give cause for preoccupation to the Ambassador of
Spain, Diego Sarmiento de Acuña, better known by his
later title as Count of Gondomar, who was perhaps a
relative of Raleigh's old prisoner of 1586.   The vain
and timid James had early been gauged by this con-
summate diplomatist, and an incident which occurred
on his first arrival in England revealed how the old
order had changed.   The Admiral at Plymouth had
insisted on the courtesies to the English flag from the

Ambassador's ship, which John Hawkins had never failed to exact in the days of Elizabeth. Gondomar had only to protest to secure an apology and the disavowal of the Port Admiral. Before many years were over he was able to thank the King for having accorded him access not merely to his Privy Council, but even to his private chamber. His first move was to offer Sir Walter a safe-conduct, for himself and one or two ships, to the mine in Guiana, which he would be free to open for his own profit. But the old adventurer was too sagacious to place his unarmed hand in the lion's jaw, and had no intention of acknowledging the sovereignty of Spain over any part of the country. The mine, he contended, was not in Spanish territory. The British claim to Guiana he held valid, in virtue of the agreements he had contracted with the original inhabitants, and if the Spaniards had entered after he had taken possession for the British Crown, they had no right to be there. James himself had so far recognised this principle that in 1604, and again in 1608, he had commissioned officers to take possession of all lands from the Amazon to the Dessequebe. The theory of effective occupation as indispensable for title had not yet been developed. On the other hand Spanish occupation was an existing fact, although the area over which it could be said to extend was undefined.

It must early have become obvious to Raleigh's clear-seeing mind that between the anti-Spanish party, who looked to him to bring about a rupture with the Escurial, and the King, who was ready either to use or to sacrifice him as a pawn in his negotiations for a dynastic marriage, his position was untenable. It is

conceivable, therefore, that he was not indisposed to
contemplate a safe line of retreat, in case the intrigues
which threatened him should preclude success. Winwood
himself presented him to the French Ambassador, the
Count des Marêts, who was able to reassure Richelieu
that their old brother-in-arms was not going to utilise
his fleet to create a diversion in favour of the French
Huguenots. It was perhaps in order to obtain this
satisfactory declaration that the envoy dilated so much
on the personal sympathies of the French Court. After
a second interview des Marêts reported that Sir Walter,
complaining of the harsh treatment he had received,
offered the French King the refusal of such results as
his expedition might obtain. The conversation, however, was only recorded, by one of the parties interested,
some weeks after it took place. It may be inferred
that, while Raleigh perceived the contingent advantages
of preserving the good-will of France, the Ambassador
too readily expanded tentative inquiries and complimentary phrases into a definite and concrete offer, to
which he does not seem himself to have attached much
importance. The researches of Mr. Gardiner in the
archives at Simancas have revealed evidence of other
negotiations with France, in which des Marêts did not
act as intermediary. A French captain of the name of
Faige was employed by Raleigh to take a message to
Montmorency, the Admiral of France, from whom he
sought authorisation to bring all captured ships and
goods into a French port. It is not clear at what period
these negotiations began, but it appears that Faige went
to France on his behalf while he was conveying his
fleet from the Thames to Plymouth, and rejoined him

at the latter port. He was again despatched with a
compatriot of the name of Belle with fresh letters,
among which was one to a M. de Brisseaux, a member
of the Council of State, in which Sir Walter expressed
satisfaction at the blow given to the Spanish party by
the murder of Concini, referred to the warrant which
he hoped to obtain, and mentioned that Faige was to
lead certain French vessels to join him in Guiana. There
is also a mysterious reference to a resolution he had
long taken if his search for the mine proved successful.
Faige and Belle, however, did not carry out this mission,
and while trading in the Mediterranean their vessel was
taken by pirates.   Faige disappears from the scene ;
Belle, who made his way eventually to Rome, was sent
by a Jesuit confessor to Spain with his evidence.   In the
records of his examination he is made to say that
Raleigh intended to investigate the mine, and if he
found it to be really valuable, he would then attack
Trinidad or Margarita.   Such a project would account
for his anxiety to reinforce his squadron with French
volunteers.   The deposition taken in 1618 was no doubt
forwarded to England, and suggested the interrogations
put to Raleigh on his return with regard to his French
commission.   He replied that he had never sought for a
commission from the King of France, adding pertinently
that "the French King's commissions are of (on) record."
He did, however, announce to his crews, after the disaster
in Guiana, that he held a French commission, and he
admitted in a letter to the King having a commission
from the Admiral of France. That he ever received a commission from the French King he again strenuously denied
on the scaffold.   The two declarations are not necessarily

inconsistent, if the manner in which they were made must be condemned as disingenuous. It must further be conceded that if no French ships joined him in Guiana, this is possibly due to the failure of Faige and Belle to execute their commission. On the other hand, there is no evidence that the French commission contained anything more than an authorisation to enter a French port under certain specified conditions, and in any case Raleigh's intercourse with the French Ambassador was carried on with the full knowledge of James. Sir Thomas Wilson reported that he asserted as much of his dealings with Faige.

An earlier negotiation, which may account for the inception of negotiations with France, was equally well known to the King. Our information on this obscure subject is derived from the despatches of the Venetian Envoy, who received the details, under promise of secrecy, from Count Scarnafissi, the Ambassador in London of Victor Amadeus of Savoy. The latter Duchy had been long perforce the faithful satellite of Spain, but circumstances had modified her political gravitation, and in 1614 a definite rupture took place. Philip then attacked the Duke's port of Oneglia, and Genoa, now wholly under Spanish influence, barred the passage of reinforcements from Savoy, and thus made its capitulation inevitable. Scarnafissi, with the full knowledge of Winwood and the King, had, through a French agent, proposed to " Sir Vat Ralle " that the squadron he was equipping, reinforced by four of the King's ships and other English and Dutch vessels, should embark French troops under the command of the Duke of Montpensier, and, effecting a junction with the Savoy squadron inside

s

the straits, strike a sudden blow at Genoa. The Spaniards, unable to divert their army from Milan, would be unable to render assistance, and a surprise could scarcely fail to be successful. Here would be a valid reason for Raleigh's anxiety to enter a French port with his squadron, and the authorisation once received might be utilised under other circumstances. It was Winwood who had brought him into relations with Scarnafissi, and the Secretary had informed him that the King, who had already assisted Savoy with subsidies, liked the business well. From a later despatch of the Venetian Envoy we learn that the King refused to entrust the execution of the project to Raleigh, whose services were dispensed with, partly because James did not wish to offend Spain too deeply, and partly because he had little confidence that such an agent would make an equitable division of the spoils. The general deduction which may be drawn from this obscure negotiation is that Raleigh, perceiving that Scarnafissi, des Marêts, and Winwood were all urging James to break the peace, and believing that Winwood's councils would prevail, was the more readily encouraged to undertake an enterprise which could hardly lead to any other result.

It was the business of Gondomar, who realised that the pretensions of Raleigh were irreconcilable with the claims of the Spanish Crown, to prove to James that the theory of "no peace beyond the line," dear to the Paladins of Elizabeth, was an obsolete and discredited doctrine, and that if the inevitable collision occurred in Guiana, the newcomers would be looked upon as aggressors by Spain. He therefore did not cease to protest against the issue of a commission. James, halting between two opinions, determined to throw the whole responsibility upon Raleigh, who had maintained that his mine was not in Spanish territory. If he had not told the truth, and a conflict arose on the spot, his head would pay the penalty. No sooner was his scheme submitted to the King, than full particulars, accompanied by a chart, were forwarded to Madrid. In 1617, when the ships were lying ready in the Thames, an Admiralty survey was made of them, and a copy given to Gondomar, who had renewed his protestations. He could have obtained the information elsewhere, but it was the King's policy to meet his objections with a deprecatory attitude of perfect frankness. In reply to his protest, Winwood was instructed to hand him a letter written by Raleigh, declaring Guiana to be the object of his journey, and undertaking to commit no outrages on subjects of Spain. Gondomar is further credited with having procured the erasure of the words "trusty and well-beloved" in the commission granted to Sir Walter. There was precedent in the Queen's commission of 1595 for the omission of the formal phrase, but none for the erasure. In the present instance the erasure involved more than a question of form. Raleigh is reported to have consulted Bacon as to the advisability of procuring an express pardon before he started, and to have received from the Lord Keeper a reply to the effect that he would do well to spare his purse, for his commission was as good a pardon from all former offences as the law could afford him. The contention that the authority delegated to him was inconsistent with the disabilities of attainder would not have escaped Gondomar, and the maintenance of the formal phrase erased would

have been hardly compatible with the King's promise
to the Ambassador that, if Raleigh returned laden with
gold acquired by an attack on Spanish subjects, the loot
should be surrendered, together with the authors of the
crime to be hanged publicly at Madrid.   After such an
assurance any further opposition on Gondomar's part
could only be matter of form, and it is not necessary to
believe that Arundel, one of the promoters, was forced
to become a surety for Raleigh's return before he was
allowed to sail.

Many of his friends now tried to dissuade him from
an undertaking which seemed foredoomed to failure.
An impression gained ground, and was shared by the
Venetian Resident, that he would make use of his fleet
for any enterprise which offered fair prospect of success.
Sir Thomas Wilson, his jailor inquisitor, records an
admission made by Raleigh himself, when questioned
by Bacon as to what he would do if he failed to find
the mine, to the effect that he would look out for the
Plate-fleet.   His rejoinder to the observation that he
would then be a pirate, was, "Who ever heard of men
being pirates for millions?"   It seems questionable
whether he would, otherwise than in jest, have made
such an admission to one who would not fail to turn it
to account.   The authority in any case is not Bacon
himself, but Wilson, who knew that some such proposal
was put forward by Raleigh as a pretext to keep his
mutinous captains together after the failure in Guiana.
A careful comparison of the evidence with regard to his
second voyage, for which the principal pieces are the
Apology and the King's *Declaration*, drawn up by Bacon,
compels the conclusion that Raleigh was not single-

hearted. In the seventeenth and the sixteenth century, to which he belonged, the standard of truth was no very exalted one, and the temptation to which he was exposed was overwhelming. Behind him were twelve years of prison; and in success, however achieved, lay his last hope of fulfilling a lifelong dream. In spite of all his assurances he was prepared to risk a conflict with Spain, believing that the anti-Spanish faction would prevail. He conceived this to be patriot's work, and while he was ready to force the King's hand, he was equally ready to promise anything to obtain the King's commission. He sailed in the pious hope, to which after his disaster he gave expression in a letter to his wife: "I hope God will send us somewhat ere we return."

But if Raleigh under temptation was not altogether truthful or straightforward, what can be urged in defence of James, who, sceptical as to the mine and profoundly mistrusting the discoverer, perceived a political advantage in not resisting the pressure of his partisans, and despatched him with a halter round his neck on an enterprise foredoomed to failure? That, knowing all he knew, and having entered into the engagements he had contracted with Gondomar, he still let Raleigh go, was the King's unpardonable crime.

By the spring of 1617 the equipment of his vessels was approaching completion. Young Walter had returned from abroad, and was to command the *Destiny*, the flagship. To this period, when Raleigh was at liberty and his son with him in London, must be assigned a story told by Aubrey on the authority of James Harrington. Father and son had been invited together to dine at some great house, and Sir Walter warned the youth to keep his quarrelsome temper under control, and demean himself with due respect to his host. Young Walter promised not to forget his manners, and, sitting next his father, was very demure and subdued, until suddenly, perhaps as the wine went to his head, he regaled the company with a scandalous adventure which had befallen him that morning. "Sir Walter, being strangely surprised and put out of countenance at so great a table, gives his son a damned blow over the face. His son, as rude as he was, would not strike his father, but strikes over the face the gentleman that sate next to him and said, 'Box about, 'twill come to my father anon!'" Whence it would appear that the euphemistic Jacobite toast of later years to the King over the Water, may be traced, by a curious irony of history, to one of the first victims of Stuart duplicity.

Sir Walter's little fleet of seven vessels sailed from the Thames in April. Among the ninety gentlemen volunteers were—Sir Warham St. Leger, son of his old comrade in Ireland; his nephew George Raleigh; his cousin William Herbert; Captain North, brother of Lord North; and Edward Hastings, brother of the Earl of Arundel. At Plymouth four more vessels awaited him with Keymis, his old retainer, who had located the mine. Here he was joined by a fly-boat commanded by a certain Captain Bailey, who, there is good reason to believe, was employed to play a similar part to that which Drake attributed to John Doughty in 1577. Money was still wanting to complete the provisioning of some of the ships, and Raleigh was obliged to sell his plate to make up the deficiency. On the 3rd of June he issued his orders to the fleet in a document which

stands for a model of "godly, severe and martial
government," and on the 12th, after being entertained
by his loyal friends in the West, he put to sea. Stormy
weather entailed a fresh start from Falmouth, and again
they were driven to take refuge in Cork, where they
lay wind-bound till the middle of August. Lord Boyle,
the prosperous purchaser of his Munster estates, made
good the precious stores consumed during this unexpected delay. He also consulted Raleigh on the
validity of certain claims put forward by his old partner
Pine, to which his opinion was at the time adverse.
One of the last acts of his life was to request Lord
Boyle to re-open this question, and not to consider it as
finally decided by his evidence.

They sailed on the 19th of August. Off Cape St.
Vincent they overhauled four French ships laden with
suspicious Spanish merchandise. Raleigh rejected the
advice of some of his captains to treat them as pirates,
and dismissed them, after purchasing a pinnace and
some nets at a fair price. On the 6th of September
they made Lancerota in the Canaries. Here their fleet
was mistaken for one of the Barbary squadrons from
whose raids these islands had suffered severely, and some
seamen who had landed were murdered. The Admiral,
however, would sanction no reprisals. Revenge, he said,
would not only offend the King, but would provoke
retaliation on a defenceless English merchantman riding
in the harbour. Bailey took advantage of this episode
to desert, and gave out that he had abandoned Raleigh,
who meant to turn pirate and had landed in a hostile
manner at Lancerota. The Spanish version of the
incident, however, afforded no support to this premature

announcement, and from Gomera, where the fleet
received much kindness from the governor's wife, the
daughter of an English mother, despatches went to
Madrid testifying officially to the exemplary conduct of
the crews.   An epidemic in the ships, which had somewhat abated at Gomera, broke out . with renewed
virulence on their departure, and death struck down his
victims with disheartening impartiality.   They buried
at sea John Pigott, the sergeant-major, and Raleigh's old
servant and true friend, John Talbot, who had remained
eleven years with him in the Tower.   He had a singular
power of holding the affections of his dependants, who
ever willingly laid down their lives in his service.
Whiddon already lay buried in Trinidad, and Keymis
was also destined to fall a victim to the phantom gold of
Guiana.   King, the last of this little group, was alone
to be with him till the end, and make the vain attempt
to save his master's life.   On the 11th of November
they made Cape Orange, and anchored in the Caliana
mouth of the river Cayenne.   Hence he sent home
Captain Peter Alley, incapacitated for further service
by sickness, with letters.   He had little but miseries to
communicate.   In his own ship forty-two were dead,
and for himself he had barely got over the most violent
calenture that ever man lived through.   But there
were some bright spots.   The indomitable spirit was
not quenched by the disastrous voyage.   Young Walter
never had so good health, and to his joy he found that
his name still lived among the Indians, who had all
proffered service.   Meanwhile, at home a greater misfortune had befallen him than he was aware of, in
the death of his constant advocate and friend, Sir

Ralph Winwood, on whose life and policy so much depended.

Leaving such ships as had not made good their repairs to follow, he sailed for the Triangle islands and organised his flotilla. Here he suffered from a severe relapse; but even if his health had not broken down, he would have been unable to take personal command of the expedition, as the companies, mistrusting the other captains, were unwilling to proceed unless he himself remained with the ships to guard the river mouths. In the absence of St. Leger, who lay sick at Caliana, the military direction was given to George Raleigh, and Keymis, as older and more experienced, was entrusted with a general supervision. Young Walter Raleigh accompanied his cousin. Precise orders were given to both leaders to do all in their power to avoid a conflict with the Spaniards, whom they believed, from the report brought back by Keymis in 1596, to be established at the junction of the Caroni and the Orinoco. Since then their settlement of San Thomé had been transferred to a site twenty miles or more down the main stream, in the immediate neighbourhood of Mount Aio and the mine. Raleigh, however, clearly believed that the town was still at the junction of the two rivers, and his orders to Keymis show that he meant the flotilla to stop short of the settlement, and place a covering party between it and the mine. They were to resort to force only if attacked. Should the mine prove disappointing in quality, Keymis was nevertheless to bring back samples, to prove that the design was not wholly illusory. If they found that troops in any considerable number had recently been despatched up the Orinoco, and that the passage to the mine could not be attempted without manifest danger, they were to be cautious about landing at all. Raleigh was aware that his men were of poor quality, and desired "for all the world not to receive a blow from the Spaniards to the dishonour of our nation." He himself would be found dead or alive at Punto Gallo on their return. On the 10th of December the flotilla started.

Diego Palomeque de Acuña, Governor of Trinidad, a relative of Gondomar, duly instructed from Madrid, was already at San Thomé, and preparing to defend the position with his small available force, when a fisherman informed him of the approach of the flotilla, which had been three weeks ascending the river to this point. Two of the slower vessels were, however, still some days' journey behind. Raleigh's account of the action which ensued is to the effect that his men, when they became aware of the unexpected proximity of the town, landed between it and the mine, intending to encamp for the night and rest till the following morning. The Spaniards had placed a portion of their force in ambush, and attacking them suddenly at nightfall, drew them on in a series of skirmishes to the town itself, which they were thus forced to take. He consistently asserted in the *Apology*, as in his un-delivered letter to Winwood, and in a later letter to Carew, that the Spaniards were the first to attack without any manner of parley. According to the Spanish version of Fray Simon, when towards noon Keymis and George Raleigh reached the spot whence the mine could be approached, the huts of San

Thomé were plainly visible on the river bank in front
of them. They therefore anchored below the town,
and at nightfall marched to attack it, with the co-operation of the boats. This account receives some confirmation from an eye-witness who was with the English,
Captain Parker, who says, "At last we landed within a
league of San Thomé, and about one of the clock at
night we made the assault." He gives in detail the
disposition of the English force after landing, which,
though it may have been made for defensive purposes,
lends colour to the assumption that they were preparing for the assault when the Spaniards suddenly
charged. The Spaniards certainly struck the first blow,
but they might plead that they only anticipated the
attack which the English were organising.

The latter, an untrustworthy rabble, were thrown
into confusion by the sudden rush of a mere handful of
men, but their officers rallied them, and the Spaniards
were driven back on the town, whence the Governor
came to their support with reinforcements. Once more
the English advance was checked, till, gallantly led by
young Raleigh, the pikemen charged. The Governor
and two other officers were killed; but Walter Raleigh
was wounded by a bullet, and still pressing forward, fell,
clubbed by the butt of a Spanish musket. "Go on," he
cried with his last breath; "may the Lord have mercy
on me and prosper your enterprise!" The death of
their admiral's high-spirited son infuriated the English.
Led by George Raleigh and Keymis, they drove the
defenders back through the town, and carried by storm
the monastery in which they had taken shelter. The
survivors fled to the woods, and made their way to a

place of refuge to which their women and children had been previously removed. The English established themselves in San Thomé, and in its church they buried the youth of so many hopes by the side of Captain Cosmer, who had also fallen in the action. Precious time was lost in waiting for the two boats commanded by Captains Whitney and Wollaston, who did not arrive until a week later. This delay enabled the Spaniards to reorganise their forces. Garcia de Aguilar, who succeeded to the command, haunted the neighbourhood of San Thomé, and in the meantime the women and children were transferred to an island in the Orinoco. At length Keymis set out in two launches for the mine. The island which the Spaniards had occupied, or a creek of the same name, lay in the passage, and they were met with a hail of arrows and bullets, which killed or disabled the whole crew of the first boat. In the face of this disaster Keymis at once decided to go back, though he was within easy reach of his destination. On his return to San Thomé he found the companies in no great heart. They were ceaselessly harassed by attacks from both Spaniards and Indians, and sickness was fast reducing the scanty numbers. No further effort was made to examine the mine. Perhaps only now, when called upon to make good his assertions, Keymis realised how slight was the evidence upon which he had guaranteed its inexhaustible wealth. George Raleigh led an exploring party a hundred miles up the Orinoco, and returned to find the garrison well-nigh out of hand. The town had been fired in several places, and stragglers cut off and tortured. It had also no doubt leaked out that among the papers found in

the Governor's house were full instructions from Madrid
with regard to Raleigh's expedition, and notification of
reinforcements already on their way. It seemed clear
that success had been compromised before they sailed,
and they decided to embark such little spoil as San
Thomé had afforded, to burn down the settlement, and
to return to the admiral with a confession of failure.

The survivors rejoined the fleet on the 2nd of March,
1618. To Keymis, in whom Raleigh had rested all his
confidence, the meeting must have been well-nigh un-
endurable. But he faced it resolutely, and told his
pitiful tale. For once, and the only time in his life,
Raleigh, contemplating the irretrievable ruin of his last
hopes, was ungenerous to a dependant. He could not
forgive his having made no effort to find the mine, which
was the occasion and the justification of the enterprise.
He told him that since his son had been killed he might
well have risked a hundred other lives to save his master's
credit. Raleigh had trusted in Keymis to his own un-
doing, and now that his faith was shattered he became
hard and stern; Keymis would have to answer for his
conduct to the King and the State. No excuses could
move him, and he refused to endorse a letter of justification which Keymis addressed to the Earl of Arundel, the
chief contributor to the expedition. On learning his
decision Keymis went to his cabin and shot himself.
The wound was not mortal, and he was able to reply to
the page sent to inquire what the report signified, that
he was only discharging a loaded weapon. He then
stabbed himself to the heart. The reproach of the man
he loved had struck home, and the secret of the mine, upon
which so much had been hazarded, perished with him.

The discontent which had long been undermining the discipline of the fleet now found open expression. Captains and crews had lost faith in their unfortunate admiral. There were not a few among them who had little credit to lose, and who saw in some act of reprisal or spoliation on Spanish ports and shipping the only hope of making good the disaster. The ringleader was Captain Whitney, for whose equipment Raleigh had sold his plate. The admiral, they argued, was a ruined man if he returned. If they could not secure his co-operation in some piratical enterprise, they were disposed to leave him and break up the fleet. Raleigh, in desperation, now held out hopes of a raid on the Mexican Plate-fleet, which could only be contemplated if they held together, meeting questions and objections by the announcement that he had a French commission, and that it was lawful to take prizes beyond the Canaries. He afterwards contended that this proposal was a mere pretext, put forward to keep the fleet in hand; and it seems that it was so understood, for Whitney and Wollaston deserted soon after he had sailed, ostensibly for Newfoundland. Carew Raleigh has stated that his father's intention had been to reorganise his expedition in Virginia, and make a second attempt to reach the mine in the following spring. The statement receives corroboration in the letter which Sir Walter addressed from St. Christopher to Winwood, of whose death he was ignorant, protesting that but for Whitney's desertion he would have returned to leave his bones in Guiana, or bring back evidence which would have convinced the King of his sincerity. With this letter he enclosed one of the compromising documents found in San Thomé. His cousin, William Herbert, carried this letter, with another to Lady Raleigh, telling the same tragic story, and alluding more than once to his approaching return. "Comfort your heart, dearest Bess," he wrote; "I shall sorrow for us both. I shall sorrow the less, because I have not long to sorrow, because not long to live."

Whatever may be inferred from probabilities, or disentangled from the confused echoes of gossip, in order to damn an unsuccessful leader as an intended pirate, no overt act against Spain could be laid to his charge after the return of the river force to Trinidad; and in spite of a mutiny in Newfoundland, having for its object to prevent the return of the fleet, he brought the *Destiny* back to Plymouth, as he had pledged his word to do, on the 21st of June, 1618, after a stormy voyage had set the crown of misery on a disastrous undertaking.

CHAPTER XVI

IN PALACE YARD

THE news of disaster had preceded him. The letters from St. Christopher had been received early in May, and Gondomar now claimed his pound of flesh. The King confirmed his pledge, and on the day on which Raleigh, broken in spirit and body, landed at Plymouth, he attended the Council in person, and listened with satisfaction to Buckingham's uncompromising attack on the traitors who, by false representations, had induced their sovereign to give his consent to the Guiana enterprise. A general approval of punishment was not enough for the Spanish Envoy, who required that Sir Walter and a dozen of his followers should be transported to Madrid for judgment. This impudent demand was strongly opposed by the Council, but James promised to surrender the prisoner, who had now been arrested, unless Philip should expressly prefer his execution in London. Satisfied with this engagement, Gondomar prepared to depart. On the eve of his journey an episode provoked by one of his servants led to a riotous demonstration in front of the embassy by the Londoners, who sustained their reputation as *hospitibus feri*. The haughty demeanour of his predecessor in her relations with foreign envoys was little to the taste of the King, who sent Buckingham to express his regret, and ordered the Lord Mayor to apologise. Gondomar was appeased, and set out in triumph, with a large train of priests released from durance at his request. The King's engagements were confirmed in a letter which Buckingham addressed to him on the 26th of July. If there was now little hope that Raleigh would escape with his life, there was no honourable issue for James from the impossible situation in which he had placed himself. He realised, however, the necessity of giving the prisoner a hearing, and of establishing some definite charge against him.

Lady Raleigh had joined her husband at Plymouth and heard from his lips the whole miserable story. His first instinct had been to come up to London and lay his case before the King, but he had scarcely set out when he was met by his kinsman, the Vice-Admiral of Devon, Sir Lewis Stukely, who had verbal orders to arrest him and to seize the ships. Pending their confirmation he took his prisoner back to Plymouth, where an examination of the contents of the *Destiny* provided him with an excuse for not returning to London. Raleigh now realised what had taken place at the Council, and perceived that any appeal to the King's sense of justice would be vain. A French vessel was lying in the harbour. The conditions of arrest were not stringently enforced, and after nightfall he was able to leave the house of Sir Christopher Harris, where he was lodged, and in company with his faithful retainer, Captain King, who had made arrangements with the French skipper, to get into a boat unperceived. But at the last his resolution changed; to fly was to acknowledge himself in the

T

wrong, and he returned to his lodgings.[1]   Stukely now received written orders to bring his prisoner to London, and after hastily selling the cargo of the *Destiny* he set out on the 25th of July.   The company included a French physician, named Manourie, who was something of a chemist and still more of a charlatan.   Raleigh welcomed him as a fellow-student, not realising that he had been engaged as a spy.

Their road lay past Sherborne, and Sir Walter now looked for the last time on the home of his happiest days, bowered in the groves his own hand had planted nearly five-and-twenty years ago.   If there was some bitterness in his soul, and if it found vent in the words which the Frenchman reported as disloyal, "All this was mine, and it was taken from me unjustly," at least the charge was true.   As they approached London his worst anticipations were confirmed, and it appeared very doubtful whether he would be afforded an opportunity of defending his reputation.   His first preoccupation was therefore to put himself right with the world, and in order to gain time he appealed to Manourie, who had won his confidence, for assistance in an artifice which in his extremity he did not consider unworthy.   He asked him for a drug which would render him so sick as to prevent his continuing the journey until he had had time to order his affairs, "For as soon as ever I come to London they will have me to the Tower and cut off my head."   This took place the day before Salisbury was reached.   He was not without hope that he might

---

[1] In the *Declaration* drawn up by Bacon it is erroneously asserted that this attempted escape was made before he was under guard, whence it is argued that his purpose to fly to France was formed immediately on his arrival in England.

obtain an interview with the King, who was expected
there, but the preparation of his defence was his first
object.   Lady Raleigh went on to London, and with her
Captain King, who was to look out for a vessel lying
in readiness in the Thames, with a view to escape
if opportunity occurred.   Sir Walter then affected a
temporary derangement of mind, and Manourie, not
unwilling to humour him in any matter which could
afterwards be used as evidence against him, administered
a drug which brought on violent sickness and an erup-
tion of the skin.   The local physicians were puzzled,
and advised that it would be dangerous to move him
for some days.   Had he not descended to an artifice,
which he justified by citing the example of David when
in danger from his enemies, the world would have been
the poorer, for during this interval he wrote his *Apology
for the Voyage to Guiana*.   Like Africanus at bay before
his enemies, he appealed to his life's record, and in this
masterly indictment of Spanish practices the old fighter
knew that he would not speak to posterity in vain.   Mr.
Gardiner, than whom no authority is more entitled to
respect, has written : "To all who knew what the facts
were, he stamped himself by his *Apology* as a liar convicted on his own confession."   These are hard words.
In judging its contents we have to consider not only how
far he had pledged himself not to force his way into
Guiana, whatever might be the conditions he found
there on arrival, but how far also James had wrung
from him a promise which it was manifestly impossible
to keep.   He had undertaken to commit no outrages on
subjects of Spain : he was not to raid or harass peaceful
settlers, as in the old buccaneering days ; but unless this

undertaking bound him to retire before a Spanish garrison
which he found in occupation of territory claimed by the
Crown of England, unless even in self-defence it bound
him to offer no resistance, the arguments of the *Apology*
have more weight than Mr. Gardiner is disposed to accord
them.   That there was a settlement at San Thomé he
knew ; that it had been moved further down stream he
did not know.   It may be argued that a few miles east
or west is of little moment in the vast area of Guiana,
and that he had by his silence on this point concealed
an important fact from the King, who, however, knew
it well enough from Gondomar.   But if he was forbidden
to resist or maintain his ground by the display of force,
why was he suffered to collect a large expedition fully
equipped for war?   If the Spaniards were, as he
maintained, the aggressors, he could not well be called
in question.   If, again, his subordinates provoked the
attack, it was necessary before condemning him to prove
he had so instructed them.   He was, indeed, as has
been said, not single-hearted, not more straightforward
than the majority of his generation.   Nor was he
ignorant of the risk he ran.   So fine an observer could
not have failed to read the shifty mind of James.   He
had sailed in the confident hope that the policy of
Winwood, Arundel, Pembroke, and the anti-Spanish
faction was in the ascendant.   Now Winwood was dead,
and the influence of Gondomar supreme.   The *Apology*
was a last appeal to the self-respect of James, and as he
penned the passages in which he defiantly maintained
the theory that there was no peace beyond the line, it
must have seemed to him still questionable whether the
King would dare to hand over the last of the Paladins

of Elizabeth to the enemy he had spent his life in
fighting.

On the 1st of August James arrived at Salisbury, and
the prisoner was hurried on to London. It was during
this last stage of the journey, according to Manourie's
evidence, that he attempted to bribe Stukely into connivance with his escape, and denounced the King in unseemly language. Against the questionable testimony
of Manourie and Stukely must be set the protest recorded
by King in his narrative, who says of his master, "In
all the years I followed him I never heard him name his
Majesty but with reverence." King had meanwhile,
through the assistance of an old servant, found out a
former boatswain of Sir Walter's, Hart by name, who
had a ketch lying in the river, which he agreed to keep
in readiness at Tilbury. Hart, however, at once gave
information to a certain Mr. Herbert, who communicated
with Sir William St. John, one of the kinsmen of Buckingham who had accepted Raleigh's money. St. John
posted off to Salisbury with his news, and on the road
met the prisoner with Stukely, who was thus warned
betimes. A farther report went to Salisbury from
Brentford, where a member of the French Embassy, De
Novion, Sieur de la Chesnée, found means of conveying
to Sir Walter a message to the effect that the Ambassador
desired to communicate with him. This visit was a
surprise to Raleigh himself, and it revealed the suspicious interest taken in his fate by France. Stukely
was now directly authorised to counterfeit sympathy,
and pretend to connive at his escape in order to discover
what secret intrigue was on foot. On the 9th of August,
two days after their arrival in London, where Raleigh was

purposely not kept in close confinement, the Envoy Le Clerc came in person and offered to help him to escape. Although he elected rather to trust in the arrangements which King had made for him, it is probable that the interview with Le Clerc confirmed him in his intention to seek a refuge in France.   There is some reason for believing that the Queen's faction, who opposed the Spanish alliance, may have been privy to this interview, and that Raleigh was encouraged to believe that, once safe from the immediate danger of Spanish vengeance, the Queen, who had always manifested her sympathies for him, would find means to procure a pardon.   Some such explanation he afterwards gave to Wilson as having inclined him to the unworthier course of flight.   Stukely, who had gained his unreserved confidence, found convincing reasons for desiring to accompany him to France, and borrowed £10 from him with which to send his servants to the country.   It was decided that the attempt should be made at once.   Raleigh, Stukely, and King left his house in Bread Street at various hours in the evening, and meeting Hart at the river-side, embarked to row to Tilbury.   At the same time another boat was seen to put off with a numerous company, and make as though it were proceeding up stream.   To Raleigh, as the wherry passed under the shadow of the Tower, the moment was fraught with great emotions.   How often in the old days had he dropped down the historic river with the ebbing tide to the ships which were waiting to bear him seaward on the quest of honour or adventure ! Now, broken by misfortune and disappointment, he was setting out, a fugitive from his country, upon a course which he could only justify to himself by the thought

that his self-appointed task was not yet done, and that
he still might fight one more battle in the cause to which
he had sacrificed his resources, his energies, and his
affections. History has few more pathetic figures than
that of the old knight-errant of the sea setting forth on
this last journey. It was not long before he perceived
that the second boat was following them. Then he
realised that the tide would not serve beyond Gravesend.
The watermen began to lag, and the miserable Stukely
affected to threaten them for not rowing faster. A little
beyond Woolwich the second boat drew up. In it was
Herbert with a crew of St. John's men. It was now
clear to Raleigh that some one had betrayed him, and he
ordered the boatmen to turn back. To the last he did
not suspect Stukely, and as he once more constituted
himself his prisoner, he bestowed on him, as a mark of
gratitude, the few objects of value he had on his person.

At Greenwich Stukely threw off the mask, and
arrested him in the King's name. Raleigh's dignified
protest, "Sir Lewis, these actions will not turn out to
your credit," was destined often to ring remorsefully in
the ears of this miserable creature, on whom the public
indignation justly fell. His reward for these services,
and the evidence collected by himself and Manourie, was
a little short of £1000. Convicted soon afterwards of
the crime of clipping coin, he received a pardon from
his royal employer, but became an outcast from society.
The old Lord High Admiral spurned him from his
presence. Even his accomplice, Manourie, whose reward
was a miserable £20, denounced the employer who had
suborned him to give false evidence. High and low
alike turned from his abject face, and he died at last, a

maniac haunted by the face of his victim, in the storm-beaten isle of Lundy, where he had sought a refuge from the reproach of mankind.

The honest Captain King accompanied his master to the Tower, and there perforce left him, as he wrote, "to His tuition, with whom I doubt not his soul resteth." A few days later Lady Raleigh was also placed under confinement in the house of a London merchant, and seals were set on her effects and property.

The only question still unsettled was how the prisoner's sacrifice could be turned to account in clenching the negotiations for the hand of the well-dowered Infanta, and Philip was invited to decide whether his enemy should be sent to Madrid, or whether punishment should be vicariously inflicted by James. The delay involved in consulting Philip's pleasure was utilised in building up the plea of justification for his death. A committee of the Privy Council, consisting of Archbishop Abbott, Lord Worcester, the Chancellor Bacon, Coke, Naunton, and Sir Julius Cæsar, was appointed to take evidence. It was no easy task to extricate the King from the difficult situation in which he had placed himself, by on the one hand sanctioning the expedition, and on the other promising Raleigh's blood to Spain if the inevitable occurred. The committee set to work on a false assumption that he had never meant to find the mine, and consequently their investigations proved inconclusive. It became necessary to find some other pretext to warrant a sentence of death. A new spy was therefore attached to his person, who was to endeavour to gain his confidence by persuading him that a frank confession might secure the King's pardon. This unenviable duty was entrusted to Sir Thomas Wilson, Keeper of the State Papers, who had since 1603 been in receipt of a pension from Spain. Raleigh's mistrustful reserve baffled even an adept like Wilson, and at his wits' end he informed the King that he knew of "no means but a rack or a halter" to make him speak. The French intrigue was the matter on which information was most urgently desired. De Novion, admitting nothing, had been placed in custody. Raleigh acknowledged having told Stukely that he had been offered a passage in a French ship, but maintained that he only did so to deceive. Eventually, however, perhaps convinced of the sincerity of Wilson's promises, he admitted in a letter to James that he had a commission from Montmorency, but not from the French King, whose Envoy had, through De Novion, offered him assistance to escape. On this Le Clerc was summoned to the Council, and, when he persisted in denying the story, all relations with him were broken off. The unsolicited intervention of France at this crisis had only done more harm than good.

In another letter addressed to the King Raleigh protested that the village of San Thomé was not burned by his directions, and pleaded his voluntary return to poverty in England as a proof of his honesty of purpose. He also composed a poetic petition to the Queen, whose voice was once more raised in his behalf, but to such a pitch of degradation had the British Court descended that her last vain appeal was made to the all-powerful favourite. To Buckingham he appears to have written also (the letter only exists in the form of a copy), explaining the motives of his attempted flight, and

making rather an abject appeal to one who was little
disposed to listen.   These letters were probably inspired
by the false hopes of clemency held forth by Wilson.
To Carew, whose influence on public opinion was considerable, he wrote in a more manly strain, recapitulating
the arguments he had used in the *Apology*.   He admitted
having contemplated the necessity of driving the
Spaniards out of their settlement before proceeding to
the mine, but maintained that he had reconsidered the
situation, and made such action subordinate to the
richness of the ore.   He had never intended the burning
of the town, but his men, when wantonly attacked, had
no option' but to repel force by force.   Finally, he had
returned to England, and placed his life at the King's
grace.   From this line of argument he never swerved in
spite of all the pressure exercised to obtain incriminating
admissions.   But one contention, repeatedly put forward
in these letters and in his conversation, outweighed in
his eyes all that might be said for or against the precise
legality of his conduct: "If it were lawful for the
Spanish to murder twenty-six Englishmen, tying them
back to back, and then to cut their throats, when they
had traded with them a whole month, and came to them
without so much as one sword among them all; and that
it may not be lawful for your Majesty's subjects, being
forced by them, to repel force by force, we may justly
say, O miserable English!"   Such language would produce little impression upon a monarch who was engaged
in composing dissertations on the Lord's Prayer, with an
appropriate dedication to Villiers, and it may have met
with little response in days of reaction from Tudor
standards of national dignity.   But to those who have

known what it means to have seen the British flag
insulted, and to be compelled to wait many years for a
tardy and hardly won satisfaction, they are of eloquent
significance in the mouth of the first apostle of Empire.

It is difficult to acquit the King of complicity in the
methods which Wilson now employed. Raleigh was
encouraged to write constantly to his wife, and their
letters were intercepted. Petty tyrannies were enforced
in the Tower. He was placed under more stringent
confinement, and threatened with the confiscation of his
favourite chemicals, supplied by the kindness of Lady
Apsley, the Lieutenant's wife. In spite of every effort
no fresh evidence was extorted. But he had undertaken
to commit no outrage on Spanish subjects in Guiana,
and his men had broken the peace. For this he was to
die, although the responsibility fell not less heavily on
the King himself. At length the Spanish agent received
the reply to Gondomar's communication, which was to
the effect that it would be more agreeable to his Spanish
Majesty that the punishment should be carried out in
England. At the same time it should be as exemplary
and immediate as the offence was notorious.

It was still necessary to find a colourable legal pretext for carrying out the orders from Madrid. The
King himself seems to have desired a trial of some sort,
but Bacon and the law officers advised him that as the
prisoner was already under sentence of death, passed in
1603, he could not be drawn in question judicially for
any crime since committed. He was accordingly relieved
from further persecution. Wilson was discharged, and
Lady Raleigh was set at liberty. The Commissioners, to
whom the question of procedure was referred, recom-

mended one of two courses. · The King might forthwith
issue the warrant for execution under the sentence of
1603, and at the same time publish a narrative of
Sir Walter's offences in print for the information of
the public.   Or the prisoner might be brought up
before the Council of State and the judges, with a
limited audience, to give semblance of publicity, and
being informed that he was already civilly dead, be
charged and heard in his defence.   At the same time
they urged a prudent reserve with regard to the French
intrigue.   This course, which they preferred as the
nearest to a legal procedure, did not, however, commend
itself to the King, who feared anything approaching a
public trial, and did not feel too sure that the Council
would so readily condemn the prisoner.   The judges
and the public audience were therefore dispensed with,
and Raleigh was finally, on the 22nd of October, brought,
not even before the Council, but before the limited body
of Commissioners.   No record of the proceedings appears
in the Council Register, but a fragmentary report exists
in the notes of Sir Julius Cæsar.   The Attorney-General
recapitulated the various charges which had been for-
mulated against him.   He had imposed on the King's
credulity by inventing the story of a mine which he
never intended to explore: he held a French commission
warranting hostilities against Spain; and his piratical
intentions were confirmed by his scheme to lie in wait
for the Mexican Plate-fleet.   The contumelious references to the King, reported by Stukely and Manourie,
furnished a theme for the eloquence of the Solicitor-
General.   Raleigh replied that he believed the King
" in his own conscience" now held him clear of all

complicity in the events of 1603.   The charges made by
Stukely and Manourie were false; the utmost he had
said was that his confidence in the King had been
deceived.   His own belief in the existence of the
mine was proved by the fact that he had spent £2000
in engaging miners and purchasing mining-tools.
The first aggression came from the Spaniards, against
whom he had not directed any attack.   He admitted
having discussed a raid on the Mexico fleet, after the
expedition to the mine had failed, but he had already
fully explained that the proposal was merely an ex-
pedient to hold his mutinous captains together.   According to the Spanish account of these proceedings, Bacon
then addressed the prisoner and informed him that he was
to die.   The Justices of the King's Bench were directed
to give execution to the old sentence.   They required
his presence in order to afford him the formal opportunity of pleading for a stay of execution, and on the 28th
of October he was brought hurriedly from the Tower,
shivering with ague, to the bar of the Court.   He contended
that his commission for the voyage was tantamount to
a pardon, but an attempt to introduce the subject of
Guiana was cut short by the announcement that he was
there only called in question for the treason of 1603.   He
then threw himself on the King's mercy, urging that that
judgment was a thing of the past, of which many present
knew the real value.   Chief-Justice Montague replied
that new offences had moved the King to revive the old
sentence, and bidding him in a few not unkindly words
prepare for death, awarded execution.   The degrading
features of the sentence had been remitted in favour of
decapitation at Westminster.

If Raleigh had not always exercised due self-restraint in pleading for a life which he passionately desired to preserve in his consciousness of power unexhausted and purpose still unfulfilled, he now resumed that quiet dignity which never failed him at crucial moments. He begged indeed a few days' respite, in which to complete some work on which he was engaged, but his appeal was as vain as had been that of Lady Raleigh and the few friends who still ventured to intercede for him. The warrant for execution had been drawn up before the summons to the King's Bench was issued, and was to be carried out on the following morning; meanwhile James was out of reach of all petitions. The prisoner was conducted to the gate-house at Westminster. The friends who there visited him were astonished to find him in such good heart, as he bade them not grudge him his last mirth in this world. The Dean of Westminster, Dr. Robert Tounson, who was delegated by the Council to attend him, testifies that he found the disposition of his mind not only brave and cheerful, but "very Christianly, so that he satisfied me then as I think he did all his spectators at his death."

It is not easy, even after all these years, to contemplate without emotion his last interview with that brave woman, who, as at the beginning she had risked all to win his love, had through their married life of six-and-twenty years made willing sacrifice of home, peace, and fortune, in constant unswerving devotion to her hero. When, late on the evening of the 28th of October, she was admitted to the gate-house, she had only just learned that the execution would take place on the following morning, and at the same time she had been assured she would be allowed the privilege of burying him. Their converse was chiefly on the means of defending his memory if he was forbidden to speak from the scaffold, and he undertook to leave her a paper of notes with his final explanations. Of their little son he could not bring himself to speak, lest the thought should unnerve him. Then midnight struck, and the hour had come to separate for ever. With a supreme effort she told him, through a blinding rush of tears, that she had obtained the disposal of his body, to which, with a brave and gentle smile, as he led her to the door, he replied, "It is well, dear Bess, that thou mayest dispose of that dead, which thou hadst not always the disposal of when alive."

Then, in the quiet and solemn silence of his last night on earth, he drew up two testamentary notes. In one he endeavoured to put right a possible injustice which he feared words of his might occasion to his former agent Pine, and appealed to Lady Raleigh to make such provision as she could for the wives of two faithful servants. In the other he formally recapitulated his answers to the charges made against him, renouncing God's mercy if he was not writing truth.

Early in the morning the Dean visited him again and administered the communion, which he received devoutly. He expressed forgiveness of all who had injured him, and steadfastly maintained his own innocence. Then he breakfasted and smoked his last pipe of tobacco. What sorcery was in those wreathing clouds of smoke, which conjured back for a moment all the scents and echoes of the far-off West,—a mirage of broad jungle plains quivering in the tropic sun, and beyond them the blue mountains that were still uncrossed? The baffled dreamer put the vision by, and, rising erect, obeyed the summons of his guards. At the door he was offered and drank a cup of sack. "It is a good drink," he quoted, "if a man might tarry by it."

The scaffold was erected in front of the Parliament House, and a great multitude had assembled to witness a scene which Englishmen have never forgiven. Not a few of the more independent peers were present, some on horseback, some in Sir Randolph Carew's balcony. Raleigh was allowed to address them, and prayed them, if his voice was feeble, if they perceived any sign of weakness in him, to ascribe it to the ague from which he had been suffering, but which he thanked God was not on him at this supreme moment. Arundel, North-ampton, and Doncaster then said they would come down to the scaffold. They shook hands with him, and he resumed his speech, which has only come down to us in inadequate reports. Dealing first with his alleged practices with France, he protested that a man's word in the hour of death, when there was no room for repentance, must carry weight, and in that knowledge he called God to witness that he never had any plot or intelligence with the French King nor with his ambassador. He repudiated the charge of having spoken in unseemly terms of the King, a charge based on the evidence of a perjured impostor. "I did never speak any dishonourable or disloyal words of the King. If I did, the Lord blot me out of the book of life. Nay, I will now protest further that I never thought such evil of him in my heart; and therefore it seemeth some-what strange that such a base fellow should receive credit." He confessed frankly that he had tried to escape, and that he had feigned sickness at Salisbury, trusting thereby to gain time till the King arrived. He re-affirmed his honesty of purpose in the voyage to Guiana, by which he had hoped to enrich the King, his partners, and himself, but all was undone by the wilfulness of Keymis. As to the report that he would not have returned unless compelled to by his company, the contrary was the true case, and he had been held a prisoner in his cabin by mutineers until he had undertaken not to bring them to England without first obtaining a pardon for four members of the crew who were under sentence. He expressed his gratitude that Arundel was present, and able to testify to his promise to return to England whether the voyage was a success or a failure. Then appealing to the Sheriff for a little more time he touched on another matter. "It was said that I was a persecutor of my Lord of Essex, and that I stood in a window over against him when he suffered, and puffed out tobacco in disdain of him. I take God to witness that my eyes shed tears for him when he died. And, as I hope to look in the face of God hereafter, my Lord of Essex did not see my face when he suffered. I was afar off in the armoury when I saw him, but he saw not me. And my soul hath been many times grieved that I was not near unto him when he died, because I understood afterwards that he asked for me at his death, to be reconciled to me. I confess I was of a contrary faction. But I knew that my Lord of Essex was a noble gentleman, and that it would be worse with me when he was gone. *For those that did set me up against him, did afterwards set*

U

themselves against me." He concluded with those moving words, which, though somewhat variously reported, are substantially similar in all the texts. "And now I entreat that you will all join with me in prayer to that great God of heaven whom I have grievously offended, that He will of His almighty goodness extend to me forgiveness, being a man full of all vanity, and one who hath lived a sinful life in such callings as have been most inducing to it ; for I have been a soldier, a sailor, and a courtier, all of them courses of wickedness and vice ; but I trust He will not only cast away my sin, but will receive me into everlasting life." And with a smile full of sweet and bitter memories he added, "I have a long journey to take, and must bid the company farewell."

The Lords then withdrew, leaving him alone with the Dean and the executioner, who prayed for forgiveness. He divested himself of gown and doublet, and moving round the scaffold besought all present to pray for him. Seeing Arundel, he desired him to beg the King that no defamatory writings should be published about him after death. He assured the Dean that he died in the faith professed by the Church of England, and was about to kneel when it was suggested that he should turn his face to the east. "What matter," he said, as he moved to comply, "which way the head lie, so the heart be right?" These were his last characteristic words. Then he knelt down, and, after praying for a short while, gave the appointed signal by stretching out his hands. The head was severed in two blows from the body, which remained motionless in the posture of prayer. The shuddering crowd turned silently

away from that scene of national dishonour, and the first
voice to find indignant utterance exclaimed, "We have
not such another head to be cut off." The body, wrapped
in his cloak, was conveyed to Lady Raleigh, who caused
it to be buried in St. Margaret's Church at Westminster.
She had previously arranged with Sir Nicholas Carew
for his interment at Beddington, but the design was not
carried out. The head was embalmed, and she kept it
with her through nine-and-twenty years of widowhood.

The public indignation which, in days when the
theory of prerogative still protected the person of the
sovereign from criticism, fell upon the instruments of
the monarch's will, was so great that James felt compelled to adopt the course originally suggested by the
Commission, and to publish a *Declaration*, setting forth
the crimes and offences of Raleigh, which it was Bacon's
ungrateful duty to compose. If later historians have to
some extent admitted that its arguments acquit the
King of a conscious act of injustice, contemporary
opinion was little modified by the terms of this defence.
His countrymen were content to leave on one side the
narrow issue of legality, and judge his case on the
broader basis which still appealed to Englishmen who
had not forgotten the great struggle of the previous
reign. They had long ceased to think of him as the
pampered favourite, the arrogant courtier. In their
eyes he stood for the greatness of England, for independence from the tyranny of priestcraft, a danger not yet
sufficiently remote to be disregarded, for the expansion
of their country's resources, for liberty of commerce,
and for the freedom of the sea. But it needed the
scaffold at Westminster to complete his triumphant

vindication, to open to his spirit that sphere of attain-
ment which it was not his fortune to take by storm in
life. There were many spots on the sun of his reputation, but the tragedy of his end revealed his greatness
and blotted out his faults. Thus by his death he
became, in a measure more than his record justifies, an
ideal to the men of a subsequent generation, who were
to engage in the great struggle for constitutional liberty.
With an almost prophetic instinct, in the last page of
his *History of the World*, he had acknowledged the debt
he was to owe to the executioner :

O eloquent, just, and mighty death ! whom none could
advise, thou hast persuaded ; what none hath dared, thou
hast done ; and whom all the world hath flattered, thou
only hast cast out of the world and despised ; thou hast
drawn together all the far-stretched greatness, all the pride,
cruelty, and ambition of man, and covered it all over with
these two narrow words, *Hic jacet* !

In the Bible which he used in the gate-house at
Westminster a few hours before he suffered, he had
penned his own epitaph. With these lines the story of
life may aptly close :

> Even such is time, that takes on trust
>   Our youth, our joys, our all we have,
> And pays us but with age and dust ;
>   Who in the dark and silent grave,
> When we have wandered all our ways,
> Shuts up the story of our days !
> But from this earth, this grave, this dust,
> The Lord shall raise me up, I trust !

Printed by R. & R. Clark, Limited, *Edinburgh*

Ingram Content Group UK Ltd.
Milton Keynes UK
UKHW022026030423
419604UK00005B/131